FROM TASHKENT WITH LOVE

Cardiff City in Europe
1964 – 1993

Mario Risoli

ST DAVID'S PRESS
Cardiff

Published in Wales by St. David's Press, an imprint of

Ashley Drake Publishing Ltd
PO Box 733
Cardiff
CF14 7ZY

www.st-davids-press.com

First Impression – 2014

ISBN
978-1-902719-41-2

© Ashley Drake Publishing Ltd 2014
Text © Mario Risoli 2014

British Library Cataloguing-in-Publication Data.
A CIP catalogue for this book is available from the British Library.

Typeset by Replika Press Pvt Ltd, India
Printed in the Czech Republic by Akcent Media Ltd

Front Cover: Cardiff City captain Brian Harris (far right) about to shake
hands with Torpedo Moscow's Victor Shustikov (far left) before the
second leg of their Cup Winners' Cup quarter-final inside Tashkent's
Pakhtakor Markaziy Stadium on 19 March, 1968. Looking on are
referee Bertil Lööw (second left) and linesman Rolf Arnshed.

Contents

Acknowledgements

My greatest gratitude goes to the former Cardiff City players who generously gave time to recall their experiences of the Cup Winners' Cup. I am especially thankful to Graham Coldrick, Bill Irwin, Freddie Pethard, Damon Searle and Derek Showers who put me in contact with several of their former colleagues. I also want to thank Val Bodden, James Gornall, Ian Haddrell, David Instone, John Lloyd, Albert Lord, Chris Parsons, Jake Payne, Tom Ross and Andrew Taylor, who all helped put me in touch with former Cardiff players. I am indebted to Richard Jeffery and Barry Jones, of the Bluebirds DownUnder supporters group in Australia, for organising an interview with Adrian Alston. Thanks also to Tim Clapham, Craig McCracken, Ceri Stennett, Tony Stephenson and the media department at the Union of European Football Associations (UEFA) for providing me with invaluable information, and to Terry Grandin and Richard Shepherd, and Laura Wagg of the Press Association for helping me with photographs. I am also grateful to the staff at Cardiff Central Library who are always so helpful and efficient, and to publisher Ashley Drake for his enthusiasm and professionalism, and for recognising this is a story which deserves to be told. Finally, a huge thank-you to a true Cardiff City legend, Peter King, for writing such a heartfelt and insightful foreword.

Mario Risoli
April 2014

Foreword

THE year was 1960 and I was a naive 17-year-old with ambitions to become a professional footballer. At the time I was playing part-time for my local side, Worcester City, in the Southern League. Among the clubs that came knocking for my services was Cardiff City, at the time managed by a lovely Welshman, Bill Jones. Along with my parents and a Worcester City director, we drove to Ninian Park to discuss a possible transfer. Words cannot explain how thrilled and excited I was to sign on the dotted line. Putting pen to paper, I had no idea the move would lead to me playing against some of Europe's greatest clubs and travelling to countries I never thought I would see.

Four years after signing for the Bluebirds, we won the Welsh Cup which meant dipping a tentative toe in European competition. For the first time in the club's history, we qualified for the Cup Winners' Cup. Britain's biggest clubs, such as Manchester United, Tottenham Hotspur and Celtic, had already experienced European nights. We, on the other hand, were a lowly and mediocre side from Division Two with no idea what to expect. As a non-seeded team, we were drawn to play that first game away against Esbjerg. I'd never heard of the place and later discovered it was a small city on the Danish coast. Esbjerg were a team of part-timers and they held us to a goalless draw at their ground. The watching South Wales journalists were deservedly critical and I imagined the pencils were already being further sharpened at half-time in the return leg at Ninian Park, when the score was still 0-0. Fortunately, we managed to scrape through 1-0. I say fortunately because I scored the goal with my head. Not a regular occurrence.

Next up for us were the Cup Winners' Cup holders, Sporting Clube from Lisbon. On their way to winning the trophy the previous year they had seen off Manchester United. Incredibly, we beat them 2-1 inside their own stadium, the vast Estádio Alvalade. I still maintain this result is Cardiff's finest in Europe. Sporting were a top club while we were on a sharp learning curve.

By the time an Achilles injury forced me to retire from the game in 1974, we had crossed swords with clubs from all over Europe - Portugal, Spain, Turkey, the Soviet Union, Cyprus, East and West Germany, Ireland, Belgium, Holland, France, Norway and Denmark. The most talked-about tie was, of course, our meeting with mighty Real Madrid in March 1971. What a night that first leg at Ninian Park was. The late and sadly missed Brian Clark scored the only goal and, years later, he told me of the many times he'd dined out on that epic result.

Of all the trips we made in Europe, the most incredible was the 1968 journey to Tashkent where we played the return leg against Torpedo Moscow. For those who don't know the whereabouts of Tashkent, as I didn't back in 1968, it's just over 1,700 miles away Moscow and close to both China and Afghanistan. We landed in Moscow, where we stayed for a few days, and I was invited to do some radio interviews along with Don Murray, our captain. The interpreter explained that the interviewer would ask questions in Russian and, after they were translated, we would reply in English. Our answers would then be translated into Russian afterwards. It appeared to go well although as this was the time of the Cold War, Don and I could have been guilty of opening up hostilities without realising!

The tie eventually finished 1-1 on aggregate and, with no penalty shoot-outs in those days, a third game was arranged.

It was to be played in Augsburg, West Germany. As usual our club doctor, Leslie Hamilton, was with us on that trip and he was interested in visiting a former concentration camp. This was the day before the game and he asked me if I would like to accompany him. I declined, for the simple reason that I did not wish to witness Man's inhumanity to Man so close to an important game. Looking back, part of me wishes that I had taken up his offer but hindsight is a wonderful thing, isn't it?

East Berlin was another memorable experience especially as we had to pass through Checkpoint Charlie. As we disembarked from our luxurious West Berlin coach, a tin-bucket of a bus came around the corner for us to board.

Machine-gun turrets, barbed wire and a 'no man's land' of at least 15 metres were evident on the east side of the Berlin Wall. Tension was in the air, the like of which we were not accustomed to, and it was not helped when a military figure in a greatcoat came to the front of the bus and, in a guttural German voice, welcomed us to East Berlin. He went on and on and on and I remember thinking that he wouldn't be out of place in an episode of *Dad's Army*. That was it. I wanted to giggle. The more he spoke, the more I wanted to giggle and as I was sitting directly down the bus, in the middle of the back seat, straight in his eyeline, there was no escape. Eventually, my suppressed laughter became too much and I leaned out of sight of 'the General' and bit on my coat sleeve in a forlorn attempt not to offend our host. I'm not sure I was that successful.

Looking back, the only Cup Winners' Cup trip I didn't enjoy was the game against FC Porto in Portugal, in 1968. That was one of the more inhospitable places we visited. As we were leaving the pitch at the end, we noticed an altercation taking place near the steps which led to the dressing rooms so we made a run for it. When we got to our dressing room we saw Bob Wilson, our number-two goalkeeper, was sitting on the bench with blood pouring from a head wound. We asked what happened and he said a policeman had hit him with a truncheon. Showered and changed, we made our way to our coach. Safe at last we thought. Wrong! The bus was pelted with stones and rocks. On the advice of our winger, Barrie Jones, who had suffered a similar fate at Millwall while playing for Plymouth Argyle, we all went down on the floor to avoid any flying glass. Thankfully, the windows didn't shatter but it was a rather traumatic end to a football match.

The manager who led us on these Cup Winners' Cup adventures was Jimmy Scoular, a tough Scot who had enjoyed a distinguished playing career. He was appointed in the summer of 1964, shortly before our first European tie against Esbjerg. I've been asked on many occasions how 'The Boss' prepared us for Cup Winners' Cup games. We did try to play a slightly different system to the norm. For instance, against Sporting in 1964, Scoular decided to omit the gifted and attack-minded Ivor Allchurch, and we adjusted accordingly. John Charles played as a sweeper behind our defence, with Gareth Williams filling the gap left by John. It meant that we were one short in midfield, having lost Gareth to the defensive line. This suited me down to the ground as I was now allowed to run wherever I wished in the centre of the park. Bliss! The system worked because we left Lisbon with an unbelievable result.

Scoular was one of four managers I served under at Cardiff, the others being Bill Jones, George Swindin and Frank O'Farrell. This meant I ended up playing for a Welshman, an Englishman, an Irishman and a Scotsman! Jones was my mentor and if, on first arriving in Cardiff, he'd asked me to jump into the Taff, I would have done so without question.

The majority of my 14 years at Ninian Park, however, were with Scoular. When he first joined the club from Bradford Park Avenue he was still 'one of the boys' as he demonstrated after the first game of the 1964-65 season. My then-girlfriend, Nikki (who became my wife), and I were planning to go to Worcester to visit my parents. We didn't own a car so we planned to travel by train. Scoular, who was still living in Yorkshire, got to hear of this and offered to drop us off in Worcester on his way back home. He also gave Bob Wilson, who had just signed from Aston Villa and was in the process of moving from the Midlands, a lift to Birmingham. I noticed a significant change in 'The Boss' during his nine-year reign and he became more and more distant from his playing staff. As the years passed, I only saw glimpses of the man who had given us that lift in 1964.

My main criticism of Scoular was his attitude towards the young lads at the club trying to make the grade. He would constantly berate them for their mistakes on the field, even in five-a-side games if they happened to be in his team. Over a glass of beer after an away game, I often chastised him about this subject. He would say, "I can't understand why they can't do it." My reply was to remind him that he was an ex-Scotland international with undoubted talent. These lads were young and still learning the trade. Nikki mentioned to me once that the wife of a Welsh Under-21 player, who shall remain nameless, told her that sometimes he arrived home in tears after being on the receiving end of one of Scoular's tirades. I didn't escape criticism but, by the time he had arrived at Ninian Park, I was an established player so any harsh comments were like water off a duck's back. In general, our relationship was one of mutual respect and I was told by a friend that 'The Boss' regarded me as a model professional which was a nice thing to hear.

Scoular could be stubborn and rather naive. For instance, Tuesday mornings would involve a full-scale practice match and as long as the first team won, which they invariably did, that was it. There was no stopping to analyse any incidents. On Thursday mornings – only two days before a game - we trained very hard, by far our hardest session of the week. When I stopped playing football and took up running, there was no way I would train hard two days before a race. That was something I learned from other athletes.

Scoular did have admirable qualities. He was, without a shadow of a doubt, committed to the cause of Cardiff City and nobody could question his dedication. When he had the time, 'The Boss' would travel to watch matches in the hope of spotting new talent, and evening games in Bristol and the Midlands were attended whenever possible.

His other asset, apart from the work ethic, was his competitive approach to all aspects of the job. For instance, Friday morning five-a-side games were 'tooth and nail' if you were involved in the same game as him. As for friendly matches, they didn't exist as far as 'The Boss' was concerned. I suppose some of that competitive spirit must have been transmitted to his players which is why we sometimes punched above our weight in Europe and overcame teams who, on paper, were technically far superior. The best example of this was our third game against Torpedo Moscow, in Augsburg.

Although we travelled far and wide throughout Europe during the 1960s and early 1970s, a later visit to a Dutch physiotherapist here in Spain, where I now live, brought home to me the fact we live in a small world. I'd picked up a calf strain while playing tennis and, as he examined me, he noticed an operational scar on my Achilles tendon. I explained it was an old football injury, one which forced me to retire earlier than planned. This physiotherapist, Gerard, told me that at 14 he, too, wanted to be a professional footballer, and had been on the books of his local club, NAC Breda. Immediately my ears pricked up because we had played that club during our European exploits. When I visited him the following week, I took along a programme from that game. Gerard looked and smiled, before pointing out one of the Breda players. "When that player retired," he explained, "he became the coach of my team." As I said, it's a small world.

Apart from achieving some great results, my lasting memories of the Cup Winners' Cup are returning home after a good result abroad. Quite a number of fans would make the trip to Rhoose Airport to welcome us. That was a nice feeling. We were proud of what we'd achieved and pleased that we'd given our fans something to cheer about.

I would like to thank Mario Risoli for inviting me to reminisce about those magical European nights from yesteryear. If, for you, this book evokes half the memories it has for me of those special times, then you are about to begin an enjoyable and emotional read.

Peter King
Alicante Province, Spain
March 2014

Preface

SEPTEMBER 5, 1962. Italian club Napoli faced non-league Bangor City at Farrar Road, the Welsh club's modest home situated in the midst of terraced houses and overlooked by Bangor Cathedral. Backed by wealthy shipping magnate Achille Lauro, the star-studded Italian side had just won promotion to Serie A, regularly attracted crowds of 80,000, and included two players – Pierluigi Ronzon and Amos Mariani - who had represented Italy. In contrast, Bangor were made up of part-timers, lay sixth in the Cheshire League and the club's entire revenue since 1945 would not have bought Napoli's Argentinian-born forwards, Humberto Rosa and Juan Carlos Tacchi. On paper, a startling fixture involving two disparate clubs, yet this tie was a typically intriguing product of the Cup Winners' Cup, a competition which pitched together the domestic cup winners from across Europe.

The preliminary-round meeting between the expensively-assembled Coppa Italia holders and the little-known winners of the Welsh Cup also encapsulated the unpredictability and drama of the European Cup's little brother. Bangor claimed a remarkable result on their sloping and muddy surface, sensationally beating Napoli 2-0. Inside the colossal San Paolo nearly three weeks later, the North Walians were just six minutes away from glory, Giovanni Fanello sealing a hard-fought 3-1 win for Napoli and forcing a play-off in London. Had the away-goal rule been in existence in 1962, Bangor would have progressed. At Highbury, the fairy tale finally ended with Napoli scraping a 2-1 victory courtesy of Rosa's late winner.

Two years after its inception, the Cup Winners' Cup had provided the continent with a remarkable and unforgettable story.

The brainchild of prominent European football journalists and organised by the committee for the Mitropa Cup – a tournament involving clubs from Italy, Hungary, Czechoslovakia and Yugoslavia – the Cup Winners' Cup was launched for the 1960-61 season. Following the success of the European Cup and the Inter-Cities Fairs Cup, the desire for a third European tournament surfaced. The new competition would involve the domestic cup winners from countries affiliated to the Union of European Football Associations (UEFA). The reception, though, was decidedly lukewarm with only 10 clubs taking part in the inaugural campaign.

The first Cup Winners' Cup match was played behind the Iron Curtain, in East Berlin on August 1, 1960. ASK Vorwärts met Czechoslovakia's Rudá Hvězda Brno in front of an 8,000 crowd inside the Friedrich-Ludwig-Jahn-Sportpark, the East German side winning the first leg of this preliminary round clash 2-1. ASK Vorwärts striker Horst Kohle, an East German international, etched his name in the history books three minutes before half-time when he scored the competition's first goal although it was the Czechs who progressed to the next round, overturning the deficit 10 days later in Brno. The trophy was eventually won by Italian side Fiorentina who beat Scotland's Rangers 4-1 on aggregate in what would be the only Cup Winners' Cup final to be played over two legs.

With clubs from Spain, Portugal and France absent, it was an inauspicious start for Europe's youngest football competition. Scepticism reigned as the likes of Atlético Madrid and Monaco declined to enter the new tournament while many of the 32 associations linked to UEFA did not have a national cup competition.The mood dramatically changed the following year. Despite the small number of entrants, the first campaign had proved a success. In the final's first leg in Glasgow, 80,000 people crammed inside Ibrox Stadium while a 50,000 crowd watched Fiorentina lift the trophy after the second leg in Florence. The apathy quickly disappeared and the credibility of the Cup Winners' Cup was given a considerable boost in 1961 when UEFA took control of the competition. All 23 clubs eligible to enter did so and, ironically, Atlético Madrid - one of the clubs which snubbed the tournament the previous year - triumphed in the final, overcoming holders Fiorentina in a replay in Stuttgart. By 1968, every one of UEFA's member associations had established a domestic cup competition so their clubs were able to participate in the Cup Winners' Cup.

The competition provided the first British success in European football, in 1963 when Tottenham Hotspur thrashed Atlético Madrid 5-1 in Rotterdam. While European Cup finals were often tight and anti-climactic affairs, Cup Winners' Cup finals rarely lacked entertainment. Slovan Bratislava caused a genuine upset in 1969, beating red-hot favourites Barcelona 3-2 in a pulsating final in Basle. Three years later, in Barcelona, Rangers clinched the trophy against Dynamo Moscow with the same result. Anderlecht – inspired by Belgium international François Van der Elst and Holland forward Rob Rensenbrink – sunk West Ham 4-2 in Brussels in the 1976 showpiece but arguably the finest Cup Winners' Cup final occurred in 1979, in Basle, where Barcelona saw off Fortuna Düsseldorf in a thrilling match which ended 4-3 after extra-time.

The competition also provided plenty of upsets. In the 1984-85 season, at the end of which they finished bottom of the Football League, Wrexham amazingly eliminated Portuguese giants FC Porto on the away-goal rule. In the 1974 final, FC Magdeburg of East Germany caused a genuine surprise by beating holders AC Milan 2-0 in Rotterdam. Real Madrid were firm favourites to win the cup in 1983 but, in Gothenburg, the Spanish giants were stunned by an Aberdeen side managed by Alex Ferguson.

During its existence, the Cup Winners' Cup produced several milestones. The 1980 final saw a European club trophy decided on penalties for the first time, Valencia beating Arsenal following a 0-0 stalemate in Brussels. The first red cards in a European final came in the competition, in 1973 when Leeds United defender Norman Hunter and AC Milan midfielder Riccardo Sogliano were dismissed during what Italian newspaper *il manifesto* called "a night of rain and rage" in Salonika.The only players to score six goals in a European match – Mascarenhas of Sporting Clube de Portugal, Borussia Dortmund's Lothar Emmerich and Levki Spartak's Kiril Milanov – all did so in the Cup Winners' Cup.

The establishment of the Champions League in 1992 sounded the death knell for the tournament. Five years later, more than one side from UEFA's most powerful associations could qualify for the Champions League, a decision that severely weakened the Cup Winners' Cup. So Barcelona, winners of the Cup Winners' Cup in 1997 for a record fourth time, now entered UEFA's elite tournament rather than defend the trophy. The biggest blow came from Holland. SC Heerenveen were the Dutch representatives in the 1998-99 Cup Winners' Cup even though they had only reached the semi-final of their domestic cup competition the previous season. The two finalists, Ajax and PSV Eindhoven, had finished first and second in the Eredivisie and thus qualified for the recently-expanded Champions League.

Having increased the number of Champions League entrants to 32, UEFA decided to abolish the Cup Winners' Cup with the 1998-99 competition being the last. By this time, the two clubs which launched the tournament 39 years earlier had disappeared. ASK Vorwärts had relocated from Berlin to Frankfurt an der Oder, a town near the Polish border, in 1971. A decade earlier, Rudá Hvězda Brno had amalgamated with Spartak ZJŠ Brno.

The 39th and last Cup Winners' Cup final was staged at Villa Park, Birmingham, on 19 May, 1999. Like the first final, it belonged to Italy as Lazio defeated Spain's Real Mallorca. Pavel Nedved, Lazio's Czech midfielder, at least ensured a glorious *adieu* for the competition with his sublime winner nine minutes from the end, hooking the ball over goalkeeper Carlos Roa from 20 yards out. '*Sei proprio forte, Lazio!*' ('You are really strong, Lazio!) declared *La Gazzetta dello Sport*, the Italian sports daily newspaper, the following day. UEFA no longer shared that view of the Cup Winners' Cup.

"The best wins, or the one who has more luck."
Didier Pironi

1

Narrow Margin
Esbjerg, 1964

'My policy has always been attack.'

Jimmy Scoular

The Hotel du Rhône. An imposing art deco-style building in the heart of Geneva's financial centre and the first hotel built in Europe after the Second World War. Designed by renowned Swiss architect Marc-Joseph Saugey, the five-star hotel, its interior adorned with silk and Italian marble, was once feted as the finest in Switzerland. President Eisenhower stayed at the du Rhône while visiting the city for the Geneva Summit in 1955. Other illustrious guests had included Hollywood stars Errol Flynn and Jayne Mansfield, jazz king Louis Armstrong, and the composer and pianist, Duke Ellington. Saugey's luxurious creation on the right bank of the River Rhône was chosen by the Union of European Football Associations (UEFA) as the venue for the 1964-65 European Cup Winners' Cup draw. Among the 30 sides plotting a path to the final at Wembley were West Ham United, one of English football's most stylish sides, and Spain's Real Zaragoza, winners of the Inter-Cities Fairs Cup the previous season. Also in the draw were powerful TSV Munich 1860 of West Germany, the talented Italians of

Torino, Czechoslovakia's most successful club, Sparta Prague, and Dinamo Zagreb of Yugoslavia, runners-up in the Inter-Cities Fairs Cup a year earlier. Then there were the holders, Sporting Clube de Portugal, champions of Portugal on 11 occasions.

Cardiff City, an average and ageing Division Two side, were Wales' flag-bearers. The Bluebirds were making their first appearance in European competition courtesy of a hard-fought victory over Bangor City in the Welsh Cup final, the one positive note in what had been a difficult season which culminated in the departure of manager George Swindin. The former Arsenal goalkeeper paid the price for a disappointing 15th-placed finish when he was sacked on the eve of the Welsh Cup final play-off following an acrimonious board meeting. His successor was Jimmy Scoular, recently – and controversially – sacked by Division Four club Bradford Park Avenue. During his playing days the muscular Scoular was a formidable wing-half, winning two Division One titles with Portsmouth, the FA Cup with Newcastle United as well as nine Scotland caps. Renowned for his tree-trunk thighs, ferocious scowl and volcanic temper, the former submarine engineer had been one of the most feared players in British football, earning the nicknames 'Iron Man' and 'Scoular the Scourge'. Yet he was more than just a hard man. A brilliant passer of the ball, he changed the course of many matches with one of his exquisitely precise cross-field passes.

Scoular moved into management in January 1961 as player-manager of Park Avenue and led the Yorkshire club into Division Three that year although they were relegated back to the league basement in 1963. Despite his admirable achievements on a shoestring budget, the 39-year-old was dismissed by Park Avenue in May 1964 following a mid-table finish. Ray Ambler, the only one of the four directors who voted against sacking the Scot, resigned from the board in protest. One of six serious candidates for the Ninian Park vacancy, Scoular was interviewed by Cardiff chairman Fred Dewey and directors George Edwards and Bob Williams at a hotel in Worcester, roughly halfway between his West Yorkshire home in Bingley and the Welsh capital. According to Dewey, a former Cardiff Corries player capped twice by Wales, Scoular "certainly impressed" during the interview and was offered the job there and then. The 'Iron Man' from Livingston was "keen on A1 fitness" but it was his numerous contacts in the British game that won over the Bluebirds hierarchy.

The Cup Winners' Cup preliminary round draw - held on 8 July and made by UEFA president Gustav Wiederkehr and the chairman of the Cup Winners' Cup Organisation Committee, Sándor Barcs, - was kind to the new Bluebirds manager who would officially begin work at Ninian Park five days later, after a short family holiday in Southsea. Cardiff avoided one of the heavyweights and were paired with the part-timers of Danish club Esbjerg, with the first leg in Denmark. These being the days before UEFA provided set dates for European ties, the clubs agreed to play the first leg at Esbjerg's Idraetspark on 9 September and the return at Ninian Park on 13 October. "We are quite pleased with this draw," commented Cardiff's secretary Graham Keenor, "and it will be nice to renew old acquaintances."

Cardiff had played Esbjerg before, during their 1959 end-of-season tour of Denmark, convincingly winning 4-0. According to Western Mail football correspondent Dewi Lewis, the visitors were so superior "they could have reached double figures". The former Arsenal and Wales forward Derek Tapscott scored twice and unfortunate Esbjerg defender Knud Clausden netted two own-goals. "Before the game City had been told that Esbjerg had been one of the best teams in Denmark," wrote Lewis. "If this is true – and one is to take this game as a real indication of their ability (or lack of it) – then Danish football must be at a very low ebb indeed." Predictably the South Wales Press expected the Bluebirds to brush Esbjerg aside and progress to the first round. 'EUROPEAN DRAW GIVES CITY GREAT CHANCE' was the headline in the *Western Mail* and Lewis wrote, "In May 1959 City won at Esbjerg by four clear goals and I would rate their present side a little stronger than it was then."

Cardiff, however, had started their 1964-65 campaign poorly. After three draws and two defeats in their opening five games, they found themselves second-bottom in Division Two. Scoular, who claimed his side were "in the middle of a transitional period", announced his squad for the Esbjerg trip on Sunday, 6 September - the day before the club's chartered flight to Denmark and the day after a 3-1 home defeat against Bolton Wanderers. The players were summoned to Ninian Park to be told who was going and who was staying behind. Scoular named a 13-man squad although he was unable to include his number one goalkeeper, Bob Wilson, who was ineligible for the first two rounds because his £2,000 transfer from Aston Villa was completed after the UEFA deadline. His place went to Dilwyn John who had last played a competitive game on 24 April, a 3-1 loss at Middlesbrough, the final fixture of the 1963-64 season.

The outfield players travelling to Esbjerg were Peter Rodrigues, Trevor Peck, John Charles, Don Murray, Gareth Williams, Barrie Hole, Steve Gammon, Peter King, Greg Farrell, Ivor Allchurch, Mel Charles and Tommy Halliday. Gammon, a wing-half, was the only survivor from the 1959 friendly. Tapscott was still at Ninian Park but out of favour, while defenders Alan Harrington and Colin Baker, both part of the Bluebirds defence that faced the Danish side five years earlier, were also

4

playing in the reserves. The squad that headed for Denmark was not short of international experience. John Charles, 32, his younger brother Mel, 29, and Allchurch, 34, were all seasoned Welsh internationals and the Swansea-born trio had starred for their country at the 1958 World Cup in Sweden. Charles senior was a superstar in Italian football and had played in the European Cup during his incredibly successful five-year spell with Juventus. He had also been involved in the Inter-Cities Fairs Cup during his brief and unhappy stay at Roma.

Dilwyn John: *I'd never heard of Esbjerg and I didn't know what to expect. It was a journey into the unknown for us. This was a European tie and all the Cardiff players were itching to be a part of it. In those days every British player wanted to play abroad and we now had that chance. Jimmy picked people who would give him their all. You had to give him 100 per cent. If you didn't, then you wouldn't play.*

Peter King: *The year before, we had played a few games in Italy as part of the deal which brought John Charles to Cardiff. We played Juventus, Roma and a team called Latina. That gave us a real insight into European football so going into the Cup Winners' Cup we weren't exactly wet behind the ears. But our knowledge of Esbjerg was less than nil. We went into the game not knowing anything about their players. There was no report on Esbjerg and the way they played. In fact, it wasn't until the season we played Real Madrid (1970-71) that we had a breakdown of our opposition in Europe.*

Don Murray: *This was our first venture into Europe so there was a lot of excitement at the club. I was only 18 at the time and I'd made my debut the previous season so I was over the moon to be included in the squad. We didn't know anything about the Esbjerg side – I'd not even heard of Esbjerg – and we didn't know about the standard of football in Denmark, but Esbjerg had won the Danish Cup so they must have been a decent side. As an introduction to European football, we had been drawn with one of the minor clubs and that was to our benefit.*

Nothing more than a small group of farms in the early 1860s, Esbjerg – situated in a desolate corner of the Jutland peninsula facing the North Sea – had blossomed into Denmark's busiest fishing port and was, in 1964, the country's fastest-growing city with a population of just over 55,000. Its centre was laid out in a chessboard pattern with Esbjerg's most famous landmark, Christian Hjerrild Clausen's medieval-style Water Tower, overlooking the city's parallel streets.

Peter Rodrigues: *I remember arriving in Esbjerg. It was a small, local airport. It was minute. There was nothing there. The main building was like a hut! It was all very relaxed and we just went straight through. There was no checking passports and going through customs or anything like that. We basically went from the plane onto the bus which took us to our hotel.*

Trevor Peck: *You couldn't exactly call where we landed an airport. It was practically a field and we had to wait a while to get off the plane because there wasn't a stairway ready for us to disembark. We had to wait for someone to bring one so we could get off. We stayed in Esbjerg for a few days. We went around the shops and chatted*

6

to the girls behind the counters. It was a quaint town and the people were very friendly.

Gareth Williams: *We landed at an angle in an old-fashioned plane out in the wild, in what was virtually a field. Esbjerg didn't have a proper airport and we had to carry our things from the plane ourselves. There was no passport control, luggage handling or anything like that. It was very primitive, unbelievable really. The airport was way out in the middle of nowhere.*

Dilwyn John: *Esbjerg wasn't a big place. We had a wander but couldn't see a great deal. We did find a place with a pool table and that's where we spent most of our time because there wasn't much else to do. We also found a nine-hole golf course which was cut into the woods and about six of us went there for a game of golf. A few of us also went to the cinema to watch 'How The West Was Won'. It was in English with Danish subtitles. Whenever that film is on television I think of Esbjerg! I remember about halfway through the film everybody suddenly started leaving, then they came back into the cinema. We discovered they were going into a big yard outside to have a smoke because you weren't allowed to smoke in public places. That was Denmark in 1964.*

Esbjerg had emerged as Denmark's strongest side in the early 1960s, winning three consecutive Danish titles from 1961-63 before lifting the Danish Cup. They would go on to win a fourth title in 1965. Nine of their players were either current or former Danish internationals. Their key players included wing-half Jens Petersen, voted Denmark's Player of the Year in 1963, right-back Jens Jørgen Hansen, who represented his country at the European Championships in Spain three months earlier, and John Madsen, widely considered Denmark's best centre-half although he had retired from international football for family reasons. Eric Gaardhøje, their goalkeeper, was another international, representing Denmark on 14 occasions. Esbjerg's last performance in European competition, in the European Cup the previous season, offered Scoular encouragement. The amateurs were crushed by PSV Eindhoven in the first round, hammered 7-1 in Holland and beaten 12-4 on aggregate. Arne Sörensen's side had also been weakened by the departure of forward and star player Carl Bertelsen, another member of Denmark's European Championship side, who joined Scottish club Greenock Morton. Scoular, though, warned his Bluebirds not to underestimate the Danish part-timers. "Don't think of them as amateurs," he told them before the first leg, "or you will be making the biggest mistake of your lives." To ensure there was no holiday atmosphere in his camp, the Scot ordered his players to be in bed by 11pm. Anyone breaking the curfew would be fined and sent home.

Don Murray: *We had John Charles in our side, one of the most famous players in the world. Wherever we went, you could be sure his face would be plastered all over the papers. It was great to have him with us. He was the player everybody wanted to see and he was the one in our side everyone abroad knew. He was a great player. The rest of us were nobodies.*

Peter King: *Esbjerg was a lovely place and the people were very friendly. The hotel we stayed in pushed the boat out for us. They would put out spreads for us on a huge table. It was basically a running buffet and we'd just help ourselves. They went out of their way to make us feel at home.*

Trevor Peck: *We had a training session at Esbjerg's ground and the pitch was quite large and in beautiful condition – better than what we were used to back home - but there was a horrible smell of fish which the wind was blowing over from the docks. Esbjerg was a busy fishing port and the smell was quite sickening. It was terrible, really awful.*

John Charles, at centre-half, was asked to marshall the Cardiff defence with Rodrigues at right-back and Peck at left-back. Williams and Hole occupied the wing-half positions with Farrell on the right wing and King on the left. Allchurch and Halliday were the inside-forwards supporting striker Mel Charles. A blend of big-name acquisitions, homegrown talent and cut-price signings, the entire Cardiff line-up had cost £78,000 to assemble and not one player was acquired by Scoular. Mel Charles, signed from Arsenal in 1961, was the costliest player at £28,000. Cardiff purchased his older brother from Roma two years later for £22,500, a deal Swindin opposed because he wanted to bring in younger players. Allchurch cost £18,000 from Newcastle United in 1962, 'Chick' Halliday £5,000 from Dumbarton in 1963, and fellow Scotsman Farrell was bought from Birmingham City for £2,000 just before the previous season's transfer deadline. John and Rodrigues, both from Cardiff, had come through the Ninian Park ranks. Rodrigues was beginning to attract attention from Division One clubs yet in the summer of 1963 he was on the verge of being released by the Bluebirds. He was given another chance after full-backs Harrington and Peck both suffered broken legs following tackles by trialist Jim Upton during a disastrous pre-season practice game. Hole, capped twice by Wales and another of Cardiff's most coveted players, had been whisked away from his native Swansea as a teenager in 1959. Williams was spotted playing for Valleys amateur side Cefn Fforest and Peck was signed from hometown club Llanelli. King, who would serve Cardiff for 14 years, arrived from Worcester City in exchange for striker Harry Knowles who rejoined the non-league outfit.

Esbjerg's shops and factories closed early to give locals the chance to watch the clash against the Welsh Cup winners and a crowd of 10,000 filled the modest Idraetspark. On a flawless surface – the *Western Mail* described it as being "as smooth as that of a billiards table" – Esbjerg almost took the lead just before half-time when their captain, Carl Emil Christiansen, watched his shot swerve just past the post. Gaardhøje had little to do, comfortably dealing with Allchurch's first-half header and then saving Halliday's attempt after the interval with Mel Charles wasting the Welsh side's best opportunity. Publicly, Scoular promised an attacking display – "I intend to go on the offensive at Esbjerg," he declared before the game – yet on the night his side played cautiously and rarely threatened Gaardhøje. When they did attack they usually fell foul of Esbjerg's offside trap which snared Scoular's forwards on 18 occasions. Cardiff's baptism in Europe turned out to be a drab, uneventful 0-0 draw, dominated by the centre-halves in each side, John Charles and Madsen. The two men Scoular hoped would unlock a well-drilled Esbjerg defence, Mel Charles and Allchurch, failed to shine.

Barrie Hole: *We'd worked on this free-kick before the game. As one of our players made a run behind the opposition's wall, the ball is passed to another player who is standing on the edge of the wall. He then had to knock it into the space where the player making the run was supposed to be. It was quite clever and we had a chance to use it in the match. It was working perfectly until the ball came to Mel. All he had to do was tap it in but he accidentally stood on the ball. Jimmy wiped the floor with him afterwards saying, 'You stepped on the ball on purpose!' and Mel was answering back, 'I couldn't help it!' That really made me laugh.*

Peter King: *Jimmy had brought this free-kick idea from Newcastle and we got a chance to try it on the edge of their penalty box but it didn't work. Jimmy gave Mel some stick after the game. It was the first time we'd seen him angry. We saw Jimmy in a new light that evening.*

Peter Rodrigues: *Esbjerg weren't a bad side. They were a reasonable standard and they were well-organised. The first leg was cat and mouse but a draw was a good result for us. The plan was to get a positive result out there and then go for them at home where we'd have our fans behind us.*

Scoular claimed Esbjerg's offside tactics "killed the game as a spectacle" but "the way the players fought" pleased him. "If we could draw all our away league games like we did this one, I would be happy," he admitted. The travelling Press was not so kind. Bryan Stiles of the *South Wales Echo* wrote, "This was a very poor game to watch and Cardiff City did their reputation very little good with their uninspiring display." In the *Western Mail*, Lewis was equally critical. "It was a bitterly disappointing performance by the Welsh side and well in keeping with what they have given this season in Football League matches."

Greg Farrell: *Before the game Jimmy sat us down and said he would be happy with a draw. I played wide right but he told me to stay back and help keep things tight. I played more in midfield that night because the boss wanted me to tuck in. It was a hard game and we mainly defended. Jimmy was happy with the result. He came into the dressing room afterwards and said, 'Well done boys'.*

Dilwyn John: *We went out there with a defensive plan. The aim was to avoid conceding a goal and we had John Charles to organise things at the back. We were quite happy to keep it at 0-0. It was a mundane match but we were pleased with the result because we always fancied our chances at Ninian Park.*

Peter King: *We got a bit of stick from the papers afterwards. They saw it as Cardiff drawing 0-0 with a side from a fishing village. Esbjerg weren't a force in Europe and they were only part-time, but we weren't a good side at that stage. Jimmy Scoular had just come in, he was getting to know us and we were getting to know him. We weren't the best side in the world by any stretch of the imagination.*

Cardiff were bottom of Division Two when Esbjerg arrived in South Wales for the second leg although they had - at the 12th attempt - just secured their first league win of the season, King and Tapscott scoring in a 2-1 win over Derby County at Ninian Park.

Esbjerg would face a Cardiff side missing their big names. Allchurch withdrew on the morning of the game with a pulled muscle and John Charles was sidelined after suffering an ankle injury during Wales' win over Scotland in a Home Championship match 10 days earlier. Charles' absence delighted the Danes who described the 'Gentle Giant' as "half the Cardiff team" in the first match. His place was taken by 19-year-old Murray who replaced Charles in the last two league matches. Scoular also drafted in left-winger Bernard Lewis with King moving to inside-forward alongside Mel Charles. Tapscott, at 32, another of Cardiff's Welsh veterans, spearheaded the attack. Just as he did in Denmark, the Scot warned his players against complacency. "They're a hard team and they'll be tough to beat," he told his charges before kick-off. "They're supposed to be amateurs but don't be fooled by the word." Another draw and the two sides would meet again in a play-off. "There will be no replay," said Esbjerg's confident president, Egon Skov, buoyed by the absence of John Charles. "We are going to win."

Don Murray: *I'd broken into the first team the previous year so when the club signed John Charles I thought it was the end for me. One of the best centre-halves in the world had joined Cardiff! I didn't see my chances of playing being very good but then John was injured in 1964-65 and I got back into the team. I did OK so when John was fit again Jimmy moved him up front and kept me in defence. I did sometimes play with John at the back, especially in Europe, and I had the privilege of playing with one of the best players the world has ever seen. To begin with, I was in awe of the man but soon settled down, and me and John became fairly close.*

Scoular's side, with Hole outstanding, showed far more purpose and ambition than they did in Denmark and it was only Gaardhøje's brilliance that kept Esbjerg on equal terms for 56 minutes. The 25-year-old teacher produced a superb save to stop Williams' shot and also denied Charles, King, Tapscott, Hole and Lewis. "The Danish 'keeper looked like a blond-headed combination of Howard Winstone and Billy Walker as he nipped along his goal line thumping shots from all angles," commented Stiles in the *South Wales Echo*, comparing the teacher with two boxers. Like Walker, Gaardhøje, who preferred to fist the ball clear rather than catch it, could certainly punch, and he moved with the light-footed style and grace for which Winstone was renowned. But the Denmark international was unable to reach King's perfectly-placed header in front of the Canton Stand, Cardiff's first European goal, and one which spared the Bluebirds a play-off in Rotterdam.

Peter King: *Their goalkeeper had a blinder at our place. He had one of those nights, he was saving everything. But I managed to score with a header, or a glancing header as the newspapers called it the next day. Greg Farrell crossed from the right and I remember thinking 'I'm going to have to head this'. I wasn't renowned for my heading ability but I just did enough to get my head to the ball and it went in at the far post. We were all relieved to go through and after the game I was jumping up and down in the dressing room with Dilwyn John who was a big mate of mine.*

Greg Farrell: *We missed a lot of chances and we should have scored more than one goal. Their goalkeeper made a lot of saves that night and he was definitely man of the match. He was flicking shots over the bar and round the post. Esbjerg weren't a bad side and they were very fit but I was confident they wouldn't beat us.*

Gareth Williams: *There wasn't any danger of us losing. We believed Esbjerg weren't good enough to beat us. They were more defensive at Ninian Park and it was a question of us having to find a way through, which we managed to do. We were all chuffed to get the win. It was our first time in Europe and we'd made it into the next round. It was something the club had never done before and we were all on a high afterwards. We also got a bonus for winning and reaching the next round.*

Bernard Lewis: *Esbjerg were nothing. It was like playing a Welsh League game. It was Cardiff's first tie in Europe and it should have been a big occasion for us but it was a nothing game really. It didn't excite anyone. Nobody had heard of Esbjerg and that's probably why there wasn't a big crowd that night.*

Totally outplayed, Esbjerg escaped with a 1-0 defeat. Gaardhøje's "wonder display" had prevented a much heavier loss. "The scoreline," wrote Stiles, "made a mockery of the thrust and power of the City's attacks and they would not have been flattered if they had beaten the Danes by three or four goals so complete was their mastery." Watched by a curious but disappointing gate of just under 9,000 – among the spectators was Coventry City manager Jimmy Hill who was said to be interested in signing Hole - Scoular's charges had sealed their place in the next round, although their European debut had failed to excite the South Wales public. That would all change within the next 48 hours.

Preliminary Round, First Leg
9 September, 1964
Idraetspark, Esbjerg

Esbjerg (0) 0   **Cardiff City (0) 0**

ESBJERG: Gaardhøje, Hansen, Jensen P, Nielsen, Madsen, Petersen J, Petersen K, Christiansen, Bruun, Jensen E, Kikkenborg.

CARDIFF CITY: John, Rodrigues, Peck, Williams, Charles J, Hole, King, Charles M, Halliday, Allchurch, Farrell.

Preliminary Round, Second Leg
13 October, 1964
Ninian Park, Cardiff

Cardiff City (0) 1   **Esbjerg (0) 0**
King 56

CARDIFF CITY: John, Rodrigues, Peck, Williams, Murray, Hole, King, Charles M, Tapscott, Lewis, Farrell.

ESBJERG: Gaardhøje, Hansen, Jensen P, Nielsen, Madsen, Petersen J, Petersen K, Christiansen, Theogersen, Jensen E, Kikkenborg.

(Cardiff City won 1-0 on aggregate)

2

Glory Boys
Sporting Clube de Portugal, 1964

'I thought our lads were superb, brilliant!'

Viv Dewey

15 October, 1964. General Election day in the United Kingdom and the populist Labour leader, Harold Wilson, was hoping his manifesto, *The New Britain*, would convince the British public to end "13 wasted years" of Conservative rule and place him in 10 Downing Street. The Conservatives and new leader Sir Alec Douglas-Home were seeking to win a fourth term in office with their *Prosperity with a Purpose* campaign. In Tokyo, at the Olympic Games, Ken Matthews won Britain's third gold medal, finishing ahead of West Germany's Dieter Lindner and Vladimir Golubnichy of the Soviet Union in the 20-kilometre walk. In Geneva, in the Cup Winners' Cup first-round draw, Cardiff were paired with the holders, Lisbon's Sporting Clube de Portugal, one of the biggest names in European football. "It is one of the plum ties," said Jimmy Scoular, "but we couldn't have picked a more difficult one."

Sporting, along with Benfica and Porto, made up Portuguese

football's *os Três Grandes* (the Big Three) and had won the trophy in Belgium the previous May, beating MTK Budapest 1-0 in a replay in Antwerp after the first game, at the Heysel Stadium in Brussels, ended 3-3. En route to the final, they destroyed Greek side Apoel Nicosia 16-1 in Lisbon – the biggest victory in a UEFA club competition - but it was their astonishing result in the next round, when they overturned a three-goal deficit to eliminate a Manchester United line-up containing George Best, Bobby Charlton and Denis Law, that made Europe sit up and take notice of the *Verde-e-Brancos* (the Green and Whites). Sporting appeared down and out following a 4-1 first leg defeat at Old Trafford but they clinched a place in the final by thrashing Matt Busby's side 5-0 inside their own Estádio José Alvalade.

The Lisbon club hired a new coach after their Antwerp triumph, with 43-year-old Frenchman Jean Luciano, who had guided Nice to the French title in 1959, replacing 'the architect' Anselmo Fernandez. However, apart from forward Geo, who had returned to his native Brazil, the Lisbon giants possessed the same players that lifted the trophy in the Bosuilstadion. They could still call on Osvaldo Silva, an explosive inside-forward from Brazil who scored a hat-trick in their remarkable second-leg win against United, and Joaquim Carvalho, outstanding in the replay against MTK and regarded by many as Portugal's best goalkeeper. Luciano also had Fernando Mendes, one of the best half-backs in the world, captain of both Sporting and Portugal and known as *o Capitao Grande* (the Great Captain), João Morais, the right-back who brought the Cup Winners' Cup to the Alvalade with his winner direct from a corner kick, and Ernesto Figueiredo, a powerful forward who scored twice in the first game against MTK Budapest.

Cardiff's form had improved since the win over Esbjerg. They had played nine league matches in between overcoming the

Danes and boarding their chartered flight to Lisbon, winning four games and drawing three. Scoular's players enjoyed a successful November, chalking up consecutive wins against Charlton Athletic, Leyton Orient and Bury, scoring nine goals in the process. Unfortunately new centre-forward Keith Ellis, who netted five of those goals, was ineligible for the Sporting tie as his switch from Scunthorpe United came after the UEFA transfer deadline, but Scoular was buoyed by the return of John Charles who had been out for more than two months with an ankle injury sustained while playing in Wales' 3-2 win over Scotland in a Home Championship clash at Ninian Park. Charles had made his comeback the Saturday before the game in Lisbon, in a 1-1 draw against Ipswich Town. He left Portman Road with a cut eyebrow which needed four stitches but, to Scoular's relief, there was no recurrence of the ankle problem.

The Cardiff manager decided to take 17 players to the Portuguese capital. Charles, Dilwyn John, Don Murray, Peter Rodrigues, Gareth Williams, Barrie Hole, Ivor Allchurch, Peter King and Greg Farrell were to make their second Cup Winners' Cup trip while Alan Harrington, Derek Tapscott and Bernard Lewis had forced their way into the Scot's first-team plans. Scoular also included three young Bluebirds – goalkeeper Lyn Davies, defender Graham Coldrick and striker George Johnston – and his two ineligible players – Ellis and Bob Wilson – because he wanted all five to gain European experience.

Peter Rodrigues: *My parents came with me on that trip. They flew out on the same plane. My grandfather was from Portugal and they wanted to look up relatives over there. When they arrived in Lisbon and got hold of a telephone directory they quickly discovered that trying to find someone called Rodrigues was like looking for somebody called Smith back home. They soon realised they were on to a loser and in the end they decided to treat the trip as a holiday. All the players were delighted to draw Sporting Lisbon but for me it was special because I was of Portuguese descent.*

Alan Harrington: *I shared a room with Peter Rodrigues in Lisbon and because of his name all the Portuguese journalists wanted to interview him so they came up to our hotel room which they were allowed to do in those days. It was funny listening to them. They were trying to find out where Peter was from and he was sat there saying, 'I'm Welsh and I've always lived in Cardiff'. They were also asking him where his parents were from and things like that. He was surprised by all the attention but I think he enjoyed it. Everyone started calling him Pedro after we got Sporting in the draw.*

Sporting were in turmoil before the first leg, lying fourth from bottom in the Primeira Liga following a wretched start to the season which saw them take just seven points from eight games and score eight goals. A 2-1 defeat at bottom club Torrense marked the end of Luciano's brief and troubled reign. The former Nice and Lausanne coach was removed from his post following a crisis board meeting with the reins handed to youth team coach - and club idol - Júlio Cernadas Pereira, better known as Juca. Once an elegant midfielder nicknamed *Cabecinha de Ouro* (the Little Head of Gold), Juca had won five titles with Sporting before a knee injury forced him to retire at 29 but the former Portugal international had already proved himself a capable coach. At the age of 33 he led Sporting to the Primeira Liga title in 1962 before winning the Portuguese Cup the following year. Juca not only had to lift a side struggling for form, he would have to do it without three players. Mascarenhas - Sporting's Angolan striker who had scored six goals in the destruction of Apoel Nicosia - and the accomplished centre-half, Alexandre Baptista, were both on the casualty list as was fringe player Bé, a Brazilian-born forward. Despite these problems, Sporting, a side put together for a cool £500,000, were still overwhelming favourites to beat the European novices from Wales. Kenneth Wolstenholme, the voice of football on the BBC, admitted before the game in the Alvalade that he could not envisage the Welsh side causing an upset.

Peter King: *We went to Lisbon with great trepidation and I remember talking to a Portuguese chap in the hotel lift. He saw us wearing our club suits and since he spoke a little English we got chatting. He said Sporting were the best side in Portugal and not Benfica who had Eusebio! We were all in awe of Benfica so you can imagine how I felt when he said that. I was thinking 'If they're better than Benfica what chance have we got?' I felt that if we came away with a 5-0 defeat that would be a moral victory. I thought we'd get annihilated. The aim was to leave without suffering a humiliating result. Some people were saying Sporting were going to put nine past us. I remember that number being mentioned.*

Bernard Lewis: *We weren't a good Second Division team. We were a bottom-half side and we'd had some bad results in the league that season. Nobody expected us to beat Sporting in Lisbon. Nobody would have put a bet on us winning out there. They were the holders and probably hadn't even heard of Cardiff City. Before the game people were saying we had no chance and that wasn't really a surprise. I couldn't see us winning in Lisbon.*

Gareth Williams: *We were on a hiding to nothing going out there. Sporting were the holders and they had taken Manchester United apart the previous season. Nobody gave us a chance in Lisbon but we weren't scared. The message in the dressing room was 'This is it – let's have a go!' The thought we might get hammered actually picked us up. It pulled us together and we were a close group. We all got on really well, we were all mates, and that probably helped us in those big European games.*

To try and keep Sporting's forward line at bay, Scoular devised a defensive strategy which sacrificed Allchurch's attacking qualities. Charles would operate as a sweeper in a defensive line which included Harrington at right-back, Murray at centre-half and Rodrigues at left-back. Hole was at left-half with Bluebirds skipper Williams, a defensive midfielder, taking Allchurch's place at inside-forward, his brief to drop back and protect the defence. Cardiff's attack relied on four players - wingers Lewis and Farrell, King at inside-forward, and Tapscott the lone striker. The tactical plan, dubbed 'the Scoular Scheme' by the Press, was designed to soak up pressure and hit Sporting with quick counter-attacks.

Dilwyn John: *We trained at Sporting's stadium before the game so we had the chance to take a look around. It definitely had the wow factor and was totally different to the grounds we were used to back in Britain. The stadium was a massive concrete bowl and just kept going back and back. It made us realise we were involved in a huge game. John Charles was used as a sweeper that night while Gareth Williams, a defensive midfielder, played almost as another centre-half. Jimmy's priority was not to concede and we went to Lisbon with a defensive plan. I always felt the sweeper idea was influenced by John more than Jimmy because he had played that role in Italy.*

Greg Farrell: *The game was seen as little Cardiff City against mighty Sporting Lisbon so before the kick-off the manager got everyone together and we had a sort of bonding session. He sat us all down and said, 'You can do this, you can do that'. He also spoke to us individually and that really lifted all the lads.*

Apathy had gripped the green and white half of Lisbon, a crowd of just over 15,300 filing into the nine-year-old Alvalade which was capable of holding 52,400 people. The holders began aggressively and it required a breathtaking piece of defending from Charles to prevent 'the Lions' taking a first-minute lead. Morais's downward header bounced over John and was heading for the back of the net when the Welsh colossus, in the words of the *Western Mail*, "popped up from seemingly nowhere" to head clear from underneath the crossbar.

Dilwyn John: *A corner came in and I foolishly went out of my six-yard box to try and get it. Crosses weren't my forte and I found myself in no man's land. One of their players headed the ball and it bounced over my head. I thought it was a certain goal but from absolutely nowhere John Charles came around the back of me, jumped and headed the ball out. I'd never seen anything like it. It was incredible. I was thinking 'Where did he come from? How did he get there?' How he read the situation I don't know. No other player could have done that.*

Alan Harrington: *John was absolutely tremendous that night. If we got a corner or a free-kick, he would go up for it. As soon as it broke down he was back in defence. To see him running up and down the pitch was unbelievable. He was in his 30s but he never flagged. He was here, there and everywhere. He was telling all the lads what to do and if a Sporting player beat you, there was John always behind you.*

Peter Rodrigues: *Jimmy Scoular felt we needed an extra defender and John was the right man to play sweeper. He had played that role in Italy so he knew the ropes. He wasn't young anymore but he was still a giant with lots of ability. John was quite a figure – upright and barrel-chested. He was dominant at the back in Lisbon and it was nice to have him in our side.*

Scoular's masterplan worked to perfection as his defence frustrated Juca's side and when they did break through, they found John in superb form, the Cardiff-born goalkeeper producing a brilliant save to stop Silva's header. Jeers and whistles seemed to greet every Cardiff touch but an eerie silence engulfed the Alvalade when, just past the half-hour mark, Farrell fired the Bluebirds in front with an inch-perfect strike. The Scot, who had drifted into the middle of the pitch, slipped the ball to Lewis on the right wing. Lewis centred to Tapscott and the former Arsenal player laid the ball back to Farrell who then beat Carvalho with a first-time shot from the edge of the penalty box. The only noise inside the stadium, noted Dewi Lewis in the *Western Mail*, came from the 30-strong travelling contingent which also included the British Midland flight crew that had taken the Division Two outfit to Lisbon.

Greg Farrell: *It was an unbelievable feeling seeing the ball go into the net. I hit it with my right foot and it went straight into the bottom corner. I had a reputation for being left-footed but I could shoot with both feet and my best goals were scored with my right foot. The goal in Lisbon was one of the best of my career but not the best. When I was playing for Bury I scored from the halfway line against Aston Villa. I had a good game in Lisbon and I gave their full-back the runaround. I was taking on their players, they didn't like it and they started coming in with two-footed tackles.*

Sporting pressed for an equaliser in the second-half but John, whose last taste of first-team action had been against Esbjerg, made two more excellent saves to thwart Fernando Pinto and then Mendes. Incredibly, and against the run of play, Tapscott extended Cardiff's lead in the 65th minute with a bizarre second. The striker, about 30 yards from goal and near the right touchline when he received the ball from Farrell, watched his cross-shot squeeze into the net off Carvalho and the post. The stunned Sporting supporters clearly felt Carvalho, who palmed the ball against the upright in a desperate attempt to push it away, was at fault and they jeered the hero of Antwerp as Tapscott and his teammates celebrated. In his 2008 autobiography *Tappy: From Barry Town to Arsenal, Cardiff City and Beyond*, published four years before his death, Tapscott admitted the goal was a fluke. It was not a banana shot inspired by Brazil's finest footballers, rather a mis-hit cross meant for Lewis whom he had spotted making a forward run.

Bernard Lewis: *The second goal was quite funny. We were under loads of pressure but defending quite well. Anyway, we managed to break away. Tappy was going down the right wing and I'm flying down the middle. He was only three or four yards from the touchline. He tried to cross the ball but sliced it and it went in. When he was interviewed later he said, "I could see Bernie Lewis running down the middle but I could also see the 'keeper off his line so I shot for the near post.' I was thinking 'You liar Tappy!' Of course it was supposed to be a cross!*

Alan Harrington: *Tappy was trying to cross the ball but he just hit it wrong. We all called him a lucky bugger when we went over to celebrate but he was saying, 'I've been practising that!' It was really funny. The ball swerved between the 'keeper and the near post and there was no way Tappy could have meant to do that. But it went in and that was the main thing.*

Dilwyn John: *I had a good view of the second goal. The papers called it Tappy's banana shot which made me smile because he wasn't known for scoring from outside the six-yard box. One of the lads whacked the ball forward and it was a case of 'Here you are Tappy, chase that'. We were just trying to relieve pressure, that's all it was, and Tappy tried to keep the ball going. I couldn't believe it when it went in. I could see the ball in the air and their 'keeper scrambling to keep it out. He fell into his net trying to save it. Tappy ran all over the place that night because he was trying to put the Sporting defenders under pressure.*

For the frustrated Sporting players, a miserable season was reaching a nadir and their already-aggressive approach in the second-half turned ugly as they hit Scoular's players with brutal challenges that went unpunished by West German referee Rudolf Kreitlein. A tailor from Bavaria, Kreitlein would later make headlines at the 1966 World Cup after sending off Argentina captain Antonio Rattin in their quarter-final match against England for repeatedly arguing with his decisions. According to Bryan Stiles in the *South Wales Echo*, some of Sporting's challenges were "more suited to the bull ring down the road". Rodrigues, Williams, Farrell and especially Lewis were floored by Portuguese tackles yet Kreitlein refused to stop play so they could receive attention.

Alan Harrington: *The crowd was angry because we were winning and it got nasty. Their players would shove an elbow in your ribs when you walked past them or give you a bang on the leg. If they were walking behind, you'd feel a boot on the back of your leg. It wasn't done in the open, it was done slyly. That was their frustration coming out but we could look after ourselves.*

Don Murray: *Sporting had some good individual players but because the game wasn't going their way they resorted to unsavoury tactics. There were two or three incidents off the ball and there were a couple of spitting incidents as well which wasn't called for at all. They were the holders and we were beating them in their own backyard which they found hard to take. They thought we were going to be a pushover but they discovered that wasn't the case. Before the game John Charles told us the Sporting players would dive and look for penalties and free-kicks, that we had to stay*

on our feet and not dive in. John gave us the experience
we needed in these games because we were so naive.

Boos and derisive whistles announced every Cardiff clearance as an increasingly desperate Sporting tried to launch a fightback. The blue wall held out until nine minutes from the end when Figueiredo smashed an unstoppable shot past John to give Sporting hope. But the Bluebirds were not to be denied and shortly before midnight, and after four minutes of extra time, Kreitlein blew the final whistle. Cardiff, in the bottom half of Division Two, had sensationally beaten the Cup Winners' Cup holders on their own soil. Sporting's furious supporters threw seat cushions onto the stadium's track in disgust.

Bernard Lewis: *I was behind Peter Rodrigues as we ran off the pitch*
and down the tunnel and he was shouting, '£100
wages this week!' We were on a £50 bonus to win that
game which was our pay for a week, or more in some
cases. We didn't hang about when the game finished.
We got off the pitch sharpish, every single one of us.
Nobody took the mickey. We could sense the crowd
was angry and we felt getting to the tunnel quickly
was the right thing to do.

Alan Harrington: *I remember seeing John Charles as we were coming*
off the pitch. We'd just won 2-1 and I noticed tears
streaming down his face. He was crying so I asked him,
'John, what's wrong?' And he said, 'We've won'. He
was really up for that game. We trained at the stadium
before the game. John was never the best trainer but
you could see he was up for this one. His tackling and
distribution were magnificent.

Don Murray:　　*Jimmy used a sweeper system that night with John Charles playing at the back and it worked. Jimmy told me before the game, 'I want you to tackle but there will be times when you don't get the ball – that's when the big man behind you will pick it up'. John made that role look so easy. In the air, nobody could touch him. He headed everything that came into the box, and he showed calmness and authority. Tappy was exceptional in Lisbon too. He ran himself into the ground although his goal was definitely a mis-hit cross. He told us he saw the 'keeper moving out so he bent the ball past him, but we were all convinced he was trying to pick out Bernard Lewis who was making a forward run. All the boys were saying, 'You mis-hit it Tappy! We know you mis-hit it!' But the ball went in and that was brilliant.*

Scoular was ecstatic and afterwards insisted the result was not a fluke but "a carefully planned victory achieved by a tremendous overall team effort". In the dressing room the manager shook hands with every one of his exhausted players and "told them they were marvellous". Farrell had spent the last 25 minutes limping around the Alvalade turf with a thigh injury. "They flogged themselves so much," explained Scoular, "that a number of them were in agony with cramp by the end of the game. They're a team of heroes...it would be totally unfair to single out any player for special mention." As for Juca's players who hoped the Cup Winners' Cup would provide some respite from a dismal domestic campaign, they were left to reflect on a humiliating defeat. "We did not play well or with luck," explained Mendes.

Greg Farrell:　　*When the final whistle went, the crowd couldn't believe it. We couldn't believe it, either. It was one of those games you dream about being involved in. We had beaten the side that had won the trophy the previous year. Back home the next day, we all bought the newspapers and to read about how we beat Sporting Lisbon was an unbelievable feeling. When we arrived at the airport, there were fans waiting for us. They were coming up to shake our hands. It was fantastic.*

Peter Rodrigues: *The hotel where we were staying had these pumpkins in the foyer and before the game Jimmy Scoular said, 'If we win tonight I'm gonna kick one of those'. When we got back to the hotel he was true to his word. He got one of the pumpkins, put it on the floor and gave it a big whack. It disintegrated everywhere. The club directors were coming through the revolving door at the time and pieces of pumpkin went all over them! But they weren't too bothered because of the result.*

Gareth Williams: *We shocked Sporting with the standard of our football that night. Quite a few of our lads played to their full potential because we had nothing to lose and Scoular got us going. He was the boss but he was also part of team, one of the lads. We did turn it on in Europe that year and that win in Lisbon was a great result for the football club, yet in the league we had some shocking results. Really, we should have done better because we had some good players and a nice blend of youth and experience.*

Dilwyn John: *We had a fabulous meal in the hotel after the game. There was a mixture of fish laid out on a big, long table and a crate of champagne. I'd never seen anything like it. We were all on a high and I must admit I got a bit*

*ratted that night. I was sitting next to Bob Wilson
and we both grabbed a bottle of champagne, stuck it
between our legs and took it back to our rooms. But we
were lucky to remain in the hotel because Scoular was
so euphoric about the result he kicked this pumpkin
which splattered everywhere. This was one of the best
hotels in Lisbon and the management weren't happy.
He had to apologise and after that they let us stay.
But Scoular was over the moon with the result. To
beat the holders at their own stadium, it was a real
feather in his cap.*

The Bluebirds returned to Rhoose on Thursday night and
were welcomed at the airport by a crowd of jubilant Cardiff
supporters wanting to pay tribute to Scoular and his 'Lisbon
Lions'. Their performance inside the Alvalade earned praise
from the Press in both countries. *A Bola*, the Lisbon-based
daily sports newspaper, praised the Bluebirds defence and in
particular their imperious 'Gentle Giant'. "What a magnificent
player John Charles is...King John has certainly not lost his
crown." In Wales, the back page of the *Western Mail* read
'MAGNIFICENT CARDIFF CITY STORM TO SENSATIONAL
VICTORY' while the *South Wales Echo* went for 'SPORTING
CRACK AGAINST CITY'S FIGHTING FURIES'. A draw at
Ninian Park would be enough to send Cardiff into the quarter-
finals to play Real Zaragoza who had already completed their
first round tie, beating Dundee 4-3 on aggregate. With UEFA
yet to implement the away-goal rule, Sporting would force a
replay in Madrid on 30 December if they won by a one-goal
margin. If they won by two goals then they, and not Cardiff,
would meet the Spaniards in the last eight. The Primeira Liga
side's preparations were hardly ideal. They flew into London
on the Monday night and travelled to Cardiff by coach, not

arriving in the Welsh capital until the early hours of Tuesday morning.

Cardiff warmed up for the decisive match with a superb 4-0 home win over Plymouth Argyle. Scoular wanted a sharp and alert John for the second leg so he played in goal against the Pilgrims instead of Wilson. He named the same team that won 2-1 in Lisbon. Charles had missed the Plymouth game with a knock picked up in the Alvalade but was declared fit for the rematch. Scoular acknowledged it was "going to be a tough task" to shut out Sporting but felt confident. The *Western Mail*'s Lewis was apprehensive. He had watched the holders train at Ninian Park and noticed their determination and focus. Mendes warned Cardiff that his side would play better at Ninian Park than they did in Lisbon, and Sporting's president, General Martiniano Homem de Figueiredo of the Portuguese Army, was confident his players would progress. "Tonight," he told journalists shortly before kick-off, "we win two-zero."

A crowd of just over 23,000 – Ninian Park's biggest for 16 months – witnessed a tense contest sprinkled with drama. As expected, Sporting pushed forward from the kick-off but once more they were held back by a Welsh barricade. The visitors were restricted to shots from outside the penalty box although they did open up the Cardiff defence twice in the first half, Figueiredo forcing John to make two excellent saves. Scoular's Bluebirds - roared on by supporters chanting 'Cardiff! Cardiff! Cardiff!' and with Hole showing why he was valued at £60,000 with the way he controlled the Bluebirds midfield - created opportunities of their own. Carvalho did well to stop efforts from Lewis, King and Tapscott. The home side should have been awarded a penalty late in the second half when Pedro Gomes handled Farrell's shot but Belgian referee Robert Schaut claimed the defender had cleared the ball with his chest.

As was the case in Lisbon, the tireless Tapscott was again the bane of Sporting, running all night and constantly gnawing away at their defence. The striker even argued with Lew Clayton when the Cardiff trainer beckoned him off so he could treat a cut on the side of his face caused by a clash with Carvalho. "He almost started to fight with me and told me to patch it up," explained Clayton afterwards. Carvalho clearly found the former Wales international an irritant. After flooring Tapscott as they both went for King's cross, the goalkeeper got hold of the striker by his right arm and right leg, picked him up and unceremoniously dropped him behind the Grange End goal line, an act which incensed Tapscott's colleagues, notably Farrell and Williams. Sporting had a chance to level the tie 10 minutes from the end when they were awarded a free-kick in a dangerous position after Murray had fouled Silva, but Pinto shot wide, wasting what proved to be their last opportunity. Aberfan boy Lewis, once an apprentice mechanic, should have settled Welsh nerves in the closing minutes only to tamely side-foot the ball at Carvalho. The miss did not matter. The game ended 0-0 with Cardiff seeing off the Portuguese challenge with what Stiles described as "raw, fighting football". It was the perfect Christmas present for chairman Fred Dewey who could expect another bumper home gate in the next round. As for the General, his pre-match confidence had been misplaced.

Don Murray: *I remember their 'keeper picking Tappy up and just dumping him behind the goal after they both went for the ball! They found it difficult at our place. Ninian was a bit of a fortress for us and it wasn't often we got turned over there. We were strong at home and got the result we deserved. It was great for the Cardiff public.*

Dilwyn John:

We didn't go out thinking 'Let's hold on to what we've got'. We played our own game. To have gone out and just defended our lead would have been the wrong way to go about it. We knocked out the holders and that put Cardiff City on the European map. It also did wonders for Jimmy's managerial career.

Peter King:

The home game was a real cup tie. We were on a £20 bonus to go through which was a big sum in those days. We were the minnows and our hard work saw us through but it wasn't a case of us having to hang on, we gave as good as we got that night. The manager sacrificed Ivor Allchurch so the system was a bit more defensive. Jimmy put me at inside-forward which suited me down to the ground because I could charge around like a headless chicken. I never saw myself as a winger, I was more of a midfield player, but you had to say Jimmy was spot on with his tactics that night. We beat Real Madrid at home in 1971 but, for me, knocking out Sporting Lisbon, especially what we did in Portugal, was Cardiff City's finest hour in Europe.

Schaut's final whistle not only ended Sporting's reign in the competition, it was also the signal for a pitch invasion by jubilant Cardiff supporters and some of Scoular's Bluebirds needed police assistance to reach the tunnel. They then made their way to the director's box to salute the crowd while in another part of the ground Mendes criticised Cardiff's physical approach as well as Schaut's performance. "It was too hard," he said. "The referee let Cardiff tackle very hard." His comments drew a rebuke from Scoular who claimed Sporting's "shirt-pulling, kicking and body checking was far worse".

Champagne was brought into the home dressing room so the players could celebrate what the *Western Mail* called "a great triumph for British soccer", and the Cardiff manager poured the bubbly into teacups. Next stop on this remarkable first European adventure: Zaragoza, Spain.

Greg Farrell: *We had a great game at home and I really enjoyed it. I remember the crowd booing the Sporting players and cheering us which gave all the lads a lift. We did outplay Sporting and they got a fright at our place. They started going into challenges with two feet because they were getting worked up. They were trying to upset us and get us sent off. When the final whistle came I ran off quickly because there was a huge pitch invasion. I went out with a few friends after the game to celebrate but I don't remember anything about it!*

First Round, First Leg
16 December, 1964
Estádio José Alvalade, Lisbon

Sporting Clube de Portugal (0) 1   Cardiff City (1) 2
Figueiredo 81   Farrell 32, Tapscott 67

SPORTING CLUBE: Carvalho, Gomes, Alfredo, Hilário, Mendes, Carlos, Sitoe, Da Silva, Figueiredo, Pinto, Morais.

CARDIFF CITY: John, Harrington, Rodrigues, Charles J, Murray, Williams, Hole, King, Lewis, Tapscott, Farrell.

First Round, Second Leg
23 December, 1964
Ninian Park, Cardiff

Cardiff City (0) 0   Sporting Clube de Portugal (0) 0

CARDIFF CITY: John, Harrington, Rodrigues, Charles J, Murray, Williams, Hole, King, Lewis, Tapscott, Farrell.

SPORTING CLUBE: Carvalho, Gomes, Alfredo, Hilário, Mendes, Carlos, Sitoe, Da Silva, Figueiredo, Pinto, Morais.

(Cardiff City won 2-1 on aggregate)

3

The Magnificos are Coming
Real Zaragoza, 1965

'These continentals have got no stamina for hard battle.'

John Charles

LA ROMAREDA. A stadium located in the south-west of Zaragoza, a city in northern Spain famous for its Moorish and medieval architecture, the capital of the Aragón region. Opened in 1957 and named after the open fields on which it was built, this utilitarian arena was the home of Cardiff's quarter-final opponents, one of the most feared sides in La Liga. Real Zaragoza were enjoying a golden period in their previously undistinguished history when Jimmy Scoular and his squad landed in northern Spain on 19 January, 1965. Since 1961 they had finished every season in the top five. They reached the Copa del Rey final in 1963 only to lose to Barcelona in the Nou Camp. A year later, they reached the final again although this time the ending was different. Atlético Madrid were beaten in the Bernabeu and Real claimed its first piece of silverware. A second Copa del Rey swiftly followed as they defeated Valencia in the final, again at the Nou Camp.

Real were coached by Roque Olsen, an Argentinian in his first year at the club who was known for his strong personality and bad temper. As they prepared for the first leg against the Welsh side, *los Blanquillos* (the White Ones) were challenging for the championship, sitting just a point adrift of leaders Real Madrid in La Liga. Their rise in Spanish football during this period was down mainly to *Los Cinco Magníficos* – The Magnificent Five – a formidable forward line containing Carlos Lapetra, Juan Manuel Villa, Eleuterio Santos, Canário and Marcelino. A right-winger from Brazil, Canário had played for Real Madrid and was part of their European Cup-winning side in 1960 while centre-forward Marcelino, inside-forwards Villa and Lapetra and left-back Severino Reija were all Spanish internationals. Marcelino enjoyed the status of national hero after scoring his country's late winner in the 1964 European Championship final against the Soviet Union and was being linked with a £150,000 move to Italian giants Internazionale, while the quick Lapetra had replaced the legendary Real Madrid player Francisco Gento on Spain's left wing. The Spaniards were blessed with some of Europe's most impressive attacking talent yet Scoular was not unhappy with the draw as he wanted to avoid West Ham United or a side from behind the Iron Curtain. He also knew what to expect since he had a player with first-hand experience of playing against *los Blanquillos*. John Charles had faced the Spanish side three years earlier in the Inter-Cities Fairs Cup while at Roma and netted the fourth goal in a 4-2 win at La Romareda. Charles was centre-forward that night but now, at the heart of Cardiff's defence, he would be expected to prevent goals rather than score them.

Scoular took 14 players to Spain – Bob Wilson, Dilwyn John, Peter Rodrigues, John Charles, Alan Harrington, Don Murray, Gareth Williams, Barrie Hole, Peter King, Bernard Lewis, Greg Farrell, Derek Tapscott, Ivor Allchurch and Graham Coldrick, all of them on a £15 bonus to avoid losing by two goals. Cardiff, though, were not intimidated by Real's impressive record. They arrived in Spain on the back of a 6-1 win over Middlesbrough, the club's biggest league win for eight years, and Wilson's pre-match remark epitomised the new post-Lisbon confidence in the camp. "Zaragoza are a good team," said the goalkeeper, "but our team is good too." Scoular chose the same system that played in Portugal with Charles as sweeper but there was one change to the side that stunned Sporting. Wilson was now eligible to play in the competition and replaced the unlucky John who had made several wonderful saves in the Alvalade.

Peter King: *Zaragoza were a good team and they had these players who were known as 'The Magnificent Five'. They were a better team than us but beating Sporting Lisbon had given us a tremendous amount of confidence. We weren't overwhelmed by Zaragoza. It was fantastic to play a side like that. Their players were so quick, and they were all flicks with great vision. It was a challenge, both physically and mentally.*

Don Murray: *Everyone was talking about their forwards. John Charles had played against them when he was at Roma and he mentioned these forwards to us before the game. He told us how quick and dangerous they were. Zaragoza were flying high in the Spanish league at the time but we had beaten the side that had put Manchester United to the sword the previous season and that gave us the belief we could do something in the competition.*

Scoular managed to annoy the Spaniards before a ball had been kicked. The club had arranged a reception for the Scot and his players the night before the game. Scoular, though, refused to cancel a training session and kept the Real dignitaries waiting for more than an hour. According to director Viv Dewey, the hosts were "certainly very shirty" about the delay but the Cardiff manager defended his conduct. "What do they think this is, a social jaunt? We've come here to play football, not to go to drinking parties."

There was some positive news before the first leg. Scoular's defence would only have to contend with four *magnificos* rather than five since Villa was out with a knee injury. He would be replaced by José Maria Encontra. Scoular's strategy at La Romareda would be the same one that had served the Bluebirds so well against Sporting, a six-man defence to absorb pressure and four attacking players – King, Farrell, Lewis and Tapscott – looking to land a sucker punch. But after just one minute his battle plan started to disintegrate. Williams conceded a needless free-kick and Lapetra fired his 20-yard effort over the Cardiff defenders and into the top corner of Wilson's goal. Real continued to attack. Wilson made a spectacular save to deny Lapetra his second of the night and Charles blocked Canário's goal-bound shot. It was only a temporary reprieve. Antonio Pais, a wing-half, doubled the lead in the 12th minute with a strike from outside the penalty area and it seemed the Zaragoza public's pre-match prediction, that Olsen's side would win by four goals, would be proved correct.

Dilwyn John: *I remember watching that game and when they went 2-0 up I thought 'Crikey, there's a cricket score coming here'. I did think we were going to take a right hammering. Their left-winger (Lapetra) was outstanding. He was tearing us to pieces and going past people at will. They looked a very good side. Their passing, control and movement were better than ours.*

Greg Farrell: *The start of that game was quite frightening. We were 2-0 down early on and I don't think I had even touched the ball. It was all Zaragoza and they were making us run around in circles. I did fear the worst when they made it 2-0. We were on the ropes and I just couldn't get into the game.*

Bernard Lewis: *We knew Zaragoza were a good team and that they were one of the top teams in Spain but we didn't expect to be 2-0 down so early on. I must admit I was really worried when they got a second. They had these great players up front and it looked as if they were going to put six or seven past us.*

Cardiff appeared to be heading for a horrible defeat but, four minutes after Pais's thunderbolt, they cut the deficit with Williams atoning for his first-minute foul by heading Farrell's cross past Enrique Yarza. "I must have jumped six feet when I saw my header going into the net," said the Bluebirds skipper afterwards. Amazingly, Cardiff equalised shortly before half-time. Farrell, discovering he was able to dominate Reija, was again the provider, this time for King who had scored his first league hat-trick only five days earlier in that win over Middlesbrough.

Peter King: *It was a header from close range and after it went in I fell like a sack of spuds and rolled over. Gareth Williams came up to me and shook my hand. There was complete silence inside the stadium because we had come back from 2-0 down. It was a deathly hush. We didn't have any fans there, it was all Zaragoza supporters.*

Barrie Hole: *I think we were all scared when they scored their second. For a while they were playing around with us. They were a quality team and they were better than us but we kept going and then they let their guard down. Our first goal silenced the crowd and Zaragoza became a bit nervous after that. It was our spirit that kept us in the game. We had gone 2-0 down in no time at all but we took them on, we didn't fall apart.*

Alan Harrington: *I'm pretty sure Zaragoza thought the game was over when it was 2-0. They thought it was going to be an easy night. They had the crowd behind them and we were chasing shadows. But they wouldn't shut up shop, they wanted to hammer us, and that allowed us to get back into the game.*

Bob Wilson: *We got to our dressing room at half-time but found the door had been locked so we couldn't get inside. It was gamesmanship. We'd come back from being 2-0 down and Zaragoza were trying to annoy us. Jimmy Scoular wasn't the type to mess about and he just kicked the door open with his foot!*

The Bluebirds repelled Real's *magníficos* in a second-half dominated by the Spanish side and the home crowd shouted *gamberros!* (hooligans!) each time a Cardiff player put in a hard tackle, although they did pay tribute to the visitors' indomitable spirit at the end by applauding Scoular's charges off the pitch. Wilson and Charles had played a pivotal role in the 2-2 draw. The goalkeeper made two terrific saves in the closing minutes which, wrote Lewis in the *Western Mail*, "brought the sporting Spanish crowd to their feet" while the Spanish daily, *El Noticiero*, described the 21-year-old from Birmingham as "the grand player for Cardiff". Charles was again immense with the Zaragoza-based newspaper, *Heraldo de Aragon*, saying he "played with perfect authority" and according to Bryan Stiles in the *South Wales Echo*, the former Juventus star was "the rock upon which wave after wave of Real attacks floundered".

Bob Wilson: *Canário tried to get me sent off. There were about 15 minutes to go and we were trying to kill time. I was rolling the ball to a defender who then passed it back to me. I'd pick it up – which you could do back then – and I'd roll it to someone else who did the same thing. Canário then stood right in front of me. I laughed so he tried to wind me up. He was looking for me to react. If I'd hit him I would have been sent off but I just laughed again and carried on. That game was one of the best of my career. I made some decent saves and the Spanish Press gave me a good write-up. One of my friends spoke Spanish and he translated a newspaper report for me. It said that I'd played well.*

Don Murray: *The game in Zaragoza was the best I ever saw John Charles play for Cardiff. We were 2-0 down early on and under the cosh. Then John actually started playing them on his own. He was absolutely tremendous, unbelievable. If it wasn't for him we would have been 9-0 down. He never stopped running, he won everything in the air, he won every tackle and he pushed us on when we were under the cosh. And this was a man coming to the end of his career. I came off the field totally in awe of him.*

Scoular was unable to contain his delight at the result. He walked onto the pitch at the final whistle to shake hands with his players and arranged a champagne party for them after the game. "Real Zaragoza are a great team," he explained, "and how my lads came back to draw 2-2 after being two goals down in the first 12 minutes had to be seen to be believed. This proves the win in Lisbon was no fluke. They (Real Zaragoza) are undoubtedly one of the best teams in Europe." His chairman, Fred Dewey, who was unable to make the trip to Spain, described hearing the result as "one of the happiest moments of my life". Scoular pointed to Williams' goal as the turning point in the game, claiming it showed his players that Zaragoza "were not unbeatable".

Peter Rodrigues: *It was my 21ˢᵗ birthday the day after the game so that made the result even sweeter. To come back from 2-0 down and leave with a 2-2 draw was fantastic and this was against a better side than Sporting Lisbon. Jimmy Scoular was upbeat, he was never down, and that transferred to the players. He was a good motivator and he got us up for that game in Zaragoza.*

Bob Wilson: *Before going to the airport to catch the flight back we went out to find somewhere to eat as we were still in Zaragoza at lunchtime. We found a bar-restaurant place near our hotel in the city centre. The locals inside noticed we were Cardiff City players and had played Real the night before. They came up and started shaking our hands and patting us on the backs which I thought was nice of them. They wanted to talk about the game and I think they were impressed with what we'd done.*

THE MAGNIFICOS ARE COMING

Gareth Williams: *We were 2-0 down in no time. I thought to myself 'What have we let ourselves in for?' We were in Zaragoza, playing in a big stadium in the quarter-finals of the Cup Winners' Cup and I think that got to us. Everyone thought we were down and out when they got the second goal but, fair play to the lads, they played really well after that. Without a doubt, we upped our game and I got a goal and Peter King got another. The result was no fluke. We could have pinched a winner in the second half but we were all chuffed with 2-2. We had a good night in Zaragoza after the game - and a few too many beers!*

The Bluebirds returned to Rhoose the following night and arrived home to both a blizzard and a heroes' reception. Zaragoza had *Los Cinco Magníficos* but, according to the *South Wales Echo*, Cardiff had *Los Once Magníficos* – 'The Magnificent Eleven'. The advantage was now with Scoular's side with the Spaniards certain to encounter a huge and vocal Ninian Park crowd a fortnight later. Real arrived in South Wales via Barcelona and London, with Marcelino and Joaquin Cortizo both included in Olsen's squad despite being suspended in Spain. Four days after the first leg Marcelino was sent off during a 3-1 defeat at Atlético Madrid following a clash with defender Manuel Etura, and was hit with a six-match suspension. As for Cortizo, the right-back was serving a 24-game ban – the most severe suspension in Spanish football history – for a tackle on Enrique Collar which left the Atlético Madrid player with a broken leg. Real claimed the duo could play at Ninian Park because the bans only applied to domestic fixtures and Hans Bangerter, the General Secretary of UEFA, confirmed they were eligible to play in European competition as the Royal Spanish Football Federation had not notified UEFA of

45

their suspensions. "Very often," explained Bangerter, "national associations consider a suspension to be valid only on their national level." Ironically, Cortizo would play a crucial role in the second-leg result.

Scoular named the same side which had silenced La Romareda while Olsen made two changes with Cortizo replacing the moody José 'Pepin' Cuéllar and out-of-form Encontra making way for Santiago Isasi, an all-action wing-back nicknamed 'the Machine'. Another draw and the two sides would travel to Nice for a play-off but a crowd of nearly 38,500 – Cardiff's biggest for four years – sensed another Herculean victory for the Second Division strugglers. The Cardiff players stood to claim a £50 bonus if they beat the Spaniards and reached the last four, and £40 if they forced a play-off on the French Riviera.

Barrie Hole:	*There was a tremendous atmosphere at Ninian Park that night. I've never forgotten it. There were nearly 40,000 people there with real excitement in the air. We fancied our chances and we really went for it. We played well – better than we did in Zaragoza. The crowd was behind us and we were really going for it. The Zaragoza players showed us more respect after what we had done in the first game.*
Greg Farrell:	*We were playing better in the Cup Winners' Cup than we were playing in the league. We were in the bottom half of the table yet we were getting these great results in Europe. When it came to the Cup Winners' Cup, we raised our game. We were the underdogs and that lifted all the players. We had nothing to lose.*

The home side created enough chances in the first half to pile the pressure on the Copa del Rey holders but they failed to beat Yarza. Williams went closest to scoring, his header beating Real's goalkeeper but not Cortizo who cleared off the line. King also had a glorious chance to put the Welsh Cup winners in front but headed straight at Yarza. Real were not entirely dormant in the opening 45 minutes and Wilson did well to stop Marcelino's close-range effort after a quick raid led by Canário. It was Canário who decided a scrappy game with a piece of South American magic 17 minutes from time. The 32-year-old dispossessed Rodrigues and darted towards goal. He fooled the Cardiff defence with a dummy before beating Wilson with a clinical finish. After Olsen's side broke the stalemate, Scoular, in a desperate attempt to snatch an equaliser, moved Charles from defence to attack but not even the former Juventus hero could secure a play-off in the south of France.

Real were relatively comfortable in the second half and in Lapetra – "a veritable will-o'-the-wisp" - they had the game's outstanding performer. Scoular's two wing men, Farrell and Lewis, were unable to make a mark on the second leg and Tapscott, who tried hard to unsettle Yarza by shoulder-charging the Spaniard, was shackled by the powerful centre-half Francisco Santamaria. Cardiff were not helped by an injury to Williams, forced to hobble through most of the second period after being hacked down by the midfielder nicknamed 'the Lion', José Luis Violeta. "I was nowhere near the ball when this Spaniard just let fly at me, kicking me on the side of the knee," complained Cardiff's captain after the game. Cardiff were out and, said Stiles, had only themselves to blame. "In Spain they set up two chances and scored from both of them. Last night they made five and missed the lot." Scoular thought his players had done enough to earn a play-off. "We missed chances in the first half and paid the penalty," he remarked.

Peter King: *Scoular had a real go at John Charles after the game because he was sold a dummy for the goal. The guy looked as if he was going wide and John went that way. He then came inside and there was now a big gap in our defence. John had tried to read the situation and went completely the wrong way. Jimmy felt that with all his experience John should have done better. He really laid into John, it was the first time he'd had a go at him and John just took it all. Zaragoza's class told in the end. They were technically superior with great vision and we were trying to break that with our work ethic.*

Alan Harrington: *We thought we'd do it at Cardiff. We fancied our chances at Ninian, just one goal and we were in the semi-final. Before the game we told the wives to go to the Royal Hotel when it was over and we'd meet them there for drinks. We still went for a drink even though we'd lost. We had a pleasant time because our wives were with us, it's just that there was no singing and dancing which would have been the case had we gone through. It was a real dampener to get so close and then lose it.*

Don Murray: *We took the game to Real at Ninian Park, they didn't batter us like they did in Spain. We created a few chances in the first half but we didn't convert them. We thought we'd done the hard part by drawing over there and that we'd do Zaragoza at Ninian Park but, unfortunately, it didn't work out that way. If I'm being honest, they just shaded it over two legs.*

Gareth Williams: *We really fancied our chances at Ninian Park. We thought we were heading for the semi-final. We were all confident and we knew we'd have the crowd behind us. We were also playing quite well at the time. We could have been two or three goals up at half-time but we didn't take our chances. Then we made a mistake and they scored. It was a heartbreaking way to go out and Scoular had a go at John Charles about the goal. John was at fault and Scoular lost it with him. That was Scoular. He said what he felt and he wasn't one for beating about the bush, but none of the players blamed John. We we were all behind him. It was a sad night but we'd had a good run.*

Real and their *magnificos* were beaten in the semi-finals by eventual winners West Ham United, losing 3-2 on aggregate. Cardiff went on to finish 13th in Division Two, losing only three of their last dozen fixtures, and beating Wrexham in the Welsh Cup final to secure another crack at the Cup Winners' Cup. The quarter-final exit at the hands of *los Blanquillos* was the catalyst for change at Ninian Park. Within 24 hours of the defeat Allchurch, Trevor Peck, John, Steve Gammon and Mel Charles were all placed on the transfer list. The Scoular revolution had begun.

Bernard Lewis: *I was sick about the result in the dressing room. We knew we were in with a chance at home but we just couldn't score. In all honesty, we weren't good enough. They were a better side, we all knew that, and over the two games they deserved to go through. We knew we weren't going to win the cup. We had beaten Sporting Lisbon but we weren't going to beat everybody in the competition.*

Quarter-final, First Leg
20 January, 1965
Estadio La Romerada, Zaragoza

Real Zaragoza (2) 2   **Cardiff City (2) 2**
Lapetra 1, Pais 12   Williams 16, King 41

REAL ZARAGOZA: Yarza, Cuéllar, Eija, Violeta, Santamaria, Pais, Canário, Santos, Marcelino, Lapetra, Encontra.

CARDIFF CITY: Wilson, Harrington, Rodrigues, Charles J, Murray, Hole, Farrell, Williams, Tapscott, King, Lewis.

Quarter-final, Second Leg
3 February, 1965
Ninian Park, Cardiff

Cardiff City (0) 0   **Real Zaragoza (0) 1**
                               Canário 73

CARDIFF CITY: Wilson, Harrington, Rodrigues, Charles J, Murray, Hole, Farrell, Williams, Tapscott, King, Lewis.

REAL ZARAGOZA: Yarza, Cortizo, Eija, Violeta, Santamaria, Pais, Canário, Santos, Marcelino, Lapetra, Encontra.

(Real Zaragoza won 3-2 on aggregate)

4

Black and Blue
Standard Liège, 1965

'Nobody gives us a cat in hell's chance.'

Jimmy Scoular

In 1965 Standard Liège were regarded as the scourge of British clubs, a reputation built on European Cup victories over two Scottish sides. Heart of Midlothian had been brushed aside in a 1958 qualifying round tie and, four years later, Rangers were dispatched in the quarter-finals. Both sides were crushed inside the intimidating Stade de Sclessin, Hearts losing 5-1 and Rangers 4-1. Now the Belgians were eyeing a third British scalp after being paired with Cardiff in the 1965-66 Cup Winners' Cup. It was certainly an unkind first-round draw for Jimmy Scoular and his players. Standard were champions of Belgium as recently as 1963 and had a decent record in European competition, reaching the last eight of the European Cup in 1959 and the semi-finals three years later.

Standard had been ousted by Anderlecht as the country's dominant side. The Brussels club won the title in 1963 and 1964 before clinching 'the double' the following year, beating their rivals from Liège in the Belgian Cup final. As league champions, Anderlecht entered the European Cup so as runners-up *les Rouches* (the Reds) were given the Cup Winners' Cup slot. Standard were still very much a force with 11 internationals on their payroll. Nine players had represented Belgium while inside-forward Velimir Naumović played for Yugoslavia and wing-half Louis Pilot was captain of Luxembourg. Jean Nicolay was Belgium's undisputed number one goalkeeper and was named the best player in the Belgian first division in 1963, winning the *Soulier d'Or* (the Golden Boot) while Léon Semmeling, a skilful right-winger, was being linked with clubs in Spain and Italy. The star of the side, however, was 23-year-old Roger Claessen, the bad boy of Belgian football. Claessen was a supremely gifted forward – strong, two-footed, good in the air and blessed with excellent technique. But his behaviour away from football – a liking for Liège's bars and nightclubs, and also the city's red light district - earned him the nickname *Roger la Honte* (Roger the Shame). Claessen also had a volatile temperament on the pitch and often clashed with officials. He was hit with a six-month ban for throwing mud at the referee during the cup final defeat against Anderlecht but was eligible to play in the Cup Winners' Cup because the Royal Belgian Football Association had not notified UEFA of his suspension.

Ninian Park would stage the first leg on 8 September and, following Cardiff's impressive European displays the previous season, expectations among the South Wales public were naturally high. Scoular, though, was fully aware of Standard's power and experience. "This will be as hard as the Zaragoza game," he warned his players before the first meeting. There had been several departures since the Real Zaragoza defeat. Ivor Allchurch had rejoined Swansea Town, Derek Tapscott had moved to Newport County and Keith Ellis had left for Lincoln City, while Mel Charles, Trevor Peck and Steve Gammon dropped into non-league football. Scoular had made only one major signing during the summer, Northern Irish forward Terry Harkin from Crewe Alexandra for £12,000.

Standard chose the seaside resort of Porthcawl as their South Wales base, their coach Milorad Pavić preferring to stay well away from the Welsh capital. "We didn't want to stay in a big city," explained the Yugoslav, a German prisoner during the Second World War. "We wanted to be where the atmosphere is invigorating." Before travelling to South Wales, Standard had only played one league game, a 2-2 draw against Antwerp, while the Cardiff players already had five league matches under their belts. Another concern for Pavić was the absence of Belgian international Paul Van Den Berg, his stylish inside-forward, ruled out with a thigh injury. Apart from two new faces, the side Scoular named to take on the Belgians was virtually the same one which had faced Sporting Lisbon and Real Zaragoza the previous season. George Johnston was now a first-team regular and the 18-year-old from Glasgow was quick to make an impact at inside-forward, scoring four goals in the first six games of the season, two coming from the penalty spot. Harkin was also handed his European debut but Scoular was missing Peter King, scorer of two crucial goals in the last Cup Winners' Cup campaign, who was out with an ankle injury. John Charles was now being used as a centre-forward and 'King John' was certainly enjoying a fruitful spell, scoring four goals in the opening five fixtures.

The Bluebirds' results at the start of 1965-66, however, had been erratic. They won the first two games, against Bury and Derby County at Ninian Park, before losing at Norwich City. They hammered Derby 5-1 at the Baseball Ground but then lost 4-1 at home against Wolverhampton Wanderers. Defensively, the Bluebirds were brittle, leaking nine goals, so for the Standard clash Scoular drafted in the experienced right-back, Alan Harrington, at the expense of young Graham

Coldrick. Bob Wilson was in goal, Don Murray – nursing an ankle injury and needing a painkilling injection to play - was at centre-half and Peter Rodrigues at left-back. Gareth Williams and Barrie Hole were the wing-halves with Greg Farrell and Bernard Lewis on the wings.

Bob Wilson: *We were at home for the first leg and, to be honest, we were a side that preferred to play the first game away and the second at home. The plan was to go away, stick the flag down and try and take a result back to Ninian Park. That's what we did in our previous European games but we couldn't do that against Standard Liège. We had to try and do it the other way round.*

Don Murray: *We knew it would be a tougher first game than the one we had against Esbjerg the previous season. Standard Liège were a much better side because the Belgian league was on a different level compared to the Danish one. They also had a player up front called Claessen who was a Belgian international and had a reputation for being a top player. He had been missing for a while but came back for the games against us.*

The onus was on Cardiff to attack and, after an early scare which saw Wilson save from Claessen, they duly delivered, taking the lead after half-an-hour. Inevitably, the goalscorer was Johnston. Farrell chipped the ball to Charles who was foiled by Nicolay but the loose ball dropped to the Scottish teenager who smashed it home although Standard equalised three minutes after the interval through Claessen.

George Johnston: *It was a great feeling to score in a European game. Most of the fans were expecting me to score that night because I was on a run. They would sing 'Give us a goal Georgie!' Up until Christmas I was in good form. Everything I touched seemed to end up in the back of the net. I scored 19 goals before Christmas that season, but after that the goals dried up. I don't know what happened.*

Terry Harkin: *I was overwhelmed by the occasion and I did OK, not great. I wasn't a confident player and I was nervous before every game. I didn't go out thinking I was as good as anybody else, it wasn't in my nature. I always went out with that wee bit of fear I was going to find it hard. I seemed to have an inferiority complex which held me back. I would look at George Johnston who was a confident lad and think 'I wish I had his confidence.' I always felt other players were better than me and that was one of my failings. All the coaching in the world couldn't have changed that because it was part of my make-up as a person. My mother was shy and quiet so I probably got it off her.*

Standard's aggression combined with Janus Aalbrecht's ineptitude soured the second-half. The Dutch referee almost lost control of the contest nine minutes after the interval when Jacques Beurlet chopped down Rodrigues who was sprinting down the left flank. The foul sparked an ugly melee. "Players rushed to the scene...pandemonium reigned," wrote Peter Jackson in the *South Wales Echo*. While Lew Clayton treated the stricken Rodrigues, scuffles broke out as Aalbrecht struggled to assert his authority. Even Charles, the 'Gentle Giant', angrily confronted the Belgians and ended up being shoved to the ground.

Peter Rodrigues: *It was a physical game and that showed the type of league Belgium had in those days. The Standard Liège players were fairly strong guys and a few of their tackles went awry. It built up and the game became tetchy. One of their players tackled me and it all kicked off. I couldn't really see what was going on because I was lying on the ground! We'd got a reputation after what we'd achieved the previous season and maybe their plan was to intimidate and put us off our stride.*

George Johnston: *There were a few hard challenges going in and then there was a bad one on Peter Rodrigues which caused a mass brawl down at the Grange End. There was a bit of fisticuffs with a few players throwing punches. Greg Farrell was involved and one or two others. I was a young kid so I kept away but it was quite ugly and at one point it looked as if it would get out of control. It was a tough game and I took a few knocks. They put a man-marker on me – he was a big, blond lad - and he roughed me up a bit. It was petty stuff like blocking and pushing. He knew I was a youngster and he got into me.*

Bernard Lewis: *There was a ruck at Ninian Park. All hell broke loose and everybody wanted to fight. I was involved at the beginning. I was 20 at the time and I lost my cool but I think everyone lost their cool. I got away from it by running over to the corner flag where the ball was. I thought it would help to try and get the game going again but the ruck took about five or six minutes to sort out.*

In the 68th minute, Standard showed their inventive side by scoring a second, Semmeling's header beating Wilson. But to maintain their lead, Pavić's men resorted to cynicism and Scoular's charges were, according to Jackson in the *South Wales Echo*, "too often kicked, shoved and stopped by Belgian boots and bodies". Aalbrecht's performance was heavily criticised after the game with the *Western Mail*'s Lewis blaming his "ignorance of the obstruction law" for the Welsh side losing their grip on the first leg. Standard's defence was rarely troubled in the second half. Harkin and Farrell never got into the game while Lucien Spronck bullied Charles out of it. The Flemish-speaking centre-half incurred the wrath of the Ninian Park crowd with his roughhouse tactics and needed a police escort off the pitch at the end.

Greg Farrell: *They were a better team than us but some of their tackles were unbelievable. They were hard that night and I had my right leg taken from me a few times. The referee didn't help us and some of their players got away with murder. In the dressing room after the game we were all talking about the way Standard Liège had played.*

Don Murray: *It was a bad-tempered game and there were a lot of nasty tackles flying about. There was one on Peter Rodrigues which was particularly bad and even John got involved. He wasn't known as the 'Gentle Giant' for nothing - he never lost his cool – but he certainly did that night. At the time the game was far more physical so you had to look after yourself. Some teams would try and rough you up and Standard were more physical than I thought they would be. That said, we didn't play particularly well.*

Scoular had to wait six weeks for the second leg in Liège and a change in the UEFA rulebook meant a 1-0 win for the Bluebirds would see them exit the competition rather than force a play-off at a neutral venue. The governing body had now introduced the away-goal rule for rounds before the quarter-finals so if the aggregate score was level after two games then the side that scored more goals away from home would go through. This meant Cardiff had to win by at least 2-0 in the Stade de Sclessin if they were to progress to the next round where Liverpool, who had just dumped Juventus out of the competition, were waiting.

The odds were heavily stacked against the Division Two club. Since the first-leg defeat Cardiff's league form had nosedived alarmingly, losing five out of seven games and conceding 21 goals, a run that plunged them into a relegation fight. To add to Scoular's problems, he had to plot Standard's downfall without his captain, Williams, who was out with a broken cheekbone. Nor could he select new striker George Andrews, spotted playing non-league football in the West Midlands, as he was signed after the UEFA deadline. Wilson's performance in the last league game before the trip to Belgium, a 2-1 home defeat against Portsmouth, also concerned Scoular who considered reinstating Dilwyn John. Wilson was at fault for Pompey's first, scored by Ray Hiron after Albert McCann's long-range shot bounced off the goalkeeper's chest. As if the Scot did not have enough to worry about, Hole had picked up an ankle injury in that game making him doubtful for the return leg. So important was the Wales international to Cardiff that he would be taken to Belgium and receive treatment at the squad's base in Spa, a town in the Ardennes that claimed to be the world's oldest health resort.

Struggling for numbers, Scoular turned to youth. Forward John Toshack, 16, and wing-half David Houston, 17, were called up for Cup Winners' Cup duty despite never kicking a ball for the first team while 18-year-old David Summerhayes - who only made his league debut on the opening day of the season as Cardiff's first-ever substitute - was told he would be flying to Liège. With 18-year-old Johnston and 19-year-old Murray also in the squad, the 14-strong Cardiff contingent heading to Belgium contained five teenagers. Scoular dropped the out-of-sorts Harkin who stayed behind to play in a reserve fixture against Shrewsbury Town. "He wanted to play in the reserves...I don't think he's playing well enough to have been included for the Liège game," admitted the Cardiff manager. There was, however, one piece of good news for the Bluebirds chief. King had shaken off his injury and was ready to play at the Stade de Sclessin.

John Toshack: *One of the other young lads at the club, David Houston, came to my school, Cantonian High, and told me I was going to Belgium! I'd never been on an aeroplane let alone been abroad so I didn't have a passport. I needed to get one of these 12-month passports which my dad had to sign. He was working on a building site somewhere and I spent a good couple of hours looking for him. I couldn't find him so in the end I had to forge his signature. To be part of a Cup Winners' Cup squad at 16 was great. I'd never played for the first team, I was on the groundstaff and playing for the Football Combination side.*

David Summerhayes: *We had a few injuries before the game in Liège and Scoular needed to fill the plane so he took a few of the youngsters over. That's the only reason I went. I doubt I would have gone otherwise. Gareth*

59

> *Williams was injured, he needed someone to take*
> *his place, and he gave the job to me. I was just 18*
> *at the time and I'd made only three appearances for*
> *the first team so the whole experience was new.*

Cardiff's choice of Spa, an attractive town 22 miles outside Liège, as their Belgian headquarters made sense. Surrounded by forests, rivers and springs, the 'Pearl of the Ardennes' guaranteed the players serenity and relaxation ahead of their Liège showdown. Scoular knew another monumental Cup Winners' Cup effort was required if Cardiff were to cause an upset and defeat – by two clear goals - a Standard side "capable of beating many of our First Division teams". Nevertheless, Scoular remained positive, pointing to the win in Lisbon 10 months earlier as evidence his side could upset the odds. However, chaos engulfed the Cardiff camp when three players – Johnston, Lewis and Toshack – were thrown into a police cell on the eve of the game. Johnston and Lewis were down to start against Standard. The group left the hotel for an afternoon walk, stopping at a café for "a sandwich and a coke". Angered by the costly bill, Johnston threw a chair into a lake, an act which resulted in the three Bluebirds being taken to a police station. "I don't think I've ever been as frightened in my life as I was then," Toshack later recalled. After what was described as "frantic negotiations" between Scoular and the local police, the trio was eventually released in the early hours.

Bernard Lewis: *We were in this big park in Spa and, for some stupid*
reason, George threw a chair into a lake. About 10
minutes later the police arrived. I remember seeing a
bloke on the phone just after the chair had been thrown
into the water and he was probably calling the police.
We were put into this vehicle, which looked like a Land

> *Rover, and then taken to a police station where we were put in a cell. We decided to stick together. When the police officer asked who chucked the chair into the lake, we all put our hands up. He said, 'Three chairs was it?' We told him, 'No, only one!' Scoular and the secretary, Graham Keenor, came to the station and sorted it out. They let us go but Scoular was really angry with us, as you can imagine.*

George Johnston: *I threw a chair into this pool and me and a couple of the other players ended up being taken to a police station. I was scared because I'd thrown the chair into the water but the lads didn't say which of us had done it. We were given a warning about our behaviour and let off with a caution. I was a young boy at the time and didn't think throwing a chair into water was such a big deal. Scoular wasn't too pleased about what happened but the whole thing didn't affect us. We played quite well on the night. To be honest, by the time the game started, I'd forgotten all about the previous day.*

Wilson kept his place in goal, despite his shaky display the previous weekend. Harrington, making his 338th appearance for his home club, was at right-back with Murray at centre-half and Rodrigues at left-back. In front of them were Summerhayes and Hole, the latter picked after being given a painkilling injection. Johnston and King were the inside-forwards with Farrell and Lewis on the wings and Charles up front.

They faced a Standard side which boasted a superb European record at home – they had won seven out of eight games inside the Stade de Sclessin - and which had been strengthened by the return of Van Den Berg.

Peter Rodrigues: *We really believed we could turn it around in Belgium. We forgot about the first leg. That result didn't matter anymore. As far as we were concerned the second game was a fresh start. We went over there looking to prove a point. We were going to give it a real go in Liège. Jimmy Scoular was a strong and forceful manager and wouldn't have it any other way.*

David Summerhayes: *Standard Liège's stadium was impressive. I remember the coach driving through gates into an outer ring and going past football pitches and baseball courts which people were playing on. It was a real eye-opener. You could only be impressed with their facilities. It certainly wasn't like the grounds we had back home. There was quite an atmosphere inside the stadium. It was a large crowd and the stands were very steep which meant the fans were right on the pitch. Standard were a big side. The guy I was up against was only a young lad but he was massive. He was practically looking down on me.*

Scoular had ordered his Bluebirds "to go all-out for goals" and they attacked Standard from the start. In a first half dominated by the visitors, Nicolay made an acrobatic save to deny Johnston, and King and Charles both went close with headers. A Rodrigues free-kick then flew just wide before Standard's goalkeeper saved from Lewis. Standard fought back in the second half and James Storme – nicknamed James Bond - missed an open goal before ending the Welsh side's brave challenge early on in the second half when he headed Semmeling's cross past Wilson. As was the case at Ninian

Park the game had a physical edge but, unlike the first leg, there were no ugly scenes. Cardiff faded towards the end and were not helped by a knee injury to Charles, who was again shackled by Spronk. The striker jarred his right knee after colliding with Joseph Vliers which reduced him to the role of a hobbling passenger for the final 10 minutes. Cardiff's gallant performance did not go unnoticed and as they left the pitch at the end they received a standing ovation by the Liège crowd. "If Cardiff had played at home the way they played here, they could have won the tie easily," said Pavić in the Standard dressing room afterwards. Scoular was understandably disappointed with the result but pleased with the performance. "We should have won...we had the chances and, apart from the first eight minutes, the better of the first half."

George Johnston: *I had a chance in the first half and their 'keeper made a great save. It was a half-volley and it was going in the right-hand corner but the 'keeper got a hand to it and pushed it behind the post. I think it was the only chance I had and if that had gone in it might have been a different game. We played well and should have beaten them. Jimmy Scoular was over the moon with our performance. He told us to go out, enjoy ourselves and do what we were capable of. That's what we did. He was so disappointed we lost but he said he was proud of all of us. We played so well we even surprised ourselves. We were unlucky out there.*

Bernard Lewis: *I had a row with their full-back which lasted the whole game. He kept kicking me on the back of my legs. It was the worst game I played in for that. A lot of stuff was happening off the ball like kicking and shoving. I was calling the full-back everything but he couldn't understand what I was saying so when we had a corner I purposely kicked him as the ball came in. He started chasing me as I was back-peddling to the halfway line. I made sure I got back to the dressing room pretty quickly at the end of that game.*

Bob Wilson: *We went out after the game and tried to get into a nightclub. We asked this guy on the door about getting in. I'm not sure if he was speaking French or Flemish but he said something and John Charles became irate. There was a bit of finger-pointing and they went nose-to-nose. A few words were exchanged and we moved off somewhere else. We were wearing our Cardiff City suits so the guy knew who we were and he was upping the price for us to go into the club.*

Standard's winning streak against British clubs came to an abrupt halt in the next round with Bill Shankly's Liverpool comfortably dispatching the Belgians, winning 5-2 on aggregate. As for Cardiff, the impressive display in Liège proved illusory and the Bluebirds spent the rest of a traumatic season fighting relegation, eventually finishing 20th and avoiding the drop by a single point. The nadir was undoubtedly a shocking 9-0 defeat at Preston North End in the penultimate fixture, a defeat which prompted a furious Scoular to snarl, "If I were a Cardiff City player, I'd be ashamed to walk down the street." There was also misery in the Welsh Cup, Cardiff losing their passport to Europe after being beaten by Swansea Town in a fifth-round replay at Ninian Park. The defeat at the Stade de Sclessin turned out to be Charles' last game for the club and also his last in professional football. Cardiff hoped the 33-year-old would recover in a month but, despite undergoing knee surgery in January 1966, the finest footballer produced by Wales never regained full fitness and he was given a free transfer at the end of the season, later joining Southern League Premier Division club Hereford United as player-manager.

Barrie Hole:

It was a hard game and the Standard Liège players were a bit naughty. They were quite feisty. I wasn't wearing shin pads and when I came off the pitch I had a look at my shin - it was covered in stud marks and needed stitches. I ended up missing the next game (at Bolton). We were a bit miffed about how physical the Belgians had been.

Peter King:

I was absolutely knackered after the game in Liège because I'd been injured and hadn't trained so much. There was a massage table in the middle of our dressing room and when I got back in I just lay on it. I was whacked. Viv Dewey then came in, saw me lying on the table and said, 'You're not injured again!' I told him I was all right and just needed to lie down because I was so tired. Standard were quite physical. It was a steel-making city and that seemed to rub off on them. We were disappointed to go out in the first round. I was gutted because I loved the excitement of European matches.

First Round, First Leg
8 September, 1965
Ninian Park, Cardiff

Cardiff City (1) **Standard Liège (0) 2**
Johnston 31 Claessen 48, Semmeling 68

CARDIFF CITY: Wilson, Harrington, Rodrigues, Williams, Murray, Hole, Farrell, Johnston, Charles J, Harkin, Lewis.

STANDARD LIÈGE: Nicolay, Vliers, Marchal, Beurlet, Spronck, Raskin, Semmeling, Paesschen, Claessen, Naumović, Storme.

First Round, Second Leg
20 October, 1965
Stade de Sclessin, Liège

Standard Liège (0) 1 **Cardiff City (0) 0**
Storme 53

STANDARD LIÈGE: Nicolay, Vliers, Marchal, Beurlet, Spronck, Raskin, Semmeling, Paesschen, Claessen, Jurkiewics, Storme.

CARDIFF CITY: Wilson, Harrington, Rodrigues, Summerhayes, Murray, Hole, Farrell, Johnston, Charles J, King, Lewis.

(Standard Liège won 3-1 on aggregate)

5

A Celtic Affair
Shamrock Rovers, 1967

'We've given better sides than Cardiff a run for their money in European competition.'

Liam Tuohy

DUBLIN. The birthplace of George Bernard Shaw, WB Yeats, Oscar Wilde and James Joyce, and the home of Guinness, the Book of Kells and the Republic of Ireland's most successful football side, Shamrock Rovers. Located in Milltown, a suburb on the city's Southside, Rovers had been crowned champions of Ireland on 10 occasions and won the Football Association of Ireland Cup 17 times, lifting the trophy for the previous four years.

The first round draw for the 1967-68 Cup Winners' Cup paired Cardiff, back on the European stage following a year's absence, with The Emerald Isle's most decorated club.

It also pitted two old Newcastle United teammates against each other. Liam Tuohy, Rovers' player-manager, had played alongside Jimmy Scoular at St James' Park during the 1960-61 season. The draw favoured the 'Iron Man' rather than the Irishman with Ninian Park staging the second leg. Cardiff were expected to progress against the part-time Dubliners

67

whose weekly wage bill was just £125 but the Irishmen were seasoned campaigners in Europe and their record served as a warning to the Bluebirds not to underestimate the Hoops. The previous season Rovers had come within seven minutes of eliminating mighty Bayern Munich in the second round of the Cup Winners' Cup, Bayern winning 3-2 in the Grünwalder Stadion, Gerd Muller breaking Irish hearts with his 83rd-minute winner. The West German giants – who also included Franz Beckenbauer and Sepp Maier - went on to lift the trophy in Nuremberg. Before that, Rovers had given two of Spain's finest sides – Valencia in 1963 and Real Zaragoza two years later - a scare in the Inter-Cities Fairs Cup, which would later become the UEFA Cup.

There had been considerable change in Cardiff's dressing room since their last European outing in Liège in October 1965. Of the side that played at the Stade de Sclessin only Bob Wilson, Don Murray, Gareth Williams, Bernard Lewis and Peter King were still at Ninian Park. John Toshack, who was taken to Belgium but not used, had since graduated to the senior team but Lewis was out of favour and would soon be offloaded to Watford. The most valuable assets had been sold. Peter Rodrigues was transferred to Leicester City in January 1966 for £42,500 and Barrie Hole headed north to Blackburn Rovers seven months later for £40,000. George Johnston had been snapped up by Arsenal in March 1967 for £20,000, Greg Farrell had also gone with Bury paying £7,000 for the winger, while George Andrews moved to Southport for £6,000.

Scoular was given a slice of the proceeds to bring in new blood with left-back Bobby Ferguson, right-back Dave Carver, left-winger Ronnie Bird, striker Bobby Brown, centre-half Brian Harris, right-winger Barrie Jones and forward Norman Dean the key signings over a 13-month period.

Unlike the previous three ties - against Sporting Lisbon,

68

Real Zaragoza and Standard Liege – Cardiff were cast in the role of firm favourites. "This time it's different," acknowledged Williams, "but we respect Shamrock." Cardiff crossed the Irish Sea on the back of a mediocre start to the season and without leading scorer Brown. Scoular's side had won three, lost three, and drawn three of their opening nine fixtures. Brown – a strong forward signed for £9,550 from Northampton Town – had netted seven goals, two from the penalty spot, but during the final training session before the flight to Ireland, the former England amateur international pulled a hamstring and was forced to stay behind. "We're going to miss him badly," said Scoular, who admitted Brown's absence was "a big blow". Sandy Allan, a Scottish forward recently plucked from Rhyl in the Cheshire League, filled the vacant plane seat.

Bobby Brown: *I was absolutely gutted to miss the game in Ireland. It was the one and only time I got a hamstring injury! It wasn't a bad one but I could feel it wasn't quite right and I didn't travel, so while the rest of the lads made their way to the airport I went back to my home in Rhiwbina. I remember being disappointed because I was missing a Cup Winners' Cup game and I'd never played in a European match.*

Scoular wanted to keep his players away from Dublin's many distractions and chose Bray, a seaside resort 12 miles outside the Irish capital, as his base. In the last three European ties, his Bluebirds had been the underdogs but now they had the pressure of being favourites, and Joe Cunningham, Rovers' 75-year-old chairman and a local bookmaker, turned up the heat on the visitors with a piece of pre-match blarney. Referring to Cardiff's recent - and controversial - League Cup defeat at Turf Moor, 'Bookie Joe' remarked, "What chance have we against a side that can go to Burnley and lose only by a disputed penalty?" Tuohy, though, was confident his players would provide a stern test and claimed Scoular would be happy to leave Dublin with a draw. "We are not overawed by Cardiff," said the former Guinness factory worker. "We believe we're on a par with several English Second Division clubs." Tuohy also pointed out Cardiff were not in the same class as Bayern, Valencia and Real Zaragoza - three "crack continental teams" Rovers had recently pushed hard in European competition.

With a 20,000-plus gate expected, Rovers switched the game from their Glenmalure Park home in Milltown to Dalymount Park in Phibsborough, on the city's Northside, a stadium which could hold more than 40,000 people. Scoular's cautious line-up echoed Tuohy's view that the Scot would be more than satisfied with a draw. A defensive wall was erected in front of goalkeeper Wilson with Graham Coldrick at right-back, Murray at centre-half, Harris as sweeper and Ferguson at left-back. They were protected by two defensive midfielders, Williams and Malcolm Clarke. Clarke, on a three-month trial from Leicester City, was given the job of containing 19-year-old forward Mick Leech, a brewery worker with a Beatles haircut and the hottest property in Irish football. Bird and Jones were on the wings with King offering support to Toshack, the lone marksman.

Don Murray: *This was now Jimmy's team. In the past his sides were made up of players he'd inherited. They had been brought in either by Bill Jones or George Swindin but now Jimmy finally had his own side. The vast majority of the players in 1967, he had signed. He always wanted to bring in younger players although he did sign Brian Harris who was in his 30s when he came*

> *to us but the quality and experience he brought from Everton made a tremendous difference. Brian was probably Jimmy's best-ever signing.*

Bobby Ferguson: *I'd played with Liam Tuohy when I was at Newcastle and was looking forward to meeting up with him again. He'd come to Newcastle from Shamrock and then went back there. He was a funny guy who looked like the actor, Barry Fitzgerald. I missed him after the first leg so I thought I'd catch up with him at Ninian Park. But I didn't play that night, the only European game I missed that season, so I never got the chance to catch up with Liam which was a real shame.*

The Rovers side picked to face Cardiff contained four Republic of Ireland internationals – centre-half Ronnie Nolan, wing-half Johnny Fullam, right-winger Frank O'Neill and centre-forward Bobby Gilbert. It would have been five had Tuohy selected himself but the 34-year-old preferred Tommy Kinsella on the left-wing. Rovers were leading the League of Ireland when the Bluebirds arrived at Dalymount Park on 20 September and the near-22,000 crowd willed a third Rovers victory in European football. With 20 minutes on the clock that victory looked a certainty. Rovers, in their green and white hooped shirts, pummelled their opponents with wing-half Fullam, who once plied his trade at Preston North End alongside Tom Finney, driving them forward. The home side won six corners in the opening 12 minutes and Wilson produced a superb save to deny Fullam. Cardiff's overworked defence was eventually broken down in the 17th minute. Kinsella's cross was diverted to Gilbert following a deflection off Williams' head and the scorer of Rovers' first goal in Munich headed the ball beyond Wilson.

Don Murray: *That was a difficult game. They had a rough and ready centre-forward called Gilbert. He was a big lad and he certainly didn't take any prisoners. The elbows were flying and he was a bit of handful but I could be physical myself. We went over there thinking the game was going to be easier than it turned out to be.*

Barrie Jones: *To get Shamrock in the first round was a fabulous draw but maybe we did underestimate them. When you play so-called lesser sides, if your attitude isn't right then you're going to struggle. Your mindset has got to be spot on. We went 1-0 down but I wouldn't have said we were in real trouble. I was impressed with the stadium. I'd been on tour to Ireland as a youngster with Swansea and I played in some awful grounds with tiny stands - they were terrible - but Dalymount Park was nice and enclosed with a good atmosphere.*

Gilbert's goal marked a turning point in the game. Instead of pressing home their advantage the Rovers charge lost momentum - "Shamrock's tornado blew itself out," wrote Peter Jackson in the *South Wales Echo* - while Cardiff ditched their negative mentality and seized control of the game. Scoular's players, and in particular Murray, were helped by Gilbert playing with a shoulder injury for the last hour. Suddenly, Rovers were under pressure. A Ferguson shot went past the upright and Bird headed Jones' cross wide when he should really have found the net. Cardiff's superiority was rewarded two minutes after the break when King netted another valuable European goal. It was one that surely delighted Scoular as it came straight from the training-ground manual. Jones dropped a corner into a space created by teammates who had pulled the Rovers defence out of position and King ran into the area to hit a half-volley past Mick Smyth, who was replacing the ineligible Jimmy Cummins, Rovers' first-choice goalkeeper. Although O'Neill's cross hit the crossbar it was Cardiff who looked the more likely winners. Williams thought he had won it for the visitors five minutes from the end when a left-footed drive beat Smyth, only to see the ball fly wide. Scoular's side, efficient if not outstanding, left Dublin with a 1-1 draw.

Bob Wilson: *We weren't expecting a great deal from Shamrock. They were better than we thought and we had a reality check over there. We struggled to get a result and we should have realised they weren't in the Cup Winners' Cup for nothing. They were a gritty side and we were fortunate to come away with a positive result.*

Bobby Ferguson: *I had a good game in Dublin and I enjoyed the occasion. It was a tough match but then every away tie in Europe was difficult. I hit a 30-yard shot which just went past the post. It was a real screamer. At the time I thought 'Bloody hell, it just missed!' I didn't get many shots in because back then the full-backs weren't encouraged to go forward.*

Graham Coldrick: *Shamrock played exceptionally well that night. They ran their socks off and they did raise their game but in the end it was a comfortable 1-1 draw for us. It was a tight ground and I remember being surprised by the size of the crowd. There were more than 20,000 at the game and I didn't expect to see that many there.*

'Bookie Joe' predicted defeat for his side in the second leg and this time his pessimism was well-founded. Rovers, after all, were without three important players. Gilbert had failed to shake off the shoulder injury sustained in the first leg, left-back Paddy Mulligan was out with an ankle injury, and the influential Fullam was nursing a knee injury. Tuohy had to reshuffle his side which meant a role for the player-manager at inside-forward. Scoular was missing Ferguson after the full-back, who had played 52 consecutive games, damaged his instep during training the day before the game, which meant a first European appearance for 23-year-old Carver, an £11,000 buy from Rotherham. Brown, however, was back and his return allowed Scoular to adopt a more adventurous approach with the south Londoner replacing the defensive Clarke at inside-forward. With home advantage and Brown in the forward line, Scoular's quiet confidence came as no surprise. "The odds must be on Cardiff," said Tuohy before the game, "but we're not without hope." That hope was extinguished during a decisive 45-minute spell. With half-an-hour gone Mick Keiran was dispossessed by King who then set up the unmarked Toshack for his first goal of the season. Keiran, a butcher by trade, was also at fault for Cardiff's second 15 minutes from the end. Belgian referee Vitan Loraux pointed to the spot after the Rovers wing-half handled Jones' cross as he challenged Brown for the ball. Brown, who had earlier squandered an easy chance, made no mistake with his penalty.

Peter King: *I laid on the goal for Tosh but I could have scored myself. I was through but decided to give it to him. After the game his girlfriend, Sue, came up to me and gave me a big kiss. I got on well with Tosh. We trained in pairs and Jimmy put Tosh with me. He was a youngster at the time and Jimmy placed him with me because I enjoyed training and liked to push myself. That's how me and Tosh built up a relationship and I became good friends with him and Sue.*

Bobby Brown: *I stuck my penalty in the bottom right corner, that's where I always put them. In the lounge after the game a goalkeeper called Pat Dunne, who was playing for Plymouth, came over to me and said, 'I should have told him (Smyth) where you put your penalties.' Pat knew because I'd stuck one past him on the opening day of the season. He used to play for Shamrock and he'd come up from Plymouth to watch his old club. We had a bit of banter about the penalty and I told him I would still have scored even if he had tipped off the goalkeeper! Funnily enough, before that season I'd never taken a penalty in my life. We needed a penalty-taker because we missed a few the previous season and nobody was keen to take them so a penalty competition was arranged which I won. Peter King then coaxed me into doing the job. He said to me, 'Nobody will moan at you if you miss because nobody wants to take them.' Anyway, I started tucking penalties away which made me wish I had taken them earlier in my career.*

Dave Carver: *The second leg was pretty straightforward because Shamrock didn't give us any trouble. We were confident we'd beat them at home. To be honest, as soon as the draw was made we all felt we should go through. It was a nice draw for us. We were no great shakes that season but Shamrock were Third Division standard.*

The scoreline flattered Rovers who had Smyth to thank for preventing a heavier loss. The goalkeeper made a series of fine saves, stopping efforts from Brown and King. Rovers visibly tired in the second half and were toothless without Gilbert and Fullam. They worried Smyth's opposite number just once, in the 66th minute, when Wilson revived memories

75

of his Zaragoza brilliance to tip away Damien Richardson's 20-yard volley. According to Jackson in the *South Wales Echo*, "City's...undoubted superiority never left the eventual result in any doubt." With a performance their manager described as "competent", Cardiff had booked their place in the second-round draw.

Peter King: *I always thought we'd get past Shamrock, even when we were 1-0 down I was confident we'd do it. I remember playing them and thinking 'We're a better side than you'. We were better. If they were playing in English football, they would have been a decent Third Division side.*

First Round, First Leg
20 September, 1967
Dalymount Park, Dublin

Shamrock Rovers (1) 1   Cardiff City (0) 1
Gilbert 17   King 47

SHAMROCK ROVERS: Smyth, Courtney, Mulligan, Kearin, Nolan, Fullam, O'Neill, Dixon, Gilbert, Leech, Kinsella.

CARDIFF CITY: Wilson, Coldrick, Ferguson, Williams, Murray, Harris, Jones, Clarke, Toshack, King, Bird.

First Round, Second Leg
4 October, 1967
Ninian Park, Cardiff

Cardiff City (1) 2   Shamrock Rovers (0) 0
Toshack 30, Brown 74 (pen)

CARDIFF CITY: Wilson, Coldrick, Carver, Williams, Murray, Harris, Jones, Brown, Toshack, King, Bird.

SHAMROCK ROVERS: Smyth, Courtney, Kelly, Dixon, Kearin, Nolan, Fullam, O'Neill, Richardson, Tuohy, Kinsella.

(Cardiff City won 3-1 on aggregate)

6

The Rat-Catchers
NAC Breda, 1967

'I think we have a very good chance against this
Second Division team.'

Robert Janse

JIMMY Scoular had to wait just over a fortnight to discover who
his side would face in the second round. The Bluebirds were
drawn with Dutch side NAC Breda, the first leg to be played in
Holland on 12 November. Known as *de Ratten* (the Rats), Breda
were relegated from the Eredivisie - Holland's top division – in
1965 for the first time in their history but the 'Pearl of the
South' immediately won promotion. In the Dutch Cup final
they were beaten in extra-time by Ajax but still entered the
Cup Winners' Cup since the Amsterdam side also won the
championship and so contested the European Cup.

It was another favourable draw for Cardiff. Breda, managed
by Robert Janse, were hardly a force in the Eredivisie. Before the
first leg they were 10th in the 18-strong division and had lost
three of their previous five league games. Their danger men
were left-winger Frans Bouwmeester, a Dutch international
who had helped Feyenoord win two Eredivisie titles, and
Jacques Visschers, a gifted striker who was so upset at scoring

just two goals during their relegation year that he considered quitting football. There was also quality in defence. Right-back Jan van Gorp had just made his first – and it would prove to be his last – appearance for Holland, in a 2-1 defeat against Yugoslavia. Since the NAC Stadion was not equipped with floodlights, the game was moved to the Philips Stadion in Eindhoven, about 40 miles from Breda. Janse's side had beaten Maltese outfit Floriana at PSV Eindhoven's 22,000-capacity home in the first round, and now the Breda manager reckoned his 'Rats' were capable of eliminating Wales' representatives. "I think we have a very good chance against this Second Division side," he said. Janse's target was to beat Cardiff by two goals in Eindhoven and then build a barricade at Ninian Park to defend that advantage.

Scoular, of course, had other ideas but he was not without problems of his own ahead of the flight to Rotterdam. Three players – Graham Coldrick, Peter King and John Toshack – were doubtful for the first leg. Coldrick was struggling with a pulled thigh muscle while Toshack and King were carrying ankle and foot injuries respectively, though Scoular still named the players in his 14-man squad. Heat equipment and "a complete medical kit" were included in the Bluebirds' luggage so Dr Leslie Hamilton, the club's medical officer, could work on the trio in Holland.

Scoular, however, was definitely without Dave Carver who had been sent off during a Welsh League game at Tredomen on 23 September. Six weeks after the incident, the Welsh FA decided to suspend the Yorkshireman for two weeks, notifying UEFA of the ban, with the suspension starting on 13 November - the day before Cardiff left for Rotterdam. It was a heavy blow for Scoular, who branded the decision "disgraceful", as Carver was a natural replacement for Coldrick if the Newport-born defender was unable to play. "The unfairness is not the suspension itself but its timing," fumed Scoular. "It comes at the precise time when we need every available player for our Cup Winners' Cup matches against NAC Breda." Cardiff asked the Welsh FA to lift the ban for one day so he could play in Eindhoven but the request was turned down. Carver's absence meant 19-year-old Steve Derrett, a local boy yet to make a first-team appearance, boarded the plane to Holland.

Dave Carver: *I mouthed off at the referee and was sent off. We waited weeks and weeks for a decision from the Welsh FA and the suspension came when we were due to play in Holland. I went to the Welsh FA hearing with Jimmy at the Royal Hotel and there were about half-a-dozen councillors there, all in their 60s and most of them had come down from North Wales. It was a right day out for them. It was a bit of a farce and Jimmy was going mad! The whole thing should have been dealt with sooner. I asked Jimmy if I could go back to Rotherham during my suspension and train with them. He agreed so that's what I did and I stayed at my mum's while I was up there. I was choked to miss the trip because I loved travelling. Some of the lads hated going away but not me. We went on tour to Australia and New Zealand in 1968 for six weeks and a few of the players couldn't wait to get back home though I loved every minute of it.*

Scoular had also lost his dependable and powerful skipper, Gareth Williams, who had been sold to Bolton Wanderers shortly after the win over Shamrock Rovers. The Bluebirds' board felt Bolton's £45,000 offer was too good to reject but while the club banked a record fee, their manager had to wave goodbye to one of his most important players. Malcolm Clarke, who had done enough to impress Scoular during his trial, replaced Williams.

Bobby Brown: *You could see the Dutch were way ahead of us. The surface we trained on was immaculate. It belonged to the electrical firm, Philips, and it was like a bowling green. It really was magnificent and it reminded me of the Bank of England pitch at Roehampton. It was nothing like what we were used to back in Cardiff. Jimmy sometimes would have us training in Jubilee Park opposite the ground which was a normal public park.*

Bob Wilson: *The training facilities in Holland were magnificent. We trained at the Philips works ground and it was fantastic. The dressing rooms were nice and there were three or four pitches. The playing surfaces were first class, absolutely lovely. They were better than most league pitches back home. You could only be impressed with their facilities.*

The night before the game the Cardiff players sat in the hotel dining room and watched Feyenoord beat Arsenal 3-2 in a friendly in Rotterdam. Elsewhere, Janse and his players were analysing footage of the Bluebirds' 3-1 defeat at Blackpool the previous weekend. A Dutch television crew was at Bloomfield Road to film the game and they handed the tape to the Eredivisie club so Janse, a sports shop owner, could study the opposition. Cardiff may have lost but the 48-year-old could see they had played well and created enough chances to have claimed their second away win of the season.

THE RAT-CATCHERS

Graham Coldrick: *After our training session we went back to the hotel to eat. We always had an à la carte menu but the hotel gave us a set menu. Jimmy said, 'What's this rubbish?' They told him this was the menu they were asked to give us by Breda and that we were to do the same for them when they came to Cardiff. Jimmy went off on one. 'We're not having this! If we can't have a proper meal then we'll pack our bags and move somewhere else!' After that they gave us the à la carte menu. I didn't agree with all the things Jimmy did as a manager but whenever we went abroad he showed us respect. Nothing was too good for us.*

King and Toshack were declared fit to face Breda so an emergency call for replacements on the morning of the game was averted, but Coldrick failed a late fitness test despite being given a painkilling injection. Watched by Scoular and Dr Hamilton, Coldrick jogged around an all-weather training pitch though it was clear the muscle injury was still bothering the full-back so he dropped out saying, "It just wouldn't be fair to the rest of the lads if I took a risk and played." Derrett, who had spent most of his embryonic career at wing-half, was named at right-back with Bob Wilson in goal, Brian Harris, the new captain, and Don Murray in the heart of defence, and Bobby Ferguson at left-back. Clarke and King were in midfield with Barrie Jones and Ronnie Bird on the wings, and Bobby Brown and Toshack up front. "It will be a tough game and tougher still if you're going to be making your debut," remarked Scoular before kick-off. "But Derrett will not let us down."

Bobby Brown: *We didn't know much about Breda but we were pleased with the draw. I nearly didn't play in the first leg. On the day of the match my left eye became inflamed and Dr Hamilton had a look to decide whether I could play or not. I thought maybe I'd got some soil in it or it was conjunctivitis. The doctor asked me if could see. I said my eyesight was fine so I played. I often had a problem with my eye and it would last five days or so and then go. The first time it happened was before that game in Holland.*

Steve Derrett: *I'd been on the fringes of the first team but never played although I'd been on the bench a couple of times. I was nervous before playing Breda. I was always anxious before a game. Dutch football wasn't very good in those days, their clubs hadn't yet done anything in Europe. It was a buzz to be playing. I was 19 and I was very excited but at the same time I didn't want to let anyone down, especially my family and friends. I did OK but there was no praise from Scoular afterwards. You didn't get that from him.*

Scoular dismissed suggestions Cardiff would play for a draw in the Philips Stadion, insisting his side would try and win the first leg - "we have no thoughts of defensive football" - but in the opening half-hour they were pegged back by the Dutch side, who were urged forward by a modest but vocal crowd, with some Breda supporters blowing hunting horns. After hitting the post, Visschers put the home side in front inside the first ten minutes when he headed Ferry Pirard's cross past Wilson. As was the case in Dublin, Cardiff were a different side after falling behind. King hit the post and Brown also struck the frame of the goal with an effort which spun off goalkeeper Peter van der Merwe's boot and onto the crossbar. The Bluebirds secured a deserved draw 22 minutes from the end when King netted his fourth European goal. For most of the night Breda's rearguard had successfully used the offside trap to snare Cardiff's forwards but it was finally unstitched by Brown and King's beautiful one-two. King passed to Brown and then ran behind Breda's defence to collect Brown's return pass before firing the ball past Van der Merwe. It was a wonderfully-worked wall pass which not only silenced the horns but earned appreciative applause from the Dutch public. They had just seen, according to Peter Jackson, "a goal of pure football science".

Peter King:	*Bobby and I played a good one-two. I gave the ball to him and he pushed it past the back four. I was through on my own and I just side-footed it past the 'keeper. My wife's cousin was based in Holland with the RAF and I got a few tickets for the game for him and his mates. I managed to spot him in the crowd because it wasn't a massive stadium and I gave him a wave. I scored later on so he was able to tell his mates he knew the goalscorer! Breda weren't Ajax. In my view they were on a par with Shamrock Rovers.*
Don Murray:	*Kingy scored some vital goals for us, especially in Europe. You would always get 15 to 20 goals a season from him. He was pretty quick and had that knack of getting into good goalscoring positions. His timing was good and he could also volley the ball well. I felt he could have gone on to play at a higher level.*
Barrie Jones:	*Breda had a good forward – Bouwmeester – who had played for one of the big Dutch clubs. At the reception after the game he came over to us, shook our hands, and said, 'I won't see you in the second game.' We asked him why not and he told us he had a fear of*

83

flying. He wouldn't get on an aeroplane. We were quite pleased about that because it meant Breda would be coming to Cardiff without their best player. He was the man who made them tick and we all thought he had been their most dangerous player in the first leg.

Despite an average performance Cardiff returned to South Wales with a satisfying 1-1 draw. Scoular was "very pleased" but acknowledged his side "could have played better". Janse conceded the Bluebirds were "harder...in better condition". Cardiff now had a fine chance of matching their 1964-65 exploits and making the last eight but Scoular - who returned home to the back-page headline 'CITY ARE ALL SET TO DEMOLISH BREDA' - was irritated by talk his charges would easily dispatch the Dutchmen in the second leg a fortnight later. "There seems to be a false impression that this will be a one-sided game, that it's a foregone conclusion," he said. "I am trying to fight this outlook because nobody at the club sees it this way." Desperate to ensure complacency did not creep in ahead of the return, especially after a 3-1 win at Carlisle United, he told his squad Breda "are in the same position as we are – everything to play for". Scoular was no doubt irked by an article in the *South Wales Echo* which gave four reasons why Cardiff "should win" – they had won at Carlisle so current form was good, they were at home, they had the incentive of meeting a big name in the next round, and they had secured a 1-1 draw in Holland with a mediocre performance.

There were two changes to the side that had drawn in Eindhoven. Gary Bell, who had scored in the win at Carlisle four days earlier, kept his place on the left wing even though Bird had recovered from his thigh injury, and Coldrick replaced Derrett at right-back. Breda were without Bouwmeester on account of his aerophobia. His place was taken by his nephew, Frans

Bouwmeester junior. Cardiff's blistering start suggested they had heeded their manager's pre-match warning. Brown put them in front after just 177 seconds, escaping Breda's offside trap as he met Coldrick's free-kick and then beating Van der Merwe. A minute later, Brown hit the post before being brought down inside the penalty area in the 19th minute. Danish referee Gunnar Michaelsen waved play on allowing Jones to double the lead. But then the home side relaxed and a bad mistake by Wilson handed Breda a lifeline just before the half-hour mark, the goalkeeper failing to catch Gerard Nouwens' harmless 30-yard shot. It would not be the goalkeeper's only error during the European campaign.

Suddenly Cardiff, so dominant in the opening 20 minutes, risked elimination. Another Breda goal would send Janse's side into the next round on away goals and Nico Rijnders tried to claim it with a hard shot on the turn which allowed Wilson to atone for his earlier mistake, the goalkeeper preserving the lead with a brilliant save. The Ninian Park crowd still feared a second-round exit but fortune favoured the home side. Five minutes into the second half Breda were reduced to 10 men for the rest of the night, midfielder Frans Vermeulen leaving the pitch with a groin injury. Minutes after an anxious Scoular left his seat in the director's box to take his place in the dugout, Cardiff – responding to their manager's touchline presence - scored twice in 90 seconds. Clarke netted the third goal with Toshack adding a fourth after Brown allowed Coldrick's low cross to roll to the teenager.

Bobby Brown: *It looked like I was going to score our second goal but I was chopped down and the ball rolled to Barrie Jones who scored instead. I think we would have got a penalty if Barrie hadn't scored. There was a bit of aggro during the game. We had a free-kick and one*

85

of their defenders went behind the wall and kicked Graham Coldrick. I had a go at him and there was a flare-up. One or two of their players were losing their cool because they were losing the game. They were a competitive side but we were better. In the end it was a comfortable win for us.

Graham Coldrick: *I played in the second leg and ripped my hamstring again. It obviously hadn't healed properly and I felt it go midway through the first half. There were no subs in those days so I carried on and that made it worse. Before half-time Dr Hamilton gave me a painkilling injection in my thigh and that, along with the adrenaline of playing, got me through. After the game the back of my leg was a dark navy colour because of the internal bleeding and they had to put cold compresses on it. When the injection wore off my leg started throbbing and the pain was 10 times worse. I was out for months and ended up missing half the games that season because of the hamstring. Eventually the club sent me to a specialist in London to get it sorted because it kept tearing.*

Cardiff were in the last eight of the Cup Winners' Cup and by the time of the draw – seven days before Christmas, in Zürich – they were the only British side left in the competition. Crusaders of Northern Ireland had been smashed by Valencia in the first round while in the second round Scottish side Aberdeen fell to Standard Liège, and Tottenham Hotspur, England's representatives and among the favourites to win the trophy for a second time, were surprisingly defeated by Olympique Lyonnais of France. As well as the Welsh Dragon, Scoular's Bluebirds were now flying the Union Jack.

Second Round, First Leg
15 November, 1967
Philips Stadion, Eindhoven

NAC Breda 1 (1)   **Cardiff City (0) 1**
Visschers 8   King 68

NAC BREDA: van der Merwe, van Gorp, van Ierland, Vermeulen, Pelkmans, Rijnders, Snoeck, Bouwmeester, Visschers, Pirard, Nouwens.

CARDIFF CITY: Wilson, Derrett, Ferguson, Clarke, Murray, Harris, Jones, Brown, King, Toshack, Bird.

Second Round, Second Leg
29 November, 1967
Ninian Park, Cardiff

Cardiff City (2) 4   **NAC Breda (1) 1**
Brown 3, Jones 19 Nouwens 28
Clarke 66, Toshack 68

CARDIFF CITY: Wilson, Coldrick, Ferguson, Clarke, Murray, Harris, Jones, Brown, King, Toshack, Bird.

NAC BREDA: van der Merwe, van Gorp, van Ierland, Graaumans, Vermeulen, Pelkmans, Rijnders, Bouwmeester, Visschers, Lauret, Nouwens.

(Cardiff City won 5-2 on aggregate)

7

The Amazing Soccer Safari
Torpedo Moscow, 1968

'I knew once John Toshack had flicked the ball
through, I would score.'

Norman Dean

Torpedo Moscow, funded by the Likhachev Automative Plant
in Moscow and the smallest of the capital's five football clubs,
were the Soviet Union's sole survivors in European competition.
They were also heavily tipped to become the first Soviet side to
win a European trophy. Torpedo had announced themselves as
genuine contenders to lift the Cup Winners' Cup following their
ruthless destruction of Czechoslovakia's Spartak Trnava in the
previous round where they waltzed to a 6-1 aggregate victory.

Their last league campaign had been disappointing. Torpedo
finished in the bottom half of the 19-strong Soviet top flight
and a mammoth 22 points behind champions Dynamo Kiev.
They did, however, provide stiff opposition for Internazionale
in the European Cup where the Russian resistance was broken
only by a Valery Voronin own-goal at San Siro. In a bid to bring
back the glory days, the hierarchy turned to a club legend,

Valentin Ivanov. A former striker who helped Torpedo win the league and cup double in 1960 as well as another league title in 1965, Ivanov was charged with leading the revival. A one-club man who scored a record 124 goals in 15 seasons with Torpedo, the Muscovite was also a national hero, playing a key role in the Soviet Union's triumph at the inaugural European Championships in France eight years earlier. At the 1962 World Cup in Chile, he was one of six joint top scorers who shared the 'Golden Boot' with four goals.

Torpedo's comfortable march into the last eight suggested Ivanov's appointment was having the desired effect and they were fancied to reach the semi-finals at the expense of a Cardiff team performing erratically in Division Two. Jimmy Scoular's side was now weakened by the loss of 13-goal striker Bobby Brown who dislocated his knee in a sickening collision with Aston Villa goalkeeper Colin Withers during the 3-0 Boxing Day win over the Midlands side. Brown attempted a comeback but the injury would end his career. Scoular replaced Brown with Brian Clark, bought from Huddersfield Town for £8,000, but the Bristolian was ineligible for the Torpedo tie as was goalkeeper Fred Davies, a £10,000 signing from Wolves, who had replaced Bob Wilson in goal at the turn of the year. Both had been signed after the UEFA deadline.

Bobby Brown: *The injury was so gruesome the referee, Jim Finney, couldn't stand over me, he had to walk away. The knee joint was at a right angle and the cruciate ligament was badly damaged. After my injury Jimmy signed Brian Clark who was thinking of packing the game in because he was in Huddersfield's reserves but he came to Cardiff and his career took off. I tried to come back and in the summer I had more surgery to clean the knee joint out. I believed I was returning to fitness, then one Saturday before a game, I was told to go and see the specialist, Dilwyn Evans, who was in the secretary's office. I thought it was a social call as I'd got to know him well after the injury. I went into the office and Graham Keenor left us alone. Dilwyn then told me the nerve in my knee could go if I damaged it again and that I should stop playing. I asked him if he was being serious and he said 'I've never been so serious in all my life' so I retired. The club gave me £500 and a job in their social department. Brian went on to score a lot of goals for Cardiff and played in some big games. I did think 'That could be me out there'. My bad luck was Brian's good fortune but it couldn't have happened to a nicer guy.*

Ivanov's Torpedo certainly did not lack quality. Anzor Kavazashvili was the Soviet Union's number two goalkeeper, the deputy to the great Lev Yashin. Victor Shustikov was a stopper in the Soviet side that reached the European Championship final four years earlier. Right-back Vyacheslav Andreyuk, midfielder Aleksandr Lenev and striker Vladimir Shcherbakov had also graduated to the international scene. The two jewels in the Torpedo ranks, however, were Voronin, one of the most complete midfielders in world football, and the inside-forward known as 'the Russian Pelé', Eduard Streltsov. Voronin was named in FIFA's All Star Team for the 1962 World Cup in Chile and UEFA's team of the tournament for the 1964 European Championships where the Soviets were narrowly beaten in the final by hosts Spain. He was a pivotal figure in the Soviet side that advanced to the semi-finals of the 1966 World Cup and the stylish architect of Torpedo's championship triumphs in 1960 and 1965. For two years running 'Valera' was named one of Europe's top 10 players by the prestigious *France Football* magazine. Voronin, though, was missing from the squad due to make the arduous journey to Cardiff. There were vague reports emanating from behind the Iron Curtain that he was out with illness or a knee injury, but the truth was very different. Voronin was serving a lengthy ban for drunkenness. By the time of the quarter-final draw, his career and life were in sad decline. His international days over and eclipsed by Streltsov at his club, the midfielder began to slide into depression and sought comfort in alcohol.

Scoular would still have to deal with Streltsov, pioneer of the back-heeled pass and widely regarded as the best outfield player the Soviet Union has ever produced. A powerful and intelligent forward blessed with a sublime touch, Streltsov should have led the Soviet charge at the 1958 World Cup in Sweden. Instead, the man voted one of Europe's top seven footballers that year was sentenced to 12 years in a labour camp 600 miles northeast from Moscow and banned from professional football for life after being convicted of raping a 20-year-old woman, Marina Lebedeva, whom he had met at a party, although the evidence was inconclusive. Streltsov had not been short of enemies after shunning moves to the Army-backed CSKA Moscow and the KGB's Dynamo Moscow. He had also insulted the 16-year-old daughter of Ekaterina Furtseva, the first female Politburo member and a favorite of Soviet leader Nikita Krushchev, when Furtseva mentioned a likely marriage with her daughter during a reception at the Kremlin to celebrate the Soviet Union's football gold success at the previous year's Olympics. Furthermore, Streltsov was marked down as a potential defector after telling close friends he was "always sorry to return to the USSR" after trips abroad with Torpedo.

Streltsov was released from the *gulag* in 1963 after serving five years of his sentence but the football ban remained so he was not allowed to play for Torpedo, instead turning out for a factory side. The following year, Leonid Brezhnev, who had replaced Khrushchev as the Soviet Union's First Secretary, lifted the ban allowing 'the Russian Pelé', now 27, to return to Torpedo. Streltsov had lost some of his power and agility, not to mention the 'Teddy Boy' hairstyle, but still possessed the craft and intelligence that had made him one of the most admired players on the planet. In his comeback season, he fired Torpedo to the 1965 title and in October 1966 he was recalled to the Soviet side. The following year Streltsov was named Soviet Footballer of the Year, an honour he would retain in 1968. Ominously for Cardiff, he had been superb in Torpedo's almost effortless win over Spartak Trnava, scoring twice in the 3-1 second-leg victory in Czechoslovakia.

According to Scoular, the Cardiff players were "delighted" to have been paired with Torpedo but he admitted this was the Welsh club's toughest test in the Cup Winners' Cup so far – tougher than Sporting Lisbon and Real Zaragoza in 1964-65. "Torpedo are really an unknown quantity," he explained. "We have no background details at all."

Scoular had some first-hand experience of Russian football having played against Torpedo in November 1959 when they visited Newcastle as part of their tour of England. He was, though, mainly relying on what he had seen from the Soviet Union in the 1966 World Cup and also their friendly at Wembley in December 1967, when they held England to a 2-2 draw.

Cardiff, however, would not be playing the return game in Moscow. With the capital in the grip of freezing temperatures, the fixture was moved 1,750 miles away to Tashkent, the capital of the Uzbek Soviet Socialist Republic and a city close to the Chinese border. Tashkent enjoyed a mild climate in February and also housed the Pakhtakor Markaziy Stadium, a

65,000-capacity concrete bowl which would stage the second leg. Scoular was inevitably concerned about the away game's impact on his side's domestic programme.

Since Cardiff and Torpedo were unable to reach an agreement on when to play the two legs, UEFA's organising committee was left to decide on the dates. The first meeting, at Ninian Park, would be played on 6 March with the return in Tashkent on 19 March. That presented Scoular with a nightmare scenario since Cardiff were scheduled to play at Middlesbrough on 16 March before facing Hull City at home on 22 March, less than 48 hours after returning to Britain. Scoular rang the managers at both clubs to see if they could play the games before their trek to the Soviet Union. As all three clubs had been knocked out of the FA Cup, the Scot asked Hull manager Cliff Britton if the fixture could be brought forward to 17 February, which was FA Cup fourth round day. Then he called his opposite number at Middlesbrough, Stan Anderson, to see if he would be happy to play on 9 March, the date set aside for the fifth round. The Teesside club initially refused, prompting an angry rebuke from Scoular who called it "the worst piece of sportsmanship I've come across in football". But his rage was soon extinguished as Boro changed their minds and agreed to his request. Hull were not so accommodating. Knowing they would have an excellent chance of winning at Ninian Park against a Cardiff side that had just travelled from the heart of Soviet Asia, they declined to switch dates.

Ivanov had no such worries as the Soviet season had ended. Torpedo's last competitive game was on 4 December, a 0-0 draw against Kairat in Almaty, Kazakhstan. Torpedo had been preparing for the quarter-final since mid-January with Ivanov arranging a couple of friendlies for his players in Sochi, a city on the Black Sea coast in southern Russia which enjoyed mild winters. Ivanov viewed Cardiff as "tough customers" and,

93

keen to discover their strengths and weaknesses, assistant coach Yuriy Zolotov flew out two days ahead of the rest of the Torpedo squad to watch Cardiff's home game against Bristol City. The Bluebirds lost 1-0 although Zolotov, who spent much of the afternoon jotting down notes, felt he had not seen the real Cardiff City. "It appeared to me the Cardiff players were holding themselves in reserve," he said, before leaving Ninian Park.

Bobby Ferguson: *I went to see Torpedo train at Ninian Park the night before the game because I was developing an interest in coaching. I watched them from behind the goal at the Canton Stand and was impressed with their training ideas and technique. Their passing drills were brilliant and they stuck in my mind for a long time. Their players loved and caressed the ball, it was fantastic to watch. Their touch and passing ability was impressive, and they were running into space and making dummy runs. I'd never seen anything like it. They used only half the pitch and players were restricted to where they could move so if you were on the touchline you could only come inside 10 yards, and if you were in the middle you couldn't go beyond a certain point. It was all about engaging, disengaging and keeping possession. They worked in tight spaces to improve ball control and their players never gave the ball away. I went away that night thinking 'Bloody hell, this lot can play!' It was clear they were a cracking side.*

Scoular ended up having to field a weakened side against Torpedo. There was no Brown and two of his full-backs, Graham Coldrick and Dave Carver, were injured. Mel Sutton and Les Lea, two midfielders signed in December, joined Davies and Clark on the ineligible list. So Bob Wilson – who Scoular felt was culpable for both goals in his last appearance, a 2-1 loss at former club Aston Villa – was back in goal. Steve Derrett was at right-back, Brian Harris and Don Murray in central defence and Bobby Ferguson at left-back with Malcolm Clarke in the holding midfielder role. Barrie Jones and Ronnie Bird were on the wings with Peter King supporting striker John Toshack. To fill the last inside-forward place, Scoular considered picking 18-year-old Leighton Phillips even though the youngster had just two substitute appearances to his name. In the end, he opted for Bryn Jones, a 20-year-old from Llandrindod Wells who had not played a competitive game since March 1967 when he featured in a Welsh Cup win over Newport County.

Bryn Jones: *I wasn't shocked to get picked because for a day or two there was talk I might play since we had quite a few players out. I didn't play well, I was crap, and I was really disappointed about that. After the game I told Terry Medwin, who was our reserve team coach, that I didn't do particularly well. The game passed me by, I just couldn't get into it. I was only 20 and I hadn't played an awful lot. There was a heck of an atmosphere because we had a big crowd and I froze a little. That's why I didn't do well but the result was more important than my performance.*

Don Murray: *We didn't know anything about Torpedo Moscow because we had no information about Russian football. In those days there was no coverage of the game over there. The results of their clubs were never printed in the papers and it was difficult to find anything on them because they were behind the Iron Curtain. Normally if you wanted to learn about a foreign side you'd go*

*out and watch them play but that wasn't possible in
this case. The only one of their players I'd heard of
was Streltsov and that's because he'd been in a labour
camp and played for the Soviet Union. Apart from that
I didn't know anything about Torpedo.*

With a semi-final place in sight, the usually frugal Cardiff board
decided to offer the players an attractive bonus scheme for the
tie. Each player would pocket £50 if Torpedo were beaten at
Ninian Park and a further £80 if they reached the last four
by winning or drawing in Tashkent. They would still collect
£30 if they lost the return leg by one goal since that result
would secure a play-off in Augsburg, West Germany. In the
first leg, a crowd of just over 30,000 watched the men in blue
enhance their Jekyll and Hyde reputation. Lacklustre against
Bristol City four days earlier, they were an entirely different
proposition against Torpedo, stunning Ivanov's players with
their fast, attacking football. It was fitting Barrie Jones, the
most impressive Cardiff forward, should score just before half-
time. Bryn Jones began the move, passing to Bird. He crossed
from the left wing, King was unable to make decent contact,
and the ball fell to Jones beyond the far post. The winger had
noticed Kavazashvili was moving to his right and headed the
ball so it curved across the goalkeeper and into the net. Cardiff
should have added to their lead in the second half as Torpedo's
early efficiency turned to panic. Harris saw his diving header
fly just over, Toshack went close with a lob and King shot wide,
as did the two Joneses.

Barrie Jones: *It was a fabulous feeling scoring that goal. Birdy
crossed the ball and Peter King got a slight touch
which deflected it to me. I headed it at the far post and
it just flew in. I used to pull Clarky's leg about this*

goal. He scored with a header against Real Madrid a few years later and I used to say to him, 'My goal against Torpedo was better than yours against Real!' Clarky was a recognised header of the ball and scored from the middle of the penalty box. Mine was at an angle, in swirling wind, and I also had Peter King in my way!

Peter King: *Torpedo were a typical Russian side - disciplined but not much flair. One of their midfielders could speak a bit of English and whenever he went for the ball with one of our players he would shout 'Mine!' or 'Leave it!' He was trying to pull the wool over our eyes so he could get the ball. He shouted these English phrases in each game against us but we never fell for it. We didn't expect a Russian to speak English during the game and it was quite a cheeky thing to do.*

Torpedo's approach at Ninian Park was surprisingly negative with Ivanov committing only two players – Streltsov and Shcherbakov – to attack although they showed more adventure in the last half-hour. They might even have salvaged what would have been an undeserved draw had Shcherbakov not slipped inside the penalty area with only Wilson to beat. The goalkeeper also made a decent save to deny Yuri Shalimov and although he was beaten by Streltsov, the Torpedo talisman was ruled to have fouled the excellent Murray before rolling the ball into the net and his effort was disallowed by the Belgian referee, Robert Schaut. Scoular hailed his side's 1-0 victory as "a great achievement" while the fancied Russians left Ninian Park with pewter tankards – a gift from the Welsh club – and damaged egos. Ivanov graciously admitted Cardiff deserved the win and was "thankful" the margin of victory was just one goal. He believed some of his younger players were intimidated by the vociferous Welsh crowd but conceded he "did not expect Cardiff to be so good". His star player, however, was confident Torpedo would produce a superior show in the second leg. "I think we will do better on the softer pitch of Tashkent," said Streltsov. "It will be much warmer there and that will suit us."

Bob Wilson: *We won 1-0 and we all thought that was a cracking result. Torpedo were a strong team with a few internationals so we were pleased. We'd also kept a clean sheet. We flew to the Soviet Union feeling we now had a chance of going through but I think everyone at the club knew we were going to be put under a hell of a lot of pressure in Tashkent.*

Now Cardiff had to make the long journey to Tashkent via Moscow, a journey the *Western Mail* dubbed the "amazing soccer safari to Asia". They had to travel without their interpreter, Ukraine-born Stefan Terlezki. A Cardiff hotelier with political aspirations and who would later become Bluebirds chairman, he fled to Britain in 1948 after deserting the Red Army although his father was a political prisoner in Siberia. Terlezki acted as Cardiff's translator in the first leg and was wanted for the journey behind the Iron Curtain, but fearing he would be detained by the KGB if he returned to the Soviet Union, he remained in the Welsh capital. A far bigger concern for Scoular was Fulham manager Bobby Robson's £60,000 bid for rising star Toshack which was tabled on the eve of the trip. Cardiff's board accepted Fulham's offer "on the grounds Toshack should be given the opportunity". Scoular knew the chances of overcoming Torpedo without his prolific goal-getter would be remote but, much to his relief, Toshack decided to stay with his home club. "I am still only a teenager and I still have a lot to learn," said the striker who discussed Fulham's approach with his father, George, and fiancée, Sue. "I believe Ninian Park is the place to learn it."

Cardiff left for Moscow's Sheremetyevo Airport on Thursday, 14 March – five days after their last league game, a 3-2 win at Middlesbrough – flying from London. They would spend two nights in Moscow, a city perishing in temperatures as low as -8°C, before flying to Tashkent on Saturday. The squad included the 11 players who had beaten Torpedo at Ninian Park, plus Phillips, Lyn Davies, Gary Bell, Norman Dean and Sandy Allan. Scoular had contacted Celtic manager Jock Stein for advice on travelling to the Soviet Union. Stein was well qualified to provide it since his side had twice visited Dynamo Kiev in European competition and he told his fellow Scot the local cuisine might not go down too well with his players. To avoid eating the Russian fare, Cardiff packed their own meat, tinned ham, cereals, chocolate, and orange juice plus a sizeable supply of anti-sickness tablets to prevent the players going down with stomach trouble.

Cardiff arrived at their central Moscow hotel after nine hours on the move. The club had chosen to stay in the famous Metropol, situated opposite the Bolshoi Theatre and close to Red Square. The five-storey art nouveau gem had been decorated by some of Russia's most acclaimed artists, notably Mikhail Vrubel. The luxury hotel was once frequented by Leo Tolstoy and Sergey Rachmaninov, and Rasputin had often been found drinking in its Russkaya Palata restaurant. Lenin delivered speeches at the Metropol, and George Bernard Shaw and John F Kennedy had stayed there. More recently, David Lean had filmed several scenes of *Dr Zhivago* inside the hotel. Now the Metropol opened its doors to Cardiff City Football Club. As soon as they checked in, Scoular and his squad were invited to the Bolshoi Ballet but, exhausted by the non-stop travelling, the offer was politely declined.

Peter King: *Brian Harris had been behind the Iron Curtain before when he was with Everton so he knew the locals wanted to buy British clothes. He took over some gear from Marks & Spencer to sell to the Russians on the black market and we did get Muscovites coming up to us and asking if we had anything for sale. Brian found somebody who wanted to buy some stuff and took him back to the hotel. He bought shirts and pullovers and his way of smuggling the clothes out of the hotel was to put them all on! He looked like the Michelin Man as he walked out.*

Bobby Ferguson: *There was this bloke hanging around our hotel and Hooky – which was Brian Harris' nickname – thought he wanted to buy stuff from us. We had brought over ties and socks and boxes of Cadbury's chocolate. We took him up to our room and laid the stuff out on one of the beds. This guy then started picking up ties and socks and I remember Hooky saying, 'Don't handle the merchandise if you can't pay the price.' He was from Liverpool and that was a typical Scouse remark! The guy wanted to buy my Trilby hat. I can't recall any money changing hands. We ended up eating most of the chocolate and giving the rest away because the people were so nice.*

Leighton Phillips: *We were given spending money in Russian roubles – I think it was roughly £8 a day – but you couldn't do anything with them, they were worthless. I remember Brian Harris using rouble notes to light his cigars.*

*The hotels we stayed in were terrible as was the food.
I ended up living on bread and coffee. We took our own
things with us but the problem was we didn't bring
cooking oil so we had to use the Russian stuff. It was
used to cook our steaks and it made them taste awful.
The hotel staff took our leftovers. They would put bits
of steak in a bag and take it home. I lost half-a-stone
on that trip and I was only 18. I was in a hell of a
state when we got back. I wasn't at all well and I think
it was down to the food I ate in Russia.*

During their brief stay in the snow-covered capital, where
the temperature plummeted as low as -13.9°C, the Bluebirds
– with a Party official always in tow - trained at the indoor
facilities of the Central Lenin Stadium, one of the world's
largest sports complexes, before taking a tour of the city by
coach, although Scoular cut short the visit to the Kremlin
and Red Square. The nervous manager ushered his players
back onto the vehicle after barely 100 yards on foot, scared
they would slip on the treacherous icy ground and pick up an
injury. He was particularly concerned about Harris who was
trying to shake off a foot problem in time for the showdown in
Tashkent.

Barrie Jones: *We trained in one of the gymnasiums in the Lenin
Stadium. It had underground training facilities
because Moscow was frozen solid in the winter. We
saw female shot-putters and weightlifters training
there. They were massive and had beards - I was
gobsmacked! People would come to the hotel where
we were staying to buy petrol coupons and you also
saw the locals queuing round corners to go into a shop
where there would be one loaf of bread on the shelf.*

It was incredible. We were given a certain amount of roubles each day as spending money but there was nothing to spend it on except balalaikas and busts of Karl Marx. Wherever we went, we were accompanied by a Party official who kept an eye on us.

Bob Wilson: *We saw everything in Moscow – the Kremlin, the Tsar's Bell, St Basil's Cathedral - although we mainly stayed in the hotel. We did see a massive outdoor swimming pool (the Moscow Pool) in the centre of the city. It was a huge thing with steam coming off it because the air was so cold and the water was heated. It looked like a giant bowl of soup. It was absolutely freezing but there were still plenty of people swimming.*

Bobby Ferguson: *There were women bus drivers in Moscow which we'd never seen before. We also came across female workers hacking ice off the pavements and putting it into sacks. The place was bloody freezing. It was so cold that if you cried the tears would freeze on your face. I've never come across cold like the cold over there. You couldn't stay out for long periods, we spent most of the time in the hotel. When we went out and spoke to the locals they always looked around before answering us. We called it 'the Moscow twitch'. They were nervous because they were talking to Westerners and they wanted to see if anyone was looking. We were watched wherever we went. In our hotel there was a person sitting at a desk on every floor to see what was going on. We'd come out of the lift and there was always someone there, watching who was going where.*

The travelling party included directors George Edwards and Viv Dewey as well as Dr Leslie Hamilton who, apart from working on Harris' injured foot, had the job of handing each player two anti-sickness tablets a day, one at breakfast and the second at supper. While the visitors shivered in Moscow, Ivanov and his players were making use of the more agreeable climate of Central Asia. Straight after the game at Ninian Park, Torpedo had made their way to Tashkent to prepare for the second leg.

Norman Dean: *Moscow wasn't a colourful place but it was still a great experience. The whole city was covered in snow. There were women on the roofs sweeping the snow off the top of their apartments while the men were at the bottom picking it up, and there would be rope around the pavements. It was very strange and we all looked at each other in amazement. We went sightseeing to places like the Kremlin, Red Square and the Lenin Stadium, which was fantastic. There were soldiers everywhere but we were a group of footballers over to play a European game so we felt quite safe.*

John Toshack: *One night we were given a choice of what to do. We could go to the Moscow State Circus or the Bolshoi Ballet. All the players chose the circus but we had two or three fans with us and one of them, Bill O'Donovan, said he wanted to go to the Bolshoi. So he went to the ballet with Viv Dewey and the rest of us went to the circus. When we saw Bill back at the hotel one of the lads asked him what the ballet was like and he said, 'It was all right but there was a bit too much dancing'. I've never forgotten that!*

Steve Derrett: *Moscow was drab. In the morning we'd stand on the steps of the hotel and watch everyone coming off the Metro. They all wore grey Army coats, and they would go one way, then in the evening they'd all go back the other way. The food in the hotel was dreadful. We tried borscht which was beetroot soup with a bit of meat and it was like sucking the sole of a shoe. We also tried their chips which were horrible but thankfully we had brought tinned ham and chocolate with us. Anything we left on our plates the waitresses would put in their aprons and it didn't take us long to work out what they were doing. They were keeping our leftovers because they didn't have anything at home so we started leaving chocolate and other bits on the table so they could take it back to their families. The hotel rooms were bleak. They had two beds and a big, old radio. It was a huge thing. All the furniture was old and of poor quality.*

Cardiff set off for Tashkent on 16 March. With the Soviet capital enveloped by Siberian weather and a heavy snowstorm forcing the closure of the city's airports the previous day, Scoular feared the club's flight would be delayed. Sure enough, what should have been a five-hour journey turned into a 14-hour marathon. The Bluebirds were held up in Moscow for six hours although the delay was down to freak weather conditions in Tashkent which had been hit by out-of-season snowfall and sub-zero temperatures. When they eventually landed in the Uzbek Soviet Socialist Republic, the mild weather usually associated with March had returned to the region and during their first full day in the Uzbek capital, the temperature peaked at a pleasant 10°C. The winter coats, so necessary for a stroll around Moscow, were no longer required.

THE AMAZING SOCCER SAFARI

Bobby Ferguson: We got to the airport to catch the plane to Tashkent and there was a delay. We were kept waiting for hours and hours and it was absolutely freezing inside the airport. There was no heating and it became so cold we were crying. When you sit for four or five hours in the freezing cold, it really takes it out of you. We were telling each other, 'Don't rub your eyes because your eyelashes will drop off.' That's how cold it was. In the end Scoular just lost it. He got hold of the Party man who was with us and said, 'Where's the plane for these boys? If it's not here in two hours, we're flying back to London...and I'll tell you something else. I'd rather be put up against a wall and shot than live in this country!' It worked because half-an-hour later we were on the plane. We did feel they were playing games with us and trying to give Torpedo an advantage.

Bob Wilson: They kept us hanging about at the airport and they even kept us hanging about on the runway. We were by the steps which took you up to the plane for a long time and it was absolutely freezing outside. It felt like it was minus 17. This big, fat woman who was in charge of collecting the tickets wouldn't let us on. She said she was missing a ticket but I don't think that was the case - she was just making excuses. Once we were on the plane we seemed to be waiting on the runway forever. The plane was moving but there was no sign of it taking off. Brian Harris hated flying, he was nervous on a plane, and he was getting irate. He threw his book on the floor and shouted, 'Get this plane in the air!'

Don Murray: *We flew to Tashkent in some old plane. We were looking at it before we went on board and one of the lads – I think it was Norman Dean – said, 'God, there's a crack in the fuselage!' Then we took off in a snowstorm which, apparently, was an every day occurrence over there but I couldn't help thinking about 1958 and Munich. It was also freezing cold inside the plane and we seemed to be flying in the clouds for ages before eventually hitting blue sky and sunshine. That whole trip was a scary experience but, thankfully, we got to Tashkent OK.*

Near the Mirzachol desert and overlooked by the Tien Shan mountains, Tashkent was once a stop on the legendary Silk Road trade route which connected China to Europe. Sacked by Genghis Khan in the early part of the 13th century, the city had experienced more recent destruction. In April 1966, an earthquake measuring 7.5 on the Richter scale flattened around 28,000 buildings – many in the Old Quarter - and 10 people were killed with almost 100,000 left homeless. Tashkent was rebuilt into a model Soviet city with wide streets, huge plazas, apartment blocks, parks and fountains although the piles of rubble still to be cleared served as a reminder of that devastating event 23 months earlier.

John Toshack: *We were taken from the airport to our hotel in this old bus. When we arrived, there were steps in front of the building and we were expecting the bus to stop so we could get out. Instead, the driver forced the bus up the steps to the hotel! He actually drove it up the steps – bump, bump, bump – and we were hanging on to the seats. I could see Jimmy Scoular sitting down the front and he was ranting and raving! We were all laughing our heads off. The bus was actually parked at an angle when we got out.*

Steve Derrett: *Tashkent was further away from Moscow than London and it was a fascinating place. There were big, wide avenues and hardly any traffic. It was really weird. Open sewers ran down the streets and we saw real poverty. The locals queued for everything and kids followed us wherever we went. They would offer us lapel badges in exchange for chewing gum or a bit of chocolate.*

Leighton Phillips: *A few of us went into a supermarket, it wasn't big but it was the main store in Tashkent. While we were in the shop all these people had gathered outside and they were looking in to see what we were doing. They couldn't afford anything and they wanted to watch what we were buying. Quite a few came in to get a closer look. It was only a small place so it became packed. These people couldn't believe the money we had - £8 must have been a bloody fortune to them. All they saw was us buying balalaikas!*

Cardiff's clash with Torpedo certainly captured the interest of the Tashkent population. The game was a 65,000 sell-out with a staggering 250,000 requests for tickets, and when Scoular's players trained on a local football field at the end of a long and dusty road, more than 1,000 curious Uzbeks turned up to watch. Cardiff and Torpedo were not the only attractions. Dynamo Moscow and their world-famous goalkeeper, Yashin, were also in Tashkent for a bout of warm-weather training allowing Scoular's charges to catch a glimpse of the 'Black

Octopus' – Yashin's nickname as he wore an all-black strip - at work.

Gary Bell:	*We had a mad coach driver in Tashkent and one morning he picked us up to take us to training. There was a bit of traffic at the front of the hotel but he didn't want to hang about so he drove the bus down these steps – and there were about 50 or 60 of them – which led from the car park onto the road. We were taken to a pitch on the outskirts of the city. It was at the end of a farm and very basic. Anyway, we started training when all of sudden oxen started wandering onto the pitch! I remember someone suggesting we use them as the wall when we came to practise free-kicks although Jimmy wasn't pleased because he took football very, very seriously. It wasn't the best preparation for a Cup Winners' Cup game but we had to make do with what we had. There were changing rooms in a corner of the pitch and next door was a hut with a sauna. Most of us hadn't seen a sauna before and the owners let us try it. We thought it was great so Don Murray said to Jimmy, 'We should have one of these at Ninian Park.' Jimmy said he'd see what he could do. Lo and behold, three or four weeks after we got back home Jimmy had a sauna put in for us. We used it regularly, especially on the weekends.*
Don Murray:	*All the locals looked like Oddjob in 'Goldfinger' – they were bald with gold teeth. They had the most expensive smiles I've ever seen. There were four of them in our hotel one night and they were drinking what looked like vodka. After two minutes of conversation they stood up and knocked back their drink. Then they sat*

down, filled their glasses up and did exactly the same thing. They chatted for two minutes, then stood up, knocked back their drink and sat down. They kept doing this and after a while one of them passed out. Two men employed by the hotel took him outside and propped him against a wall. The other three carried on until another one passed out. He too was carried outside so two were left. They did the same thing until just one guy was left. It was fascinating to watch!

John Toshack: *The food out there was terrible. It was like dog food. The only thing we could eat were these big bread rolls. We called them discuses. To get something to eat we would queue outside Jimmy Scoular's room for rations and he would hand out corned beef, ham and chocolate. We just couldn't eat the local stuff.*

Ivanov made two changes to the side that had been so disappointing at Ninian Park, drafting in Mikhail Gershkovich, one of the Soviet Union's emerging strikers, and midfielder Aleksandr Stenischev. Scoular opted for a defensive line-up with Dean replacing Bryn Jones at inside-right with orders to play as a defensive left-half rather than as a forward. The versatile Dean was on the transfer list after struggling to make an impact following his £6,000 arrival from Southampton but he had impressed Scoular in the wing-half role against Fulham reserves, the last Combination game before the trip to Moscow. Harris was picked despite not being 100 per cent fit, as was Bird who needed treatment on his ankle after slipping on the hotel staircase. "If our system works," said Scoular, boosted by the news Torpedo would still be without Voronin, "then we are in with a chance." Cardiff had brought a record of the Welsh national anthem with them so it could be played before the game and also a Welsh flag to be flown at the stadium.

Barrie Jones: *I don't think the Uzbeks knew what the whole thing was about, they came to the game out of curiosity. It was a lovely atmosphere because they appreciated it when you did something well. The changing rooms were basic and I've never forgotten the toilets – you had to stand up to do your business. And the toilets didn't have flushes, you had to get water to flush it away. We weren't in the best frame of mind for that game and that's because we were staying in a horrible hotel and we'd done a lot of travelling. All we ate was ham with huge bread rolls which were like discs. Torpedo deserved to win. We had been a much better side at Cardiff, but we dug in.*

As expected, Torpedo went for the jugular straight away with the superb Wilson called into action after 50 seconds to scramble away Shcherbakov's close-range shot. Before Gershkovich's goal in the 33rd-minute, the Cardiff goalkeeper had been tested nine times. There was nothing Wilson could do to stop Gershkovich levelling the tie. The ball bounced kindly for the striker as he wriggled clear of Dean and Ferguson and that allowed him to curl it over Wilson who had come off his line to try and block the shot. Cardiff were more dangerous after the interval. Toshack saw a header fly just wide following a King cross and Bird squandered a wonderful chance 12 minutes from the end. The winger had the Torpedo goal at his mercy after being set up by Jones but his shot was saved by Kavazashvili. Ivanov's side made one, last surge in the final minute and it needed a superb stop by Wilson to deny Streltsov what would have been a dramatic semi-final clincher. His side may have lost but Scoular was delighted his travel-weary players had restricted Streltsov and his colleagues to a 1-0 win, forcing a third game on neutral soil. "Very few critics gave City a chance of surviving in the Soviet Union, particularly after their marathon journey. The feat of Jimmy Scoular's men must rank with the club's finest achievements in Europe," proclaimed the *Western Mail*.

Bob Wilson:
Torpedo gave us a right battering. They threw everything at us, especially in the last half-hour. We really had to stick the flag in because we were under pressure all the time. There are periods in a game where you think 'OK, we'll get a break for a couple of minutes now' but it didn't happen in that game. We never had the chance to come up for air. They were always coming at us and we had to have 10 men behind the ball all the time. We would get the ball away and then it would come straight back at us. But we'd got a play-off which we were pleased with and it was after this game that the Press started to take notice of us.

Bobby Ferguson:
Brian picked up an injury during the game, a haematoma, so Dr Hamilton gave him an anti-inflammatory injection to soak it up. He had a bad reaction to it. I think he was allergic to whatever the doc gave him. I was sitting next to Hooky and his eyes started swinging around, I thought he was going to pass out. The doc gave him another injection and it sorted him out straight away. Then we got on the coach to go back to the hotel and when we arrived we saw a big crowd of Uzbeks standing outside. They were waiting for us and a lot of them were holding bottles.

We thought there was going to be trouble and that they were going to throw the bottles at us because we had taken Torpedo to a play-off but when we got off the coach they started patting us on the back and giving us the bottles which had vodka inside. It turned out the Uzbeks didn't like the Russians and had supported us, not Torpedo!

Norman Dean: *We'd lost 1-0 but we'd forced a play-off so we were quite happy. We had an evening meal and then went back to our rooms. We took a bottle of vodka up with us and a few of us met up for a drink in one of the rooms as we were pleased to get another game. We were chuffed to have lost by just one goal because Torpedo were one of the top Russian teams and we were just a mid-table side in our Second Division. A few of us liked a bit of a sing-song – me, Brian Harris, Barrie Jones, Malcolm Clarke – and we started to sing. We weren't being rowdy, we were talking and having a little sing-song. Suddenly two guards carrying guns burst into the room. They told us to stop and disperse. If we didn't then we'd all be in trouble. We didn't argue with them. We all went back to our rooms after that.*

Barrie Jones: *Our bus driver out in Tashkent was mental but he was a wonderful lad, an absolute superstar. Any money we had left over we gave to him. We had nothing to spend it on and we couldn't change it back so it made no difference to us. The driver couldn't believe it when we gave him this money. He was kissing and hugging us. Everyone got a cuddle off him. We must have given him six years' wages!*

Cardiff began their marathon journey home the next morning, leaving the hotel at 5.30am to catch a flight to Moscow just before noon. With time to spare in the Soviet capital, the players were taken to see Lenin's Tomb in Red Square. "I'll go home, tell the kids I saw Lenin and they will want to know if I saw Paul and Ringo too," joked Harris as he made his way into the mausoleum. After returning to the Hotel Metropol for a meal, they were driven to the airport for their evening flight to London.

Bobby Ferguson:　　*There was a massive queue to see Lenin's Tomb, it must have been half-a-mile long. Our liaison officer took us right to the front and said that when we got to the tomb we mustn't laugh, cough or smoke, and we had to take our hats off. We were to be completely silent and make sure we had solemn faces when we walked around the tomb which was basically a glass coffin. There were guards around it with bayonets pointed at the crowd so we did what the interpreter said. When we flew back from Moscow it was on a BOAC plane. The captain said over the speaker, 'Congratulations to Cardiff City on their marvellous result'. The plane was full and all the passengers applauded. It was a great feeling to be on a British plane with British pilots and British stewardesses. We'd roughed it in Moscow and Tashkent so it was good to be on a nice plane and given decent food. The journey home didn't seem anywhere near as bad as the one out. I didn't notice, probably because I was still half-cut after drinking the vodka from the Uzbeks! They gave us bottles of the stuff and we drank it neat all night.*

Peter King: *We shook hands with the liaison guy at the airport and started singing the Vera Lynn song, 'We'll Meet Again'. He cried his eyes out! He was a nice bloke, a smashing guy in fact. He came to the hotel when we were first in Moscow and said he had tickets for the Bolshoi Ballet, which was like getting tickets for the FA Cup final, and also tickets for the Moscow State Circus. We went to Lenin's Tomb and he broke into the long queue, about 20 yards from the entrance, so we could slip in. The people dutifully stepped back. He came with us everywhere. There were other people following us around as well but we didn't know who they were.*

From London, Cardiff – minus their boots which had gone missing en route from Tashkent - headed back to South Wales by coach, stopping in Reading for an evening meal. They finally reached the Welsh capital at 2.15am on Thursday, 21 March, having travelled virtually non-stop for 26 hours. To play Torpedo in Tashkent, the Bluebirds had clocked up a total of nearly 7,000 miles and, after arriving home, it was no surprise when Scoular admitted his players were "very, very tired". Unhappy with the demands the game in Tashkent had placed on his squad, he compiled a report of their exhausting expedition to Central Asia and asked the board to give it to the Welsh FA so they could bring the matter to UEFA's attention. Viv Dewey supported his manager's view. "We have no complaints whatever about the Russian hospitality. It was very good," said the chairman's son. "But I personally feel it is unreasonable to expect a club to make such a long journey for one competitive match." Unbelievably, Cardiff faced Hull at Ninian Park just 41 hours after returning from the Soviet Union. The side contained seven players who had done battle with Torpedo. The players' boots were found by Aeroflot, the Russian airline, and returned in time for the game but the arduous journey had taken its toll. Unsurprisingly, Scoular's players lost 3-2.

Steve Derrett: *We played Hull on the Friday night and we had no chance. It was lashing down with rain and we were 3-0 down at one point. As far as Scoular was concerned, it was a game we should have won but we could hardly lift our legs. On the Tuesday we'd played a game thousands of miles away and didn't get back home until the early hours of Thursday. We had to change our watches twice on the way home, first when we landed in Moscow from Tashkent, and again when we got back to London from Moscow. We'd been away for nearly a week and eaten shit food yet he still expected us to play well on the Friday night. Looking at it sensibly, there was no way in the world we could have won that game.*

Scoular discovered SV Hamburg awaited his Bluebirds in the semi-finals if they overcame Torpedo in the play-off on 3 April. The chosen venue was the Rosenaustadion in Augsburg, a historic city 35 miles from Munich. The Scot, however, suffered a serious setback before flying to Bavaria. Murray, who had done an impressive marking job on Streltsov in the previous two games, had torn ankle ligaments on the Saturday before the play-off, in a 3-1 defeat at Millwall. The Scotland Under-23 international was forced off before half-time at The Den and was, according to Scoular, "touch and go" for the play-off. Cardiff did everything in their power to help Murray, who had not missed a game since October 1966, recover for the rematch with Torpedo and Streltsov. The centre-half was given a course of chymoral injections over three days to reduce the swelling and a heat-ray lamp was taken to West Germany so the injury could be treated until the day of the game.

Cardiff flew to Munich although they were delayed at Rhoose Airport for three hours by a blizzard so severe the club organised a plane to be put on stand-by at Liverpool's Speke Airport. The late arrival meant they were unable to train at the 55,000-capacity Rosenaustadion that evening. Scoular's main concern, though, was devising a contingency plan in the event Murray was ruled out. Another centre-half, 21-year-old Richie Morgan, was included in the squad but the former Cardiff Corries player had never played a first-team match and pitching Morgan against the Soviet Union's Player of the Year would be a colossal gamble. The other option, which was seen as the more likely, would be to put the fit-again Coldrick at centre-half, a position he had played before, with Derrett at right-back. When Murray failed his late fitness test at the Rosenaustadion – "No good, boss. I'm out," said the disconsolate defender to his manager after limping around the athletics track encircling the stadium - Scoular sprung a major surprise and chose Morgan at centre-half with Coldrick remaining at full-back. 'This is your chance, son," Scoular told Morgan after a disconsolate Murray, despite an intensive course of injections, announced his withdrawal.

Don Murray: *I picked up an injury at Millwall and we left it until the morning of the game to see if I could play. I had a fitness test and I knew after running a few yards down the track that I was out. Richie came in and did tremendously well. Streltsov was a handful but Richie played him brilliantly and we were under a lot of pressure in that game. I sat next to Jimmy on the bench and that was an experience! Every ball that was kicked, he was up and down, swearing like a trooper. He kept thumping me in the leg during the game and saying, 'What about that!' Jimmy really lived and breathed the game.*

Richie Morgan: *To be fair to Scoular, it took a bit of bottle to put me in for that game. It was a quarter-final play-off and he had alternatives. He could have moved Graham Coldrick, who was experienced, to centre-half but he picked someone who was still a reserve player. I went into management myself and I don't think I would have been so brave. He told me on the morning of the game that I was playing. He said in his broad Scottish accent, 'I'm giving you a chance and if you bottle it, then the team will suffer.' He said I had the ability and he wanted to see if I had the bottle to go with it. He also told me that if I was overawed and the occasion was too big for me, then we'd lose. I didn't have much time to think about the game which was a good thing. I was 21 and my debut was going to be in a quarter-final play-off in the Cup Winners' Cup. It was a fairytale, real 'Roy of the Rovers' stuff. It was a gamble for Scoular and a shock for me. It was fortunate I had a passport so I could travel. Brian Harris had been injured just before the game in Tashkent and I was put on stand-by. I ended up staying at home because Brian recovered but at least it meant I got a passport sorted, so I was OK to go to Augsburg.*

The Welsh press were pessimistic about Cardiff's chances of winning without Murray, the team's defensive lynchpin. In the *South Wales Echo*, Peter Jackson described the Scot's absence as "a sledgehammer blow to City's hopes of winning this quarter-final decider". Dewi Lewis feared Streltsov would dominate Murray's young and inexperienced stand-in. "It is asking a lot of a lad who has not had any Football League experience to hold a centre-forward rated as one of the best in Europe," he wrote in the *Western Mail*. Murray, however, backed Morgan's shock selection, insisting, "He won't let us down." Interestingly, Hamburg technical director Georg Knöpfle - in Augsburg to run the rule over his side's next opponents – went against popular opinion and predicted a Welsh victory, even though Voronin was back for Torpedo and Cardiff were missing their first-choice centre-half.

Peter King: *Both teams turned up at the stadium on Tuesday night for a training session. Torpedo went first and we watched them from the touchline. They finished off by playing one-touch inside the penalty area and it was really impressive. They were superb at it. Jimmy Scoular tried to get us to do the same thing. He said to us, 'Right, after we've done our warm-up we'll play one-touch.' So we did our warm-up -which hadn't changed for about eight years – and then all 15 or 16 of us moved into the penalty area to play one-touch. We split into two teams, some of us wearing bibs, and started playing but we were terrible! It was embarrassing. We were so bad that the people watching started to laugh. After 10 minutes or so Jimmy Scoular told us to pack it in because we were making fools of ourselves!*

Coldrick and Morgan were the only changes to the side which played in Tashkent with Wilson in goal, Ferguson at left-back and Harris as sweeper. Bird and Barrie Jones were the wide men with Clarke and King in midfield, and the versatile Dean supporting Toshack up front. Scoular was looking to overcome one of the favourites to win the Cup Winners' Cup on neutral soil with four reserve players as Wilson, Morgan, Bird and Dean were not first-choices in Division Two fixtures. As for Torpedo, Ivanov kept faith with the same players who had won in Tashkent apart from David Pais who made way for Voronin, brought in from the cold as the desperate Ivanov searched for a solution to his Cardiff problem. The tie would be settled in Augsburg. If the two sides were still deadlocked after extra-time then West German referee Helmut Fritz would decide the quarter-final with the toss of a coin.

Richie Morgan: *All the lads were good to me, especially Brian Harris. He knew what I was going through after Scoular told me I was playing and he took me under his wing. He realised I'd probably be nervous in the afternoon so when most of the lads went to sleep, we played cards for a couple of hours. He was trying to take my mind off the game and keep me calm. He knew the nerves might take over the closer we got to the game and was brilliant with me on the pitch as well. He talked me through the game and was always there if I made a mistake. I'm sure I made a few glaring errors but Brian used his skill and experience to cover them up. He was a great professional and he shouted at me all the time – where to go, when to tackle, when to hold off. He did a superb job for me as well as for the team. Brian was playing for a Second Division side but he was still a First Division player.*

Cardiff were hit by two storms early on; a Bavarian blizzard, which soon passed, and a Russian cyclone, which did not. Just as they did in Tashkent, Torpedo wasted no time applying pressure to Scoular's defence but once again they found Wilson in imperious form. The Bluebirds' second-choice goalkeeper produced two terrific saves, first palming away a Vorinin header before stopping Streltsov's strike after the forward had shaken off Morgan. Lenev also went close with a drive that flew just past the post. Cardiff gradually edged their way into the contest and Jones forced Kavazashvili into action with a thunderous shot. Torpedo failed to heed the warning. Four minutes before half-time the crowd of nearly 26,000 saw 'Dixie' Dean fire the Bluebirds ahead after the Russian defence had been opened up. Toshack outjumped Vladimir Pakhomov, Torpedo's gangly centre-half, to head Coldrick's long ball to the unmarked Dean who controlled the ball with his chest before beating Kavazashvili with a sublime half-volley. Afterwards, Dean said he knew he would score as soon as Toshack flicked the ball on.

Norman Dean: *A cross came in and Tosh nodded it down. The ball bounced nicely but I had to be patient. I volleyed it from about 10-12 yards out. That was one of my strong points as a player, I could hit the ball and hit it with both feet - something we were taught at Southampton. Me, Martin Chivers and Mick Channon always practised shooting, volleying and crossing and we were taught to hit the target.*

Richie Morgan: *Norman Dean was the best I've ever seen when it came to volleying the ball. I've never watched anyone do it better than him. He had great technique, he could volley from anywhere. It was quite unbelievable. A lot of people can volley the ball but it could go way off target. With Norman it was controlled volleying. What did surprise me that night was the crowd. Because we were playing in West Germany I thought we'd get the backing of the Augsburg crowd but we didn't and that has stuck in my mind. As we were from a Western country I thought they would have supported Cardiff but instead they were with the Russians and I never quite understood that. Maybe they felt Torpedo were the better side or maybe they thought we were English - it was only two years after England beat West Germany in the World Cup final – and didn't understand we were a Welsh club. They weren't openly hostile to us but if you had to say which side of the line they were coming down on, you would have said Torpedo Moscow.*

Graham Coldrick: *It was a good time to score, just before half-time. To see the ball go in was a brilliant feeling, absolutely brilliant. I went down the right, looked up and saw Norman in the box. I whacked it over, Tosh flicked it on to Norman who was on the penalty spot. He let it drop and then hit it on the half-volley. I was an overlapping full-back so I used to go forward quite a lot. Torpedo were comfortable on the ball. They knocked it about and played one-twos but they started to get frustrated. I thought Richie would have been overawed by the occasion but, fair play, he did well that night.*

Watched by their worried coach, who had left his seat on the touchline, Torpedo pressed forward in the second half but the Cardiff defence, brilliantly led by Harris, held firm. Morgan repaid Scoular's faith in him by shackling Streltsov, and frustration eventually overtook the Soviet superstar. First, he caught Morgan in the kidneys, which left the Cardiff player spitting blood. Then, he stood on the defender's throat after being tackled by the young debutant. Lew Clayton and Dr Hamilton both rushed onto the pitch to treat the stricken player who was struggling to breathe while Fritz called for a stretcher. Morgan – who, in a post-match interview, said he feared he "was dying" - soon recovered and continued to control Streltsov for the remaining half-an-hour. "I couldn't get my breath," continued Morgan, "and my face must have gone blue."

Richie Morgan: *I made a sliding tackle on Streltsov and as he got up he stood on my throat. For two or three minutes I struggled to breathe. I can't remember too much about it although Dr Hamilton ran onto the pitch to see me. It probably looked more dramatic than it was. It could have been a lot worse but I was OK after a few minutes. In those days they just threw water on you and slapped you on the back. Some people said it was an accident, some said it wasn't. I always gave Streltsov the benefit of the doubt. He was a big, strong player. He didn't have a lot of pace and that suited me but he was sharp in the air and he came at me time and time again. I'd watched Streltsov at Ninian Park but Torpedo were quite defensive that night so I didn't learn too much about him. The play-off was different, they went on all-out attack, but Bob Wilson made one brilliant save after another and Barrie Jones had the game of his life. He had amazing control and he held the ball away from Torpedo.*

Bobby Ferguson: *Streltsov was a big forward with a thick neck, it was like a bull's. He'd been in a labour camp for five years but was still a powerhouse and he had a hell of a battle with Richie in Augsburg. Richie was a tough boy and he put in a strong tackle on Streltsov. They both went to ground, Streltsov got up quickly and kicked Richie in the throat. You could kill someone doing that. Richie couldn't breathe because the muscles in his throat went into spasm and you could see his diaphragm going up and down. The doc came running onto the pitch and stuck his hand down Richie's throat because he thought he might have swallowed his tongue. He was doing all kinds of things to get Richie breathing again and he finally got the air going through him. It was quite a frightening experience. Richie had a blinder that night, he hardly gave Streltsov a kick, but he was lucky to survive that incident.*

Torpedo's pressure was relentless and, with Wilson helpless, Gershkovitch looked certain to wipe out Cardiff's lead but he miskicked in front of goal. Scoular's men escaped and they should have killed off Torpedo midway through the second-half when Jones only had Kavazashvli to beat, but the winger fluffed his shot which hit the goalkeeper and then bounced out for a corner. The tension became unbearable as the game neared its climax. Ferguson cleared Yenev's shot off the line after the winger had gone past Wilson before the Bluebirds' goalkeeper produced an astonishing save in the closing seconds to prevent Gershkovitch securing extra-time. Wilson catapulted across his goal "in defiance of gravity" to palm away the forward's close-range effort which proved to be the Russians' last attempt. After five minutes of stoppage time, Fritz blew the final whistle. Cardiff, 15ᵗʰ in Division Two and fighting relegation, had beaten Torpedo 1-0 and were in the semi-finals of the Cup Winners' Cup. Scoular's players danced in delight and embraced each other. Morgan – dubbed 'Morgan the Mighty' by the *South Wales Echo* for subduing Strelstov – ran 40 yards to hug his goalkeeper.

Bob Wilson: *I thought the German crowd would cheer us and boo the Russians but they supported Torpedo and you noticed it when you walked off the pitch. They booed us off at half-time and full-time. I could have understood it if we were playing in East Germany but we were in the West. We were coming off and we could hear the crowd booing so me and Malcolm Clarke gave them the V-sign. We'd won and it was our way of saying 'Up yours!' That was one of my better games. I had a busy night and I made a couple of good saves. Jimmy didn't like giving players too much praise but he came over to me in the dressing room, tapped me on the shoulder, and said, 'Well done.'*

Bobby Ferguson: *I had to clear one off the line late on. The forward went around Bob and tapped the ball towards the net. I came in from the blind side and just got back in time to clear it. It was about six inches away from going in. The Torpedo guy had the shock of his life because he hadn't seen me, he was more concerned about Bob. It was a hell of an achievement to knock Torpedo out because they were a powerful side. Bob made a save near the end which was unbelievable. He pushed away a shot from about six yards out. Bob made some cracking saves during that European run. Quite a few times I thought 'Oh, that's a goal' because the shot was so well-struck I didn't think he'd get to the ball but he did.*

Graham Coldrick: *Torpedo put us under a lot of pressure and Bob Wilson made quite a few saves that night, some of them outstanding. He kept us in the game, really. He made a hell of a save near the end. The fella whacked it and Bob dived to his right, got his fingers to it, and pushed it over the bar. It was unbelievable. They had a lot of possession, especially late on. It was backs against the*

124

wall stuff but we held out. That was a hell of a result because a lot of people had Torpedo down as favourites to win the trophy.

Scoular was unable to hide his emotions after his side's extraordinary win. "I almost feel lost for words. I can only say the lads were simply magnificent," he said. "I couldn't have asked any more from them." Harris – who briefly regretted moving to Ninian Park after a nightmare debut, a 7-1 defeat at Plymouth Argyle in October 1966 – said he felt as proud as when he won the FA Cup with Everton two years earlier. The defeated Ivanov was philosophical about the result. "I've always said one goal would decide it but I thought we would have got it," sighed the Torpedo coach. The Soviets would have to wait a little longer for a European finalist while Cardiff advanced to meet Hamburg, and AC Milan played Bayern Munich in the other semi-final.

Richie Morgan: *We played Torpedo over 270 minutes and they only put one goal past us. That was a great achievement because they were a strong side with a lot of quality players. I'm sure when the draw was made they saw us as something of a pushover. They thought they would win so they were a bit shell-shocked when they lost in Augsburg. They didn't show any emotion as they walked off the pitch. We pinched a goal and then didn't give them a lot of space to play. We had a bank of 10 men behind the ball, even Tosh came back to defend. If it had been a flowing end-to-end game we might have struggled. Afterwards Scoular didn't say anything to me apart from 'Well done son'. That's the way the man was. He played me because he expected me to do the job so I'd only done what he expected me to do.*

Peter King: *I was 25 on the day we played Torpedo in Augsburg*
               so the win was a nice birthday present. Richie had an
               absolute blinder, Brian couldn't have played any better,
               and Bob played out of his skin. There was a difference
               in class between us and Torpedo. Their players had a
               lot of technical ability but we got the result because of
               hard work and we also had that bit of luck you need.

Cardiff arrived back at Rhoose the following night, just before 10pm. They were greeted by "a sea of cheering people wearing blue and white". Hundreds of supporters had turned up at the airport to provide Scoular and his players with a heroes' reception. "We might not have got many cheers from the German spectators at the match but this certainly makes up for it," commented Cardiff's manager. His players were also lauded in the Press. 'IT'S WUNDERBAR, WUNDERBAR' screamed the back page of the *South Wales Echo* while the *Western Mail* declared 'MIGHTY TORPEDO FALL TO WELSHMEN'. But on the weekend, against Blackpool at Ninian Park, the heroes of Augsburg returned to reality. Scoular fielded exactly the same side that stunned Torpedo – Murray was still injured – and they lost 3-1, leaving them just four points above the drop zone.

Barrie Jones: *Jimmy Scoular played exactly the same team on the*
                 Saturday against Blackpool and we lost. Whenever we
                 had a good result away in Europe we seemed to lose the
                 following Saturday. We'd struggle because we'd been
                 celebrating a success in the Cup Winners' Cup. What
                 we should have done was fly straight home after the
                 game so we could come in on the Thursday and get
                 ready for the game at the weekend. Jimmy Scoular
                 did change it in the end and we started coming back
                 straight after the game.

Richie Morgan: *We stayed in Augsburg overnight and we had a good night after the game! We had a celebration in our hotel, then we went out. I think some of the more seasoned pros celebrated far longer than I did. For me, euphoria and tiredness kicked in and I went to bed. We played Blackpool on the Saturday and lost and I'm positive the Wednesday night contributed to that. We didn't get back to Cardiff until Thursday evening so we only had Friday to prepare for Blackpool. Today, sides would come straight back after the game so you're in your own place ready to prepare for training on Thursday. We did stay up that season but the European run didn't help our league situation.*

Quarter-Final, First Leg
6 March, 1968
Ninian Park, Cardiff

Cardiff City (1) 1   **Torpedo Moscow (0) 0**
Barrie Jones 43

CARDIFF CITY: Wilson, Derrett, Ferguson, Clarke, Murray, Harris, Jones
Barrie, Jones Bryn, King, Toshack, Bird.

TORPEDO MOSCOW: Kavazashvili, Shumakov, Shustikov, Yenets, Pakhomov,
Lenev, Nepomilujev, Shcherbakov, Streltsov, Brednev,
Pais.

Quarter-Final, Second Leg
19 March, 1968
Pakhtakor Markaziy Stadium, Tashkent

Torpedo Moscow (1) 1   **Cardiff City (0) 0**
Gershkovitch 33

TORPEDO MOSCOW: Kavazashvili, Shumakov, Shustikov, Yenets, Pakhomov,
Lenev, Stanishev, Shcherbakov, Streltsov, Gershkovitch,
Pais.

CARDIFF CITY: Wilson, Derrett, Ferguson, Clarke, Murray, Harris, Jones
Barrie, Dean, King, Toshack, Bird.

(1-1 on aggregate)

Quarter-Final, Play-off
3 April, 1968
Rosenaustadion, Augsburg

Torpedo Moscow (0)   **Cardiff City (1) 1**
                             Dean 42

TORPEDO MOSCOW: Kavazashvili, Nepomilujev, Shustikov, Yenets, Pakhomov,
Lenev, Stanishev, Shcherbakov, Streltsov, Gershkovitch,
Voronin.

CARDIFF CITY: Wilson, Coldrick, Ferguson, Clarke, Morgan, Harris,
Jones Barrie, Dean, King, Toshack, Bird.

8

Champagne With Tears
SV Hamburg, 1968

'That's football, you never know where you are from beginning to end.'

Uwe Seeler

LIKE their Welsh opponents, Hamburg advanced to the semi-finals after surviving a play-off. Olympique Lyonnais forced a third game after wiping out the Bundesliga side's 2-0 advantage in the second leg at the Stade de Gerland. But with the deciding game staged at Hamburg's Volksparkstadion, the Germans had a precious advantage and they repeated the first-leg result with Uwe Seeler – their irrepressible forward and West Germany's captain - scoring both goals, the second from the penalty spot. Bundesliga champions in 1960, Hamburg had been crushed 4-0 by Bayern Munich in the domestic cup final the previous season, but UEFA allowed them to enter the Cup Winners' Cup since Bayern automatically qualified for the 1967-68 competition as holders. As with Cardiff, their success in Europe was in contrast to their dismal domestic form. Before the first leg they were a disappointing 13th in the 18-strong

Bundesliga and had lost their last three league fixtures. With Karlsruhe and Borussia Neunkirchen well adrift at the bottom, there were at least no relegation worries for *die Rothosen* (the Red Shorts).

Hamburg were installed as favourites against Cardiff although coach Kurt Koch would be without his two most influential players – Seeler and stopper Willi Schulz – for the first leg at the Volksparkstadion on 24 April. The pair, ever-present members of the West German side that finished runners-up in the World Cup two years earlier, were both injured four days before the first game, in a 4-1 defeat at Borussia Mönchengladbach. Schulz, rated one of the world's best central defenders and voted best sweeper of the 1966 World Cup, was ruled out with a knee injury and Seeler was sidelined with a thigh problem. With Koch seeking a two-goal lead to take to South Wales, it was the loss of 31-year-old Seeler - twice voted West German Player of the Year - which really hurt Hamburg. So important were Schulz and Seeler to *die Rothosen* that Koch assigned four staff to treat the two internationals, all to no avail.

The absence of Schulz and Seeler – with 108 international appearances between them – improved Jimmy Scoular's chances of leaving Hamburg with a result. Following the Tashkent trip, Scoular saw his charges slump to four consecutive defeats but, after a draw and two wins in the space of eight days, the Bluebirds manager could travel to West Germany with some optimism. Cardiff halted the alarming slide at St Andrew's where they held promotion-chasing Birmingham City to a 0-0 draw before beating both Queens Park Rangers and Carlisle United 1-0 at Ninian Park. Don Murray was now back from injury - the defender returned to action in the win over Rangers – but Richie Morgan was still included in the squad for Hamburg. The unlucky Graham Coldrick was again injured so Dave Carver, who had played in the last three league games, took his place while winger Les Lea, now eligible to play in the competition, made his first European trip. Cardiff flew to Hamburg-Fuhlsbüttel Airport from London. Scoular normally allowed members of the Press and supporters to travel with his squad but, on this occasion, he insisted on club personnel only. The Scot wanted no distractions as he prepared his players for one of the most important games in the club's 69-year history, and within an hour of checking into their Hamburg hotel, he took his squad to the Volksparkstadion for a training session.

Richie Morgan: *We trained at the stadium which was on a flight path so there was only so long we could have the lights on. After training for about an hour-and-a-quarter Scoular decided to finish off with a five-a-side game. He loved his five-a-sides. While this was going on a fella came over and said, 'Mr Scoular, the lights need to be switched off.' Scoular said, 'OK, we won't be much longer.' We carried on playing and in the end they switched the lights off. It went from being very bright to very dark and for a few seconds we couldn't see a thing because our eyes hadn't adjusted to the change, and out of the darkness we heard this Scottish voice shout, 'You bastards! Just wait until you come to Cardiff! We'll turn the fucking lights off there!' That was typical Jimmy Scoular.*

Cardiff's performance in Augsburg had been criticised by sections of the German Press which accused the Bluebirds of an overly-physical approach. Koch's players were told "to make sure they wear shin pads" and Holger Dieckmann, Hamburg's utility player, added his voice to the chorus, claiming Cardiff had been aggressive against Torpedo. *Die Rothosen* were

131

expecting the same treatment and they would also have to break through the Welsh wall minus Seeler who had scored seven of their 16 goals in the Cup Winners' Cup run. But even without the player affectionately called *Uns Uwe* (Our Uwe) by Hamburg supporters, they still posed a formidable threat. The Dörfel brothers, striker Gert and winger Bernd, and midfielder Werner Krämer were all West German internationals while Franz-Josef Hönig was a forward with a decent goalscoring record. Hamburg were aiming to take a two-goal lead to Ninian Park. "Anything under that," remarked the club's technical director Georg Knöpfle, "won't be enough for the return leg." As an added incentive, the Bundesliga club offered their players a 1,000 Deutschmark (£400) bonus to beat the Division Two side. The Cardiff bonus was nowhere near as generous. Scoular's men would receive an £80 windfall if they won inside the Volksparkstadion, £50 for a draw and £25 if they lost by one goal.

Don Murray: *Uwe Seeler was involved with Adidas at the time and he came to our hotel before the game with a couple of other people from Adidas. They wanted to make out we were wearing their brand for the game – we all wore different makes - so they took our boots, blanked out the logos if they weren't Adidas, and then painted three white stripes down them which was the Adidas design. The game was being shown on TV and I think the club must have made a few bob from Adidas. Even if you wore Adidas boots, like I did, they still took them and whitened up the stripes!*

Richie Morgan: *The game was on TV and the club had obviously done a deal with Adidas. They wanted to give us their boots to wear but there was no way we were going to change, so the Adidas people took our boots and painted three white stripes on them, to make it look like we were all wearing Adidas boots. The game was shown in black and white and there weren't close-ups like there are today so they could get away with it. Anyway, all this stuff turned up at our hotel. In return, they gave us a suit carrier, a kit bag and a key ring. We were like kiddies because we'd had something for nothing. We thought we'd arrived. Looking back, I laugh about it.*

Dave Carver: *This German fella came to our hotel on the morning of the game and painted white stripes on all our boots. Most of us wore Adidas boots anyway. The funny thing was the paint hadn't dried by the time we got changed for the game and I remember putting my boots on and getting this white paint all over my hands! For painting stripes on our boots we all got a new pair from Adidas which was nice.*

Scoular kept his line-up for the first game a close secret until the eleventh hour. He toyed with the idea of playing a five-man defence with Morgan as the extra defender but decided to stick with the system that served him well in Augsburg. Bob Wilson was in goal, Carver at right-back, Brian Harris and Murray in the heart of defence and Bobby Ferguson at left-back. Lea was on the right wing at Ronnie Bird's expense with Malcolm Clarke, Peter King and Norman Dean in midfield, Barrie Jones on the left wing and John Toshack up front. "The players realise this is a chance of a lifetime to reach the final of a major European tournament," said the Cardiff manager. "I'm sure they will run until they drop."

Bobby Ferguson: *Jimmy was clever. Before we went to Hamburg he got us together and said he wanted to show us something. He told us he had a friend who lived in Hamburg who'd sent him a newspaper article. It had comments from someone at Hamburg who saw us play Torpedo Moscow in Augsburg. He was giving a run-down of Cardiff City and he said, 'They are a team of terrorists'. Those were his very words! He was basically saying we were a team of kickers and pushers. As a side we didn't take any prisoners but you couldn't call us a team of terrorists. This was Jimmy's way of motivating us and it did get us going. That article really did gee us up. I've never forgotten that description of us – a bunch of terrorists!*

Cardiff walked out into the Volksparkstadion – built mainly with ruins from Einsbuttel, a district of Hamburg destroyed by Allied bombing during the Second World War – with nearly 65,000 people against them. Rockets were lit, horns were blown and banners were waved as the German crowd greeted *die Rothosen* but, after just four minutes, the stadium became "as hushed as a funeral parlour" with Dean giving the Bluebirds a shock lead with their first attack of the night. King passed to Clarke who found Dean with a diagonal ball through the middle. The former Southampton player evaded one German challenge and then moved towards Hamburg's 18-yard box. From just outside the penalty area, Dean used his right foot to squeeze an accurate shot between Hamburg's Turkish goalkeeper, Arkoç Özcan, and the post. As Dean and his teammates celebrated, the only noise that could be heard inside Hamburg's arena emanated from the 50 travelling supporters.

Norman Dean: *I expected to play up front but Jimmy Scoular picked me at right-half. I was quite happy as long as I was playing. We attacked down the right and a good ball came in. I was about two or three yards outside the box, on the left hand side, and I pushed the ball forward and then hit a low shot which went into the bottom corner. I celebrated by running around the penalty box with my arms in the air and I could see the other lads coming towards me. Dave Carver was the first to get to me. After going 1-0 up, the manager pushed me further back but I did get another chance to score with a header. I was about 10-15 yards out but I just couldn't get up enough and it came off the top of my head and went over the bar. That would have put us 2-0 up.*

Dave Carver: *Scoular put steel into us and that meant we never had a complex playing teams like Hamburg. We were never, ever fearful. Scoular wasn't the best tactician but he made sure we never went onto the pitch feeling inferior to our opponents. We never thought 'Bloody hell, we're playing Hamburg.' We always went out believing we could get a result and that was down to the manager.*

Dean's goal was the cue for a relentless Hamburg onslaught. Wilson produced a fine save to stop a Hönig strike and then Harris headed Gert Dörfel's swerving free-kick against the underside of the crossbar after his goalkeeper failed to reach it. Before that, Jones crossed for Dean but he was unable to guide his header on target. Hans Schulz looked certain to score an equaliser just before half-time but Wilson, again in brilliant form, raced off his line to foil the midfielder. The script stayed the same in the second-half with the Bluebirds defence working overtime to keep out the home side. Hamburg shots either went high or wide or were saved by the outstanding Wilson. Cardiff kept 10 men behind the ball with Toshack cutting an isolated figure up front.

Bobby Ferguson: *Dean scored a cracker and after that it was backs to the wall. We were getting slaughtered and we just tried to hang on. We had been under pressure in Augsburg but more so in Hamburg. We just couldn't get out of our own half and we hardly crossed the halfway line. There was a hell of a pressure on our defence. Technically, Hamburg were much better than us. We just battled and battled. Bob had a blinder in goal and he made some fantastic saves, just as he did in Augsburg.*

Bob Wilson: *The game in Hamburg was probably the best performance of my career. We were under pressure but we all accepted that was going to be the case and everything went well for me that night. I wasn't in the first team at the time - Fred Davies was - so one week I'd be playing a side such as Lovell's Athletic and the next I was in the semi-final of the Cup Winners' Cup at the Volksparkstadion. It was amazing really, unreal.*

John Toshack: *Hamburg kept coming and coming and coming. I felt like John Wayne in 'The Alamo' and the lads at the back produced a terrific display. Brian Harris was outstanding during this run. He relished those games, probably because they took him back to his time at Everton where he played in some big games like the FA Cup final. He was experienced which was invaluable in the European games. He brought confidence to*

*the whole team, especially the defence, and he was a
calming presence at the back. Brian was in his 30s
when he came to Cardiff but he could read the game
and he formed a good partnership with Don Murray
who was strong in the air.*

Wilson was eventually beaten in the 69th minute, right-
back Helmut Sandmann the unlikely Hamburg saviour. Gert
Dörfel's corner fell to Sandmann after bouncing between
Murray's legs, and the defender, unmarked and seven yards
from goal, slammed the ball past Wilson. After 70 minutes of
resolute defending, Cardiff had been unstitched by a routine
set-piece. In the *South Wales Echo* Peter Jackson described the
German equaliser as a "simple affair which left City defenders
looking at each other and wondering 'How did that happen?'"
Hamburg now sensed a winner and they almost claimed it
five minutes from time. Spanish referee José Maria Ortiz de
Mendibil penalised Murray for dangerous play inside the
penalty box and awarded the Germans an indirect free-kick
in between the penalty spot and Wilson's six-yard box. Cardiff
erected a barricade with every player standing in front of the
goal. "It looks as if they're lining up for a photo," observed
BBC commentator Kenneth Wolstenholme. The wall did its
job. Krämer's low shot was blocked on the line by Ferguson
before being cleared by Harris. Mendibil played four minutes
of stoppage time but Hamburg were unable to conjure a late
and dramatic winner.

Don Murray: *Hamburg threw the kitchen sink at us after Norman
scored but we defended brilliantly. I remember this
free-kick against us. The ball came to Bobby Ferguson
who was on the line and it got stuck between his legs
and there was Brian Harris to kick the ball away!*

137

We were really under the cosh and Bob Wilson kept us in the game. His performances in Augsburg and Hamburg were two of the best by a goalkeeper that I've ever seen.

Bobby Ferguson: *One of the Hamburg players had a shot in the last few minutes. It was a screamer, it fizzed along the ground. I'd sat down on the touchline and the ball got jammed under my backside. I looked up and saw an avalanche of people coming towards me, like a herd of buffalo! I was trying to get the ball from under my legs so I could clear it and in the end Brian managed to kick it away.*

Cardiff left the Volksparkstadion with a 1-1 draw and, inevitably, Scoular's players were now dreaming of Rotterdam. 'CITY HAVE ONE FOOT IN THE FINAL' declared the back page of the *South Wales Echo* which hailed the Bluebirds defence for defying the "German blitzkrieg". Harris later likened the game to the film, *Zulu*, and claimed Hamburg were a better side than Torpedo Moscow. "I'm confident we can now get to the final but I'm not in any way overconfident....they will give nothing away at Ninian Park." Scoular, who admitted he would have been "happy" with a 1-0 defeat, expected the second leg to be just as difficult. "The only significant difference," he remarked, "is that the pressure is now on Hamburg." Sections of the German Press were pessimistic about the Bundesliga side's chances in the Welsh capital. "Only a miracle can see Hamburg through to the final," was the verdict of *Bild*, the country's biggest-selling newspaper.

Les Lea: *If it wasn't for Bob we would have lost in Hamburg by two or three goals. He made some top-drawer saves that night, he was out of this world. We were under tremendous pressure in the second half and we just couldn't get the ball out of our own half. It was a relief when we did get it clear but then it came straight back at us. Our defence was excellent and we also had a bit of luck. Jimmy Scoular was pleased after the game. He had a smile on his face and said one or two nice things to us. He wasn't like that often because he expected a performance from us every time but that night he couldn't say a word against us.*

Bob Wilson: *After the game we went to the Reeperbahn for a few drinks. That's where all the bars were. You could describe the Reeperbahn as Amsterdam-plus. We went into bars and they'd have these naughty shows. It was dancing and cabaret. Girls would come over and ask you to buy them a drink. Then one of the other lads would come in and say, 'You should see what they're doing at this club down the street!' and we'd move on to that club. I'd never seen anything like the Reeperbahn before. There weren't just men drinking in these bars, there were women too. We had a few beers and watched some shows. It was harmless fun. A few of us never went to bed that night.*

The clubs had agreed to play the second leg a week later, on May Day. Another stalemate – the away-goal rule did not apply to the latter rounds – and the two sides would contest a play-off in the Danish town of Vejle, in the southeast of the Jutland peninsula, on 16 May. Cardiff anticipated a sell-out at Ninian Park and printed 60,000 tickets while extra staff were hired to deal with the huge number of postal applications. On the pitch the Bluebirds geared up for the return game with a 1-1 draw at Blackburn Rovers. With one eye on the semi-final, Scoular rested his defensive pillars, Harris and Murray. Hamburg, meanwhile drew 0-0 at home with champions Eintracht Braunschweig. Willi Schulz and Seeler were again absent but Koch hoped both men would recover in time to play at Ninian Park. Seeler, nicknamed *der Dicker* (the Fat One) by his teammates, stayed behind in Hamburg for an extra day for further fitness tests under the supervision of club doctor Kurt Fischer.

Peter King: *We had a league game at Blackburn before the home leg and the manager wanted to rest some of his senior players. Lew Clayton said the boss wanted to see me, Don and Brian in his office, one at a time. So I went in and Scoular said, 'Do you need a rest on Saturday because the Hamburg game is coming up?' I told him no. He said, 'Are you sure?' I replied that I'd rather play. Don and Brian felt it was beneficial to have a rest but I played and the boss made me captain. That was the only game I was captain during my time at Cardiff City.*

Bobby Ferguson: *On the morning of the game Jimmy Scoular took us to St. Pierre (Golf and Country Club) in Chepstow because he wanted to get us out of Cardiff and away from the Press but I thought that was a mistake. We got there at about 9.30am and had a big lounge to stay in but no bedrooms where we could have a rest. Instead we were hanging around a golf club all day. We didn't know what to do with ourselves. It was a lovely day and we had a walk around the course but that's not really what you want to do before a game. You wanted to relax, to switch off, to rest and have a sleep so you felt refreshed afterwards. I liked a kip before a game and I'd wake up feeling like a new man but before that match with Hamburg I felt as if I'd been on the go all day, I didn't feel as fresh and sharp as I wanted to be. We also spent an hour on the coach getting from Chepstow to Ninian Park. I don't think going to St. Pierre affected the result but it was still the wrong thing to do. It was a crazy idea. Scoular should have treated it as just another game and we should have stayed at home, had two or three hours kip, and then made our way to the ground for 5pm.*

Scoular named the same side that defended so heroically in Hamburg. He could have selected Coldrick as he had recovered from his hamstring problem but the full-back had not played since 12 April and there was also the risk he might suffer a recurrence of the injury during the game. With only one substitute permitted, Scoular did not want to waste it on an injured player, while Carver, the man who had replaced Coldrick, was in fine form. Willi Schulz was again ruled out but Seeler was declared fit with Heinz Libuda making way for the team captain, the only change to the side held at the Volksparkstadion. Cardiff had home advantage but now faced a Hamburg side led by a world-class forward. "I want the fans to keep cheering even if, at times, things don't work out," said Scoular beforehand. "If they stay right behind us all the time, they can see us through."

Bob Wilson: *We felt we could go all the way. After drawing in Hamburg, we had our eyes on Rotterdam. We thought 'We've got this far, now it's all on the day.' We'd got a result at their place so we had a good chance. We were at home, we were a side that could hold our own, and we were always capable of scoring. Personally, I thought we'd do it.*

On a beautiful spring evening, a crowd of 43,070 squeezed into Ninian Park, the vast majority willing Scoular's players to make history, and Stadion Feijenoord beckoned after 10 minutes when Dean claimed another extraordinary European goal. As was the case in Hamburg, Clarke was the provider. He slipped the ball to Dean who was standing just inside the penalty area and, with his left foot, the 23-year-old unleashed a first-time shot which Özcan was powerless to stop. Ninian Park erupted but the mood quickly changed as the Bundesliga side took just five minutes to respond. Gert Dörfel's pass fell to Hönig and the Hamburg player who most impressed Scoular in the first leg, lashed a superb first-time strike past Wilson.

Cardiff soon recovered and, during an exhilarating 26-minute spell, they bombarded Özcan's goal in search of a second. The Turk made an excellent save to deny Jones before Dean shot wide with the goal at his mercy after Özcan and his defence failed to clear a Jones cross. King then flicked on Carver's long ball to Dean who had ghosted behind the Hamburg defence but Özcan once more rescued the visitors. He made another impressive save just before half-time when Toshack headed Harris' free-kick into the penalty area. Jürgen Kurbjuhn's sliced clearance dropped straight to Dean who watched the former Beşiktaş and Austria Wien goalkeeper tip his header over the target. The first leg roles had been reversed. Now it was Hamburg on the back foot with Cardiff, making a mockery of their league position, launching one attack after another.

Les Lea: *Hamburg were favourites to win, even at Ninian Park, but as the game went on I felt we'd get the result. After half-an-hour I thought we had a great chance of beating them. The game was in our hands and maybe we underestimated them in the second-half. Personally, I didn't have a great game. We didn't want to concede so I kept falling back. I didn't want the opposing full-back coming down the line so I twisted my game around. It was a difficult game for a winger and I was too wary that night.*

Bobby Ferguson: *We were at home but we were still the underdogs because they were full of internationals and Seeler was back. To be honest, Hamburg were better than us all over the pitch but we had a team spirit which was essential. If you have spirit and belief, then you've got a chance. It was always going to be a battle but we stuck together and fought like hell. Everybody worked hard for each other.*

The interval provided Hamburg the opportunity to regroup and they were a more dangerous unit in the second half, taking the lead in the 56th minute courtesy of Seeler's audacious strike from just inside the 18-yard box. The Hamburg captain scooped Gert Dörfel's pass off the ground with his right foot and then used his left to lob the ball over the tall goalkeeper who was off his line. 'What a goal! Oh, what a great goal by Seeler!" were the words of BBC commentator Wolstenholme. The band of Hamburg supporters chanted 'Uwe! Uwe!' The momentum was with Koch's side and they almost claimed a third, Gert Dörfel hitting the post after being put through by Krämer.

Bob Wilson: *We seemed to be giving them too much room in the middle of the park in the second half. They were dominating that area and that's why they went 2-1 up. I think Seeler had a bit of luck with his goal. It was*

143

a swing and hope. Maybe I'm doing him an injustice but I'm not sure he meant it. He had his back to goal and just swung at it. I thought it was going over the bar but it dropped into the top corner of the net. You've got to hold your hand up, it was a good goal from his point of view and a bad one from ours. Seeler did a similar thing against England in the 1970 World Cup. That was the type of player he was.

Peter King: *Seeler kicked the ball over his shoulder from the edge of the box. It was a great looping shot and there was nothing Bob could do about it. I don't care how good Uwe Seeler was, it was a fluke. I've got no qualms saying that. I don't think he was attempting to score from that position. I think he was just trying to kick the ball into the middle.*

Cardiff's resilient streak surfaced once more and, with 12 minutes remaining, Harris levelled the tie in front of the Grange End with what proved to be the only goal of his Ninian Park career. Kurbjuhn fouled Jones and the winger's subsequent free-kick was headed into the far corner of Özcan's net by Harris. The equaliser sparked a pitch invasion by jubilant Cardiff supporters which delayed the restart. Dutch referee Laurens van Ravens would add on that time at the end. Scoular's players were now in the ascendancy and pressed for the goal that would send them to Rotterdam. Kurbjuhn cleared a Dean effort off the line and Toshack was just inches away from reaching Dean's pass.

The second leg then went into stoppage time, van Ravens playing the time it took the police to clear the pitch after Harris' equaliser. With nearly a minute-and-half of stoppage time played, and just as it seemed the semi-final was heading for a play-off in Vejle, Hönig collected a loose ball inside his own half. The Hamburg number 10 surged forward with Jones in pursuit. Hönig crossed the halfway line and continued to run until he was 25 yards from Wilson's goal. Seeler and Gert Dörfel were both to his right, but there appeared to be little danger as neither player was in a threatening position while Cardiff's back four were in front of Hönig. So the German fired a shot. It should have been a comfortable save for the goalkeeper but, to the horror of the Cardiff players, dugout and supporters, the ball spun over Wilson's hand and rolled into the net. Wilson scrambled back in a desperate bid to stop his side's exit but he had no chance of remedying his error. With only seconds left, Hamburg had booked their place in the final.

Barrie Jones: *Hönig picked the ball up inside his own half and started running with it. I chased after him and looking back, I wish I'd kicked him. I didn't think of fouling him because I didn't think he'd score. He was stretching when he hit the ball so it wasn't a blinding shot. It wasn't as if he got into his stride and blasted it. Hönig was knackered as well because it was the end of the game. I saw Bob get to it and I actually turned away because I thought he'd saved it. I was looking for space to get the ball. Then I looked back and saw the ball was in the net and Bob was lying on the ground looking distraught. We were unlucky to lose that game. We should have gone to the final in Rotterdam because I felt we were the best over two legs. We were the far better side in Cardiff and deserved to win. I had no luck in semi-finals. I lost in the FA Cup semi-final with Swansea, I lost in the League Cup semi-final with Plymouth, and I lost the Cup Winners' Cup semi-final with Cardiff.*

Bob Wilson: *Hönig shot and I dived to my left. I tried to punch the ball away with my right hand. I tried to palm it away for a corner. I got my hand to it but only my last two knuckles. I just didn't catch it right. You could say it was a mistimed punch, a misconnection. The ball went up and bounced into the net. I could sense the crowd's disappointment and there was nowhere to hide. I wanted the ground to open up. That's the thing about being a goalkeeper – if you make a mistake there's nobody to bail you out. I really thought we were going to win that game and when it was 2-2 I thought we'd get the winner. I'd had all these good games in Europe but I knew I was going to be remembered for letting in a nasty goal. I just wanted to jump into the Taff that night. It was such a sad way for the campaign to end. I felt it had all been for nothing. My wife, Maureen, was in the Grandstand watching the game. She didn't see the goal because she left a few minutes before the end so she could get a seat in the players' lounge which got busy after games. One of the journalists – he wasn't one of the local guys - said she was pale-faced as she left as if she had a premonition of what was going to happen. It was a load of cobblers! I wasn't happy about those comments but there was no point complaining.*

Hönig's last-gasp strike was effectively the final kick of the game. As soon as Dean touched the ball for the restart, van Ravens blew the final whistle. Cardiff's remarkable Cup Winners' Cup journey was over. The Hamburg players embraced each other while their shattered and dejected opponents made their way to the dressing room. Wolstenholme neatly summed up the second leg's final act. "Is there a crueller blow in football than that?" Seeler conceded *die Rothosen* were "very lucky" to win. "It's a game of 90 minutes and we won it in the last second. What more can I say?" Scoular refrained from criticising Wilson in public – "my sympathies are with Bob Wilson because if a goalkeeper makes a mistake then more often than not it is fatal" – but, in the privacy of the dressing room, he told the 24-year-old Brummie he would never play for him again. 'Iron Man' Scoular would keep his word. The former decorator remained at Cardiff until January 1970 but was never picked.

Bobby Ferguson: *We were on top and pressing for the winner when they got the third goal. Both sides had settled for the play-off and I'm pretty sure that guy didn't think he'd score. It was hit in hope, he did it to waste time. I had a good view of what happened. Bob dived for the ball and that put backspin on it. It was incredible the way the ball moved. It shot forward and then went behind Bob. I couldn't believe it when the ball went in. We were all down in the dressing room. We just sat there in disbelief. I sat there for quite a while before I went for a bath. Jimmy Scoular was ranting and raving at Bob and said to him, 'You'll never play for me again.' Brian Harris was convinced we'd make it to the final and had bought a bottle of champagne. It was in the dressing room after the game but went down like a lead balloon. Bob was really low after the game. I told him to forget about it and said he'd been magnificent in Augsburg and Hamburg. I saw him quite a bit because he lived two doors down from me in Rhiwbina. I don't think he ever got over that mistake. Scoular never gave him the chance to get over it.*

Don Murray: *We were all absolutely gutted. We were so close but we fell at the final hurdle. That was one of the worst moments of my career along with the defeat at Sheffield United in 1971 which cost us promotion. I felt for Bob. Nobody could blame him because if it wasn't for him we wouldn't have got that far in the competition. If an outfield player makes a mistake then someone else can cover up. If a goalkeeper makes a mistake then it usually ends in a goal. After that game Jimmy should have put his arm around Bob but that wasn't in his nature. All the players went up to Bob and said, 'We wouldn't have got this far if it wasn't for you.'*

Gary Bell: *I watched that game from the stands and I could see the guy (Hönig) running with Barrie Jones chasing him. He got the ball in our half and kept going and going. I was thinking to myself 'Just kick him, Jonesey. Just kick him.' They would have had a free-kick but it would have been far out. Barrie didn't kick him, he wasn't that sort of player, and the guy scored with virtually the last kick of the game. It was so cruel. It was a bumpy pitch and that probably didn't help Bob. I was in and around the dressing room after the game and Scoular said to Bob, 'You'll never play for this club again'. That was terrible, really. It was because of Bob's performances that we got as far as we did. It was said in the heat of the moment but that was Bob's last game for the club.*

Afterwards, and inside a silent and dimly-lit Ninian Park, Wilson faced the media. "I feel sick," he said, "and I'm sick of people coming up to me and saying 'bad luck'." Despite

148

the heartbreaking defeat, Harris uncorked the champagne although he remarked, "It doesn't taste the same with tears in it." The defender thought his equaliser had at least secured a play-off in Denmark, but then came Wilson's mistake. Recalling the game in 1999, Harris - who died in 2008 – said, "It was sickening because we didn't deserve to lose. We played well that night. It was the manner of the goal more than anything. Unfortunately, Bob made a right mess of it but that's a goalkeeper's life. He took the plaudits from the first leg, he had to take the stick from the second. If it was a superb goal you couldn't have any qualms about it, but it wasn't. We didn't deserve to lose and we didn't deserve to lose like that."

Bob Wilson: *If Jimmy Scoular said something to me I don't remember it. I was numb after the game. I was blocking everything out and I didn't want to see anybody. Even if he had said something sympathetic I wouldn't have noticed. All I can remember was Bobby Ferguson, who was also a neighbour, saying, 'Come on, let's go out' and we went to a quiet pub with the wives for a few drinks. I'd never felt so dejected in my life. It was a horrible feeling and it lasted for weeks. It was something you couldn't walk away from. It turned out to be my last appearance for Cardiff. I knew after the game it was the end for me at the club. Fred Davies was the number one and I knew I'd eventually be off somewhere else. I did take some consolation from what happened in the Challenge Cup Final between Wakefield Trinity and Leeds at Wembley a few days later. I was watching that game on TV and in the last minute Wakefield had a conversion right in front of the posts. Don Fox only had to put the ball over the bar and Wakefield would win the cup but he missed.*

I remember thinking 'I know how you feel Don'. That showed mistakes could happen to anyone, it wasn't just me.

Les Lea:

Our dressing room was like a morgue afterwards. Brian Harris opened a bottle of champagne and I had a glass. I think most of the lads did. After the game I went to a friend's house and my old P.E. teacher, Mr Tomlinson, was there waiting for me. He'd come down from Urmston to watch me play. I had no idea he was there. I'd not met him since I left school at 15 and was thrilled to see him again because he was a lovely man. He said he thought we were unlucky and he did lift my spirits. It took me ages to get over that game. We all thought about it for a few days but nobody wanted to say anything because it was such a sore subject and we didn't want to upset Bob.

Norman Dean:

We were all slumped in the dressing room after the game. For about 10 minutes nobody spoke. Usually you'd have a bath and get changed but everyone just sat there, silent. Then there was a knock on the door. My mum and two sisters had come down from the Midlands to watch the game. I had no idea they were there. So I had a bath, got ready and took them into the city centre for something to eat. I was glad they had turned up because it was a good outlet after what happened. But it took me a while to get to sleep that night because I kept thinking about the game. Bob was sick afterwards but none of us blamed him. What was annoying was the fact we allowed the player to run 30 yards before he shot. I felt so sorry for Bob. He did us proud in the previous three games.

Cardiff nursed a post-Hamburg hangover until the end of the season. Their final two home games - against Huddersfield Town and Charlton Athletic – both ended 0-0 and in between they lost 1-0 at Norwich City. Scoular's side finished the campaign in 13th place, their exertions in the Cup Winners' Cup had clearly affected their league form. However, the run to the semi-finals was good for the Bluebirds' bank account with the Welsh club banking £24,000. They also retained the Welsh Cup, demolishing Hereford United 6-1 over two legs. Hamburg may have wriggled past Cardiff but they were comfortably beaten 2-0 by AC Milan in the final at the Stadion Feijenoord where Swedish forward Kurt Hamrin scored twice in the opening 20 minutes.

Steve Derrett: *We were on a huge bonus to reach the final. We would have got £1,000 each. That was a life-changing amount. Win or lose, that was the bonus and the club would also have sent us to Majorca for a holiday and our wives and girlfriends would have joined us. But nobody was thinking about that during the game. It doesn't matter how much is on the table – it could have been a million pounds – it doesn't make you play any better. That mistake cost Bob his career at Cardiff City. Everyone was devastated but none of the players blamed Bob because he had been superb in Tashkent, Augsburg and Hamburg. It was just a mistake on the day, one of those things.*

John Toshack: *To lose in that way was tragic. If it was a great goal or a well-worked goal...but to lose it that way made it even more difficult to stomach, and Ninian Park was a miserable place after the game. Poor old Bob, he had been outstanding in all the matches, then he made one mistake. For a Second Division side to have come so close to reaching a European final, it was unheard of, and for me, the highlight of my first five years of professional football was that particular European run.*

Semi-final, First Leg
24 April, 1968
Volksparkstadion, Hamburg

SV Hamburg (0) 1   **Cardiff City (1) 1**
Sandeman 69   Dean 4

SV HAMBURG: Özcan, Sandeman, Kurbjuhn, Dieckmann, Horst, Hellfritz, Schulz H, Krämer, Libuda, Hönig, Dörfel G.

CARDIFF CITY: Wilson, Carver, Ferguson, Murray, Harris, Dean, Jones, Clarke, King, Toshack, Lea.

Semi-final, Second Leg
1 May, 1968
Ninian Park, Cardiff

Cardiff City (1) 2   **SV Hamburg (1) 3**
Dean 10, Harris 78   Hönig 15, 90 Seeler 56

CARDIFF CITY: Wilson, Carver, Ferguson, Murray, Harris, Dean, Jones, Clarke, King, Toshack, Lea.

SV HAMBURG: Özcan, Sandeman, Kurbjuhn, Horst, Hellfritz, Dieckmann, Schulz H, Krämer, Seeler, Hönig, Dörfel G.

(SV Hamburg won 4-3 on aggregate)

9

Battle of the Das Antas
FC Porto, 1968

'In Portugal, we know only how to attack.'

José Maria Pedroto

FOUR years after the unforgettable victory over Sporting Lisbon, Cardiff were again presented with Portuguese opposition in the shape of FC Porto, their first round opponents in the 1968-69 competition. Ninian Park would stage the first leg on 18 September with the return in the 65,000-capacity Estádio das Antas on 2 October. José Maria Pedroto's side had beaten Vitoria Setubal to lift the Portuguese Cup yet it was the first piece of silverware in a barren, and at times, traumatic decade for the Oporto club. While the Primeira Liga title had become the property of the Lisbon giants since 1960 – Benfica winning eight with Sporting breaking the sequence in 1962 – Porto almost went bankrupt in 1965 and, in a desperate bid to raise money, director Anibal Abreu virtually begged Benfica to buy their best players. Porto had finished third in the last three seasons and the Portuguese Cup triumph was their first trophy since they were crowned champions of Portugal nine years earlier. The previous season they were dumped out of the Inter-Cities Fairs Cup in the first round by Hibernian, the

Scottish side winning 3-0 in Edinburgh and losing the return 3-1. "I think Cardiff should beat them," proclaimed Hibernian manager Bob Shankly - brother of Liverpool's Bill – after learning of the draw.

After a shocking start to the campaign, blamed on a six-week, end-of-season tour to Australia and New Zealand where they played 14 games, Cardiff's results had dramatically improved. They dropped to the bottom of the table after losing their first three fixtures – against Crystal Palace, Charlton Athletic and Norwich City – but a 3-3 draw at Bury stopped the rot and with the forward pairing of Brian Clark and John Toshack banging in the goals, Cardiff won their next four games although they went into the first leg on the back of a 3-0 hiding at Huddersfield Town.

Porto's side included three members of the Portugal squad which finished third at the 1966 World Cup. Américo, their goalkeeper, was the understudy to Joaquim Carvalho. Right-back Alberto Festa played in three World Cup games including the semi-final against England but was now sidelined after being hurt in a car crash. Like Américo, midfielder Custódio Pinto, one of Porto's star men, did not make an appearance in England. Feeling unwell before the first leg, Pedroto named the intelligent link player as a substitute. Pedroto – nicknamed *Zé do Boné*, the Portuguese name for the comic-strip character Andy Capp, as he usually wore a flat cap – promised his side would not be negative at Ninian Park. "We know only how to attack," said the 39-year-old coach after arriving in Cardiff via Lisbon and London. Porto's main weapon was Brazilian striker Djalma, scorer of 26 goals during the last campaign and the highest-paid player at the das Antas. Their left-winger, Francisco Nóbrega, had made four appearances for Portugal and scored both goals in their 2-1 cup final win over Vitória Setúbal.

As the Primeira Liga season had kicked-off just 11 days before the first leg, Cardiff possessed a fitness advantage over *os Dragoes* (the Dragons) but Jimmy Scoular was wary of the Porto threat and warned his players the game would be as tough as their previous Cup Winners' Cup battles. "I will be happy if it's 1-0 in our favour," confessed the Cardiff manager. Three players were handed their European debuts – goalkeeper Fred Davies, midfielder Mel Sutton and striker Brian Clark. Unhappy with Graham Coldrick's display at Leeds Road, where Cardiff were soundly beaten 3-0 by Huddersfield Town, Scoular picked Steve Derrett at right-back. Brian Harris and Don Murray were the two central-defensive pillars. Gary Bell, a left-winger converted into a left-back, was now preferred to Bobby Ferguson who was axed after the Charlton Athletic defeat. Ronnie Bird and Barrie Jones were the two wingers and Peter King – who had recovered from a pulled chest muscle – joined Sutton in the middle of the park behind Clark and Toshack. Norman Dean, who made such an astonishing impact in the previous Cup Winners' Cup crusade, had left Ninian Park before Porto's visit, joining Division Three club Barnsley. His goalscoring exploits against Torpedo Moscow and Hamburg during the march to the semi-finals were not enough to convince Scoular he was worth a first-team spot and 'Dixie' moved to Oakwell in a £10,000 deal, with Cardiff making a £4,000 profit.

Fred Davies: *Jimmy Scoular was up for this game and he really wound us up beforehand. He got us together and said Porto have got all these international players and they're this and they're that. He also said they were softies. That was the way he motivated us. It was my first European game because I was ineligible the previous season so Bob Wilson had played in the Cup Winners' Cup. He made a mistake and was crucified for it but he didn't make that mistake on purpose. Me and Bob got on well – goalkeepers mainly do get along because we work together.*

Norman Dean: *After the season I'd just had, I was disappointed when Scoular let me go. He said Barnsley had come in for me and that he was willing to sell me. I knew I could do a job for Cardiff if he'd let me, even in midfield. I felt I proved a point in those Cup Winners' Cup matches. I showed him I could play in big games but managers have their own ideas. When I was at Southampton we won promotion to the First Division and I scored 11 goals in 18 appearances, which wasn't bad! I really felt I could have done a job for Cardiff.*

Cardiff were unhappy with the choice of referee for the first leg, fearing Gaspar Pintado Viu, of Spain, might favour his Iberian neighbours. Despite their body checking and pulling shirts and shorts, Porto were unable to disrupt the home side's rhythm, their defence struggling to cope with Toshack's aerial ability. Clark wasted two early opportunities to score before Toshack beat Américo after 23 minutes. The 19-year-old, who almost had his shirt ripped off him by centre-half Bernardo da Velha earlier in the game, headed Jones' cross past the diving goalkeeper and into the top corner. Clark almost doubled the lead before the interval, hitting the post after a fine run.

Porto were being overrun and, in response, Pedroto threw on Pinto at half-time with 19-year-old Pavão making way. Yet it was Cardiff who continued to call the tune and after squandering a wonderful chance at the start of the second half, Bird converted a spot-kick after Toshack was fouled by Porto's other centre-half, Acácio Carneiro. The Bluebirds were cruising and a third goal would surely have killed the tie but, to Scoular's dismay, the Portuguese were allowed back into the contest on the hour. Davies came too far off his line to try and clear a free-kick and Pinto beat him to the ball, heading it into the net. Pinto then equalised with a controversial second, a goal Harris afterwards described as "diabolical". Cardiff claimed the ball was over the by-line when Nóbrega crossed and as the Bluebirds defence stood still, waiting for the sound of a whistle which never came, Pinto headed *os Dragoes* level. "Perhaps we shouldn't have stopped and played to the whistle," admitted Harris afterwards. "But to all of us at that very split second, the ball was so obviously out of play that it was only a question of awarding us a goal kick." Unhappy with many of Pintado Viu's decisions, as well as his reluctance to penalise Porto for their "shirt-grabbing stunts", Harris, as the Cardiff captain, tried to open dialogue with the official from Barcelona. "He didn't speak English, I don't speak Spanish so we really got nowhere." Toshack tried to restore the lead only to see Américo make a brilliant one-handed save. So the visitors claimed a 2-2 draw, a result that had seemed so unlikely after 51 minutes. With two away goals and the second leg in their das Antas cauldron, the odds were firmly in favour of Porto.

Barrie Jones: *Porto equalised with a disputed goal. The ball went over the line by a yard. I'd chased the guy to the by-line so I had a great view. It was over by a good yard before he knocked it into the box. I think Don and the other lads at the back stopped and the fella scored. The ref gave the goal. There was outrage, it was unbelievable. That was a bad decision because the ball had clearly gone over the line. Even Pinto knocked it in thinking 'I'll argue about this after'. We were 2-0 up at one point and I thought we were comfortable. I couldn't see us throwing it away. We were flying and I don't think Don had a kick, but they were a good side and Pinto was a good player. They raised their game when they went 2-0 down. You had to give Pinto credit because they were two great headers.*

Steve Derrett: *We were cruising at home, then we went to sleep. We eased off when we went 2-0 up and they scored twice and came away with a 2-2 draw. Scoular was really angry with us after the game. We should have finished them off at Ninian Park, then the return would have been a formality. Instead we had to go over there and try and get a result. We were doing well at the time. We were playing well and winning games so we should have put the tie to bed at home.*

Scoular was incensed by Pinto's equaliser and Pintado Viu's performance. The referee, he said, failed to punish the Portuguese side's "rugby tactics" and claimed a British official would have sent off three Porto players. "I've played football all over the world," remarked the Bluebirds manager, "and I've never seen anything like the shirt-tugging and body checking by Porto. This is not football." A Spanish referee, he continued, should not have been awarded a game involving a Portuguese side. Cardiff even sent an official letter of protest to UEFA regarding the appointment of Pintado Viu and two Spanish linesmen, Francisco David and Andrés Barragan, for the game. "I think the nationality of Porto and the nationality of the referee were too closely related. If they can have a Spanish referee, why can't we have an English referee over there? We should be allowed one," said Scoular.

Cardiff arrived in northern Portugal a fortnight later buoyed by two consecutive league wins – against Carlisle United and

Bristol City – which had lifted them to sixth in Division Two and two points behind leaders Charlton. The day before flying to Oporto, Scoular and his players gathered at Ninian Park to watch a recording of the first leg and their dominant first-half display convinced the Scot his side was capable of stunning Porto in front of their own public. However, his call to UEFA for an English referee to take charge of the return - to protect his players from Porto's cynicism – was predictably ignored. Frenchman Robert Héliès, once a goalkeeper on St Etienne's books, was given the second leg.

Cardiff's problems in Portugal began well before a ball had been kicked. Scoular wanted to stay in Vila do Conde, a fishing port five miles outside Oporto, but had to change plans when he learned Porto were staying in the hotel he had earmarked. When they arrived at the replacement hotel, in the centre of Oporto, they discovered it was in the process of being renovated. Workmen, drilling and hammering greeted the Bluebirds and when Lance Hayward, the club's assistant secretary, opened his room window, he saw a bag of cement being hauled up on a pulley. The noise was too much for Scoular, who described the hotel as "a shambles", and he moved his squad down the road, to a hotel where Cardiff supporters and the Press were staying.

Graham Coldrick: *We got to the hotel and went to our rooms, then headed downstairs for a cup of tea and some toast before going to training. Jimmy Scoular said, 'Don't unpack your bags – we're not stopping here!' We got our suitcases and moved to another hotel. Jimmy wanted us to have a kip in the afternoons and the building work would have disturbed us. No way was he having that. There were cement mixers all over the place and all this work going on. It was more like a building site than a hotel.*

Barrie Jones: *It was a bit like the hotel in 'Carry on Abroad'. It was terrible. Jimmy said to us, 'Get your bags, we're going somewhere else'. He liked good hotels and good food, and he wanted his players to be comfortable. If it was a poor hotel, or the food wasn't up to scratch, he'd change it. Jimmy was great like that.*

Scoular took 17 players to Portugal, the XI that played at Ninian Park plus Wilson, Coldrick, Les Lea, Leighton Phillips, Richie Morgan and Dave Carver. Cardiff suffered a major setback before the game when Harris, who limped out of the 3-0 win at Bristol City four days earlier with a groin strain, was ruled out. Scoular had been desperate for his inspirational captain to play in Oporto, providing him with an electric heat pad to use at home and flying out ultrasound equipment so he could receive treatment in Oporto, but the veteran defender failed a late fitness test. Derrett took Harris' place in central defence with Coldrick named at right-back, and Lea replaced Bird. The Welsh side were treated to more Portuguese gamesmanship before the match. Scoular was originally told the kick-off would be at 9.30pm but was then informed it had been moved back to 9.45pm. When Cardiff arrived at the Estádio das Antas they were informed the kick-off was 9.30pm so a quarter-of-an-hour's preparation had been lost. In the build-up to the game, Scoular had been asked about Porto's spoiling tactics and whether he was worried his players would react. "Porto are a niggling side but we've never been involved in any trouble," he replied. "We've learned from our experience during the past four years to cope with the problems of European football."

Mel Sutton: *The Porto players were highly strung. Any contact and they would make the most of it. They would go down and then roll about. We weren't used to that sort of thing and we didn't expect the other players to do it. That game was volatile. There had been tension at Ninian Park and that transferred to the second leg. It was a niggly game, the crowd wasn't nice, and the referee wasn't helpful to us.*

Barrie Jones: *The crowd was horrible and so were the Porto players. They thought they were miles better than us, that they were going to beat us comfortably, and that we weren't good enough to be on the same pitch as them. They were fouling us and kicking us. If you went past the full-back, he'd run back and kick you. They were cynical and they were kicking us from the start. They were a horrible lot.*

Porto were backed by a vocal 60,000 crowd and the das Antas erupted with joy in the eighth minute when Djalma beat Davies with a crisp, close-range finish after collecting Nóbrega's pass. Nine minutes later, the Welsh side thought they had been given a glorious chance to equalise when Héliès pointed to the spot. Clark looked certain to score after Toshack headed down Jones' cross but the striker was barged in the back by full-back Valdemar Pacheco. Héliès awarded a penalty and while Clark placed the ball on the spot ready for Toshack, the designated penalty-taker in Bird's absence, Porto players "hustled and manhandled" the Frenchman, urging him to consult his linesman. Even though no flag was raised, Héliès – to the disbelief of the Cardiff players – changed his mind and awarded the home side a free-kick. "From that moment on," opined Peter Jackson in the *South Wales Echo*, "it was painfully obvious City would not have a referee of sufficient strength. Porto had got away with murder." The night further darkened for Cardiff in the 37th minute when they were reduced to 10 men, Héliès dismissing Coldrick for a foul on Porto midfielder and captain Eduardo Gomes. The defender was later fined £10 and suspended for a week by the Football Association of Wales.

Graham Coldrick: *Thirty-seven minutes - it has always stuck in mind. You couldn't meet a nicer fella than Peter King, he wouldn't say boo to a goose. He fouled this lad (Gomes). It wasn't anything malicious but he got up and had a real go at Peter. That just sent me over the top. I detested that sort of thing. I tried to talk to the Porto player but he didn't know what I was going on about so I said, 'I'll have you'. He came flying down the wing and I just went into him – whack! He went through the air like Superman and the ref sent me straight off.*

Steve Derrett: *The referee gave us a penalty, he actually pointed to the spot. The Porto players started pushing and shoving him and then he gave them a free-kick. I realised at that point we weren't going to go through. Then Graham Coldrick was sent off so Mel Sutton had to play right-back. I've never forgotten this one moment when the ball was bouncing between Mel and a Porto player, close to our bench. The referee was near the two players and Scoular shouted out, 'Mel! Now's your chance – kick the fuckin' ref!' Quite a few of us heard it!*

Mel Sutton: *The ball was going along the touchline, near where Jimmy was sitting. The referee was standing close to the touchline and as I went in for the tackle, Jimmy shouts at me, telling me to go for the ball and the*

162

referee! He wasn't happy with the referee and that's the way he was. We all had a good laugh about it later on.

Scoular made his feelings public when Héliès blew for half-time, the 43-year-old sprinting onto the pitch to remonstrate with the referee. Héliès, he felt, had reversed the penalty decision "out of fear". Scoular finally had something to smile about six minutes into the second half when Toshack silenced the das Antas crowd by heading home Derrett's free-kick. Porto, however, exploited their numerical advantage 13 minutes from the end when Pinto, Cardiff's tormentor in the first leg, restored their lead following Djalma's quickly-taken free-kick. The Welsh side would force extra time with a second equaliser and, four minutes from the end, Héliès again pointed to the spot after Pinto pushed Toshack as he went to head another Derrett free-kick. The Porto players inevitably protested but this time there was no volte face. Bird, a spot-kick specialist who had tucked away a penalty in the first leg, was now on the pitch, as a replacement for fellow substitute Leighton Phillips, but Scoular wanted Toshack to take the kick. He was made to regret that call, the agile Américo saving the striker's effort with his forearm. The das Antas exploded with joy. Cardiff, semi-finalists five months earlier, had fallen at the first fence.

John Toshack: *I wasn't the best with penalties, I missed a few during my career. I missed as many as I scored! I remember missing one against Coventry when I was 17 and another in Hungary when I was playing for Wales. If you look at players who've missed penalties – people like Michel Platini and Roberto Baggio – then I'm not in bad company. Birdy usually took our penalties but*

I ended up taking the one in Oporto. It was a difficult place to play and it was pretty hostile that night. Porto had got a draw at our place and their players were desperate to win at home. The das Antas was one of the most hostile places I've been to. I went there as manager of Sporting Lisbon and we got a 0-0 draw. We ended up having to stay in the dressing room for two hours! There was always an atmosphere there and it wasn't nice.

Peter King: *Before the game we went onto the pitch to have a look at it. Tosh was our penalty-taker and he walked up to the goal and said, 'Kingy, we'll get a last-minute penalty and I'm gonna stick it in the corner and we'll win'. Anyway, we got a penalty at the end and it was in the same goal where me and Tosh were talking before the game. Up stepped Tosh who was still a young lad. He put the ball to the right of the goalkeeper but it was saved. Really, one of the more experienced boys should have taken that penalty. When the final whistle went Tosh burst out crying. I tried to console him and put my arm around him.*

It was Bird, not Toshack, who placed the ball on the spot yet it was the teenager who was given the pressure-packed job of taking the penalty. As Bird had taken a penalty at Ninian Park, Scoular felt Américo would know where the winger would place his kick so he chose Toshack. His penalty was struck well but Américo dived the right way. The young Wales international "broke down in anguish" at the end, his team-mates trying to console him. In the dressing room a distraught Toshack sat on a bench, clutching a bottle of mineral water while he stared at the floor, his eyes filled with tears.

Barrie Jones: *Porto went berserk when we got a penalty near the end. All hell broke loose. It wasn't a good penalty, Tosh wasn't a great penalty-taker. He'd taken them before and missed. Birdy was good with penalties and was confident taking them. If he was on the pitch then he should have taken it and I think he would have scored. Tosh missed but had he scored to make it 2-2, I reckon we would have been lucky to get off that pitch.*

Dave Carver: *Tosh was devastated about missing the penalty. He was someone who always kept his emotions in check, even when he was a youngster, but he couldn't control them that night. He was really upset. He was in tears in the dressing room. Tosh was a confident lad and that's why he took penalties but he wasn't a great striker of the ball. The only good thing about that trip was Porto giving us all a nice bottle of port.*

Cardiff's troubles continued after the final whistle, as they headed towards the concrete steps which led to the stadium's underground dressing rooms. Despite the presence of police, some on horseback, hundreds of "frenzied" Porto supporters invaded the pitch after Héliès had blown his whistle for the last time and one made a beeline for Scoular. The police intervened, wielding their truncheons indiscriminately and several of the Cardiff contingent were hit. Director Viv Dewey – who, along with Hayward, was made to watch the game on the bench with Scoular and the playing staff – was struck on the hand and neck. Davies was hit on the shoulder and Scoular on the arm while Clark was shocked when he saw Murray's bare back covered in welts. But it was Wilson who took the heaviest blows. The back-up goalkeeper returned to the safety of the dressing room with blood spurting from a three-inch wound on his head and his back covered in weals inflicted by a police baton. "It was horrifying," said Dewey afterwards, "and the most horrifying aspect of it all was that instead of protecting us, the police attacked us." A 20-yard trail of blood, belonging to Wilson, ran from the bottom of the steps to the door of the visitors' dressing room.

Fred Davies: *I was at the other end of the pitch to the steps which led to the dressing rooms so I had to walk the length of the pitch to get to them. I could see it kicking off as I was making my way over there and by the time I got to the steps, World War Three had broken out! Porto fans were on the pitch and wanted to have a go at Jimmy. The police started hitting people with batons. I was struck on the arm but Bob got it much worse. Porto were a good side but they dived a lot and over-reacted to tackles. They were rolling about every time they were tackled which upset Jimmy and he wasn't afraid to let anyone know how he felt.*

Bob Wilson: *This lad got over the fence and started making his way towards Scoular so four or five of us went to defend him. We were by the steps leading down to the dressing room area. The police then charged into us and started hitting us. I saw policeman's trousers in front of me and I thought 'I'm not going through this for nothing' so I kicked him in the balls. The next thing I knew I was rolling down the steps because I'd been hit on the head by a truncheon. I didn't see what happened to the police guy but Don Murray told me he went down. I didn't feel anything when I was hit on the head because I was pumped up with adrenaline but I knew it was bleeding because there was blood on my hands. There*

*were red welts on my back as well. Our trainer, Lew
Clayton, got someone from Porto to look at the head
wound. He made a sign that it needed stitches and he
wanted to take me into the home dressing room to
get it done but I said there was no way I was going
in there and told him just to put a plaster on it. Doc
Hamilton then put some stitches in and I combed my
parting the other way so they were hidden. When I
got on the coach I was shaking and that was down to
concussion and shock. On top of that I had this fear
the bus windows were going to shatter because Porto
fans were throwing stuff. I was scared glass was going
to fly everywhere. I remember when I got home, my
wife had heard one of the Cardiff players was hit on
the head and she said to me, 'I knew it was you!'*

Scoular had abandoned the policy of staying overnight after
a European away tie, believing it had an adverse effect on his
side's performance the following Saturday, so Cardiff flew out
of Oporto straight after the game. "In one way the penalty
miss might have been a blessing in disguise," wrote Jackson.
"Porto's fans had become so ugly in their mood – so had
their players – that I shudder to think what sort of violence
would have erupted had extra time been played, let alone City
winning." The *Western Mail*'s Clive Phillips said the city famous
for port wine was "overflowing with soccer shame". He wrote,
"I dread to think of the outcome in that vast Antas Stadium...
had Cardiff won."

Don Murray: *The game in Oporto was like a minor war. It was very
heated and there were lots of incidents all over the
pitch. As we were walking off at the end their fans
were throwing cushions at us. A couple of the lads*

threw them back which didn't help. It just inflamed the situation. There were punches and boots flying as we went down the steps. We needed a police escort out of the stadium and I remember a firecracker hitting the coach window. I thought we'd been shot at. We all had to duck down as the bus drove away from the stadium. It was horrific.

Barrie Jones: *Porto had won yet their fans were still causing trouble by our coach. We stayed in our dressing room for ages after the game. It must have been an hour-and-a-half, waiting for everything to calm down but there were still lots of Porto fans waiting for us when we got to the coach. We weren't violent to their players and we'd lost yet they were throwing stones at our bus. We were all crouching down as we were being driven away from the stadium. I sometimes think what would have happened had we won! It was a horrendous experience. We were being hit as we left the pitch and we were trying to get off as quickly as possible. I was kicked as well. It was awful. If it happened today, Porto would be banned from Europe.*

Enraged by the events in Oporto, Cardiff lodged a second protest with UEFA. They complained about the lack of protection on and off the pitch, the confusion over the kick-off time, Héliès reversing his penalty decision, and the das Antas ball boys wearing the same colours as the Porto players. The club sent its letter to the Football Association of Wales and requested the governing body to "register the strongest possible protest to UEFA against the lack of protection given to our players and officials which resulted in their sustaining physical injuries and also against the gamesmanship to which they were subjected".

Copies were also sent to the Football League and the Football Association. The Welsh club's complaints, however, could not be corroborated as there was no UEFA observer at the das Antas so, instead of being expelled from the competition, Porto escaped with a warning. "Had we had a neutral report and had it confirmed what Cardiff City had said, the most serious action would have been taken by UEFA," explained Hans Bangerter, UEFA's General Secretary. There were so many ties on 2 October, continued Bangerter, that it was not possible for an observer to be at every game. Cardiff were unimpressed with UEFA's verdict which was delivered more than five weeks after the second leg. "I don't think the punishment, if you can call it a punishment, meets the crime," said chairman Fred Dewey.

Richie Morgan: *I watched that match on the bench which was probably the safest place to have been. It just kicked off. The game turned nasty and so did the players. At the end we got attacked by their fans but the police didn't protect us. Everybody wanted a piece of us, we were the villains over there. Bottles were thrown onto the pitch and there was a lot of damage to our coach. I was drawing the curtains on the bus and a brick was thrown at the window. What happened in Oporto was swept under the carpet. Nothing was said. Outside of Cardiff, it received very little coverage. If it happened today, UEFA would hold a big investigation.*

Porto's second-round elimination at the hands of eventual winners Slovan Bratislava provided some consolation for the aggrieved Bluebirds. Pedroto's men were crushed 4-1 on aggregate by the Czechs who went on to beat Barcelona in the final. Out of Europe, Cardiff poured their efforts into a promotion charge, the first of Scoular's reign, but inconsistency in the second half of the season – from Boxing Day onwards they suffered eight defeats - cost them a top-two finish and they eventually finished fifth though they claimed the Welsh Cup for the third consecutive year.

Graham Coldrick: *Looking back, what I did was stupid and in the end it cost us the game but what he (Gomes) did wound me up. Scoular had a go at me when we got home. He said what I did was stupid and it was, I wouldn't deny that. I believe we would have won that night had I stayed on the pitch. I said to Scoular, 'What would you have done if you were in the same situation?' He told me, 'That's beside the point. What you did cost us the game.' I got suspended by the Welsh FA and when that happened you didn't get paid so all the lads used to put so much a week into this fund in case any of us got suspended. If we did get banned, then we'd get money from the fund which covered our lost wages.*

Steve Derrett: *We flew straight home after the game in Porto, thank God. It was a horrible, horrible game and we weren't treated fairly. The Porto players were horrendous but we wouldn't back down and gave as good as we got. The police came on at the end and lashed our boys. Bricks and stones were thrown at our coach after the game and to disperse the fans a policeman got his gun out and started firing over the crowd! I've never been back to Portugal since and I wouldn't go back there if someone paid me. What happened that night left a sour taste.*

First Round, First Leg
18 September, 1968
Ninian Park, Cardiff

Cardiff City (1) 2   **FC Porto (0) 2**
Toshack 24, Bird 51 (pen)   Pinto 57, 60

CARDIFF CITY: Davies, Derrett, Bell, Sutton, Murray, Harris, Jones, King, Clark, Toshack, Bird.

FC PORTO: Américo, Sucena, Bernardo, Valdemar, Acacio, Rolando, Pavão (Pinto), Chico, Djalma, Gomez, Nóbrega.

First Round, Second Leg
2 October, 1968
Estádio das Antas, Oporto

FC Porto (1) 2   **Cardiff City (0) 1**
Djalma 8, Pinto 77   Toshack 52

FC PORTO: Américo, Sucena, Bernardo, Valdemar, Atraca, Lisbao, Pavão (Rolando), Pinto, Djalma (Mesquita), Gomez, Nóbrega.

CARDIFF CITY: Davies, Coldrick, Bell, Sutton, Murray, Derrett, Jones, King, Clark, Toshack, Lea (Phillips, Bird).

(FC Porto won 4-3 on aggregate)

10

Men in Brown
Mjøndalen, 1969

'We are not optimistic.'

Kåre Nilsen

MJØNDALEN. A tiny sawmill town in south-east Norway, 28 miles outside the capital Oslo, and Cardiff's first-round destination in the 1969-70 Cup Winners' Cup. The draw had been kind to Jimmy Scoular, pitting his side against the amateurs of Mjøndalen Idrettsforening who plied their trade in the Norwegian second division. Kåre Nilsen's team – which included two students, a gardener, lorry driver, bookkeeper and furniture dealer - were beaten 3-0 by Lyn Fotball in the Norwegian Football Cup final but qualified for the competition since the Oslo club entered the European Cup as league champions.

Cardiff had lost just one of their opening nine league fixtures – their best start to a season since 1959 - and were expected to make light work of a bunch of amateurs making their first-ever appearance in European competition. Scoular, who would take his side to the modest Nedre Eiker Stadion for the first leg, insisted his players had no intention of taking the Norwegians lightly. "To underestimate any opposition is unwise," he said.

Mjøndalen, insisted Scoular, would be treated exactly the same as Torpedo Moscow and Hamburg. Cardiff arrived at their base in Drammen, Norway's ninth largest city and seven miles from Mjøndalen, after a seven-hour journey. The flight to Oslo took nearly five hours which included a 45-minute stop in Amsterdam to refuel. Scoular had taken over 16 players, with Jim Eadie, signed from Scottish club Kirkintilloch Rob Roy, replacing Bob Wilson as back-up goalkeeper. Wilson, who had been involved in every Cup Winners' Cup trip since Sporting Lisbon in 1964, was left at home. The first round clash in the 15,000-capacity Nedre Eiker Stadion was billed as "a blind date" by the *Western Mail* as Scoular confessed he knew nothing about the opposition apart from their shirt colour. "I've no idea what system they operate or what type of game they play – but I do know they wear brown shirts."

Gary Bell: *I missed the game out there because of food poisoning. I ate something dodgy on the plane, something that didn't agree with me. When I got off the plane I felt unwell. I got to the hotel and started throwing up. I tried to do a bit of training on the day of the game but I kept being sick and felt drained so I went back to the hotel and stayed in bed. Nobody else went down with it which was strange.*

Mjøndalen had been one of Norway's top sides during the 1930s when they won three Norwegian titles and three Norwegian Football Cups but the club fell into decline after losing their top-flight status in 1950. The cup final appearance the previous season and a recent cup quarter-final win over First Division leaders Rosenborg hinted at a brighter future. Nilsen's part-timers were also given a lift 24 hours before their duel with the Bluebirds when fellow Norwegians Skeid

Fotball knocked Munich 1860 out of the Inter-Cities Fairs Cup, following up their 2-2 draw in Bavaria with a surprise 2-1 win in Oslo. Skeid's surprise victory had not gone unnoticed at Cardiff's hotel. "Norwegian football can't be as bad as some would make out," commented Scoular although Nilsen remained pessimistic about his side's chances against the Welsh Cup holders, saying, "I hope we don't lose by too many."

Leighton Phillips: *We stayed in a beautiful place surrounded by fjords and mountains. It was stunning. I remember our first morning over there. It was a lovely, crisp day. There wasn't a cloud in the sky. The air was so fresh. I kept breathing it in because you just wanted to inhale it. The Mjøndalen fans were friendly. There was a nice atmosphere at the game. You wouldn't have thought it was a Cup Winners' Cup tie.*

Mjøndalen came to a standstill for the first leg. Paper mills and timber yards shut early and a crowd of 18,000 – nearly quadruple the town's population – squeezed inside the Nedre Eike Stadion, the club erecting temporary stands to accommodate the extra numbers. Before the game, a band of King Olav's Guards marched through the streets of Mjøndalen to mark the club's first game in European football. Cardiff's clash against the men in brown shirts was one of three ties involving British and Norwegians clubs on the same night. In the European Cup, Leeds United faced Lyn Fotball at Elland Road and 254 miles away in Trondheim, Southampton played Rosenborg in the Inter-Cities Fairs Cup.

To replace the sick Gary Bell, Scoular moved Dave Carver to left-back so Steve Derrett, who broke into the Wales side the previous season following some fine displays for his club, could slot in at right-back with Brian Harris and Don Murray, his trusted central defensive pairing. Fred Davies was in goal. Scoular decided to rejig his midfield, axing the out-of-form Barrie Jones for the first time since the player joined Cardiff in March 1967, and handing his number seven shirt to Leighton Phillips who lined up alongside Les Lea, Mel Sutton and Peter King. Scoular told Jones he was dropped less than three hours before kick-off. Brian Clark and John Toshack, already with seven goals between them, led the offensive charge. "We shall play attacking football throughout and will certainly not ease up should we get on top," declared Scoular. "If we are capable of putting in 10 goals then we will."

Steve Derrett: *Mjøndalen was a lovely trip, the total opposite to Oporto. The weather was nice and Norwegian teams were poor in in those days so it was like a mini holiday for us. When we arrived at the ground, there were children dressed in national costume carrying baskets of apples. They were handing apples out before the game. It was a big occasion for Mjøndalen - it was their first-ever time in Europe and they saw Cardiff City as a big club because we'd played a lot of games in the Cup Winners' Cup and reached the semi-finals in 1968. People remembered that and we were well-respected.*

By now, Scoular's priorities had changed. His focus was firmly on the league – "our bread and butter" - and trying to win promotion, not achieving glory in the Cup Winners' Cup. Cardiff had reached the semi-finals in 1968 but that memorable run came at a price as it had a detrimental effect on their domestic form. Now in his sixth season with the Bluebirds and having rebuilt the side in his image, Scoular wanted to achieve what the board of directors had hired him to do – end Cardiff City's exile from the top flight. "If I had to choose, I would sooner be beaten here by Mjøndalen than at Sheffield United on Saturday," he told the Press before the first leg. His players, though, were determined to avoid an embarrassing result in the county of Buskerud. In the late afternoon sunshine, and in a stadium overlooked by mountains and pine trees, Clark put Cardiff in front inside three minutes with his first European goal, prodding King's pass beyond Runar Nilsen, a 28-year-old plumber. The visitors had to wait until the 36th minute for their second. An error by office clerk Torbjörn Loe let Clark in and he placed the ball into the gaping net after dribbling past Nilsen. Three minutes before half-time Toshack joined his strike partner on the scoresheet when he headed home Carver's cross.

The only positive for Mjøndalen came a minute before the interval when shop assistant Jan Olsen made it 3-1, beating Davies with a right-footed drive after a mistake by Derrett.

Barrie Jones: *At that time there was a huge gap between Norwegian football and ours. Mjøndalen were hopeless and the game over there was like a practice match for us. But we were a good outfit that year. The beauty of that Cardiff side was the team spirit. We all got on, both on and off the pitch. It was a good bunch of lads and we were all mates. On the pitch we believed in our ability and everybody knew their job. We had flair players, we had fellas who could score goals, we had a strong defence and we had a good goalkeeper. If that team had stayed together I'm convinced it would have won promotion.*

Dave Carver: *The standard of the opposition wasn't high. We'd had harder games in the Welsh Cup and I had no doubts we'd*

*go through. The ground wasn't up to much. There were
what looked like portable stands down the sides of the
pitch, I think they were erected just for the game. The
pitch wasn't good. It was non-league standard. I ended
up breaking Les Lea's toe in that game. We both went
for the same ball and I accidentally trod on his boot!*

Cardiff showed no mercy in the second half although they
had to wait until the 71st minute to add to their tally when
Lea netted with a 20-yard drive. Three minutes later Sutton
claimed his first Bluebirds goal before Clark set up King with
11 minutes left. Mjøndalen were unable to cope with Cardiff's
breaks and it was a question of how many goals Scoular's
men would score before the final whistle. At the end, the
Norwegians had conceded seven with Toshack completing
the Cup Winners' Cup massacre two minutes from time with
another header. "Boxing's equivalent would surely have been
a humane first-round stoppage by the referee," wrote Peter
Jackson who claimed the manner in which "Mjøndalen's
hopeless amateurs" were ripped apart was "enough to make
a Viking turn in his grave". Even Scoular admitted he was
"disappointed" by the Norwegian effort.

Peter King: *One of the Mjøndalen players came up to me in the
second half and said, 'Please don't score any more
goals.' I didn't pay any notice because you could never
feel sorry for the opposition. We tried to score as many
as we could. They were a lovely bunch of players but
they weren't the best team in the world and they knew
before kick-off we were going to beat them.*

Les Lea: *They weren't in the same league as us and we were
on top for the entire 90 minutes. I didn't expect us to*

177

score seven. As the game went on they started making mistakes at the back and that's when we knew it was going to be an easy ride. I felt sorry for Mjøndalen and their fans because it was a big occasion for them and they'd been kind to us but you had to have a killer instinct. It was Mjøndalen's first time in Europe and they lost 7-1 which must have been horrendous for them. I actually broke my toe in that game. Someone (Carver) stamped on it and I felt it go but I played on. I had no idea it was broken and afterwards I had a job getting my boot off because the toe was so swollen.

With his side all but guaranteed a place in the next round, Scoular wanted his players to make history in the second leg and break the European record of 18 goals scored over two legs, held by two Portuguese clubs – Sporting Lisbon, who thrashed APOEL Nicosia in the Cup Winners' Cup in 1963, and Benfica, who swept aside hapless Stade Dudelange, of Luxembourg, in the European Cup in 1965. "We have a public to entertain," was Scoular's ominous message to the Norwegians before the game in Cardiff. To etch their names in the UEFA record books, the Bluebirds had to put 12 past Mjøndalen at Ninian Park and to increase his side's firepower, Scoular picked three forwards with Sandy Allan lining up alongside Clark and Toshack. Allan had only made four first-team appearances since arriving from Rhyl but boasted an impressive goal-a-game record for the reserve side which had earned him the nickname 'Handy Sandy'.

A goal spree could not be discounted. Cardiff, and especially Toshack, were on a high after beating Division Two leaders Queens Park Rangers 4-2 in a thrilling encounter at Ninian Park which saw Toshack score the first hat-trick of his career.

Mjøndalen, meanwhile, were fielding an even weaker side than the one thrashed in Norway a fortnight earlier. Nilsen, their first-choice goalkeeper, was rested for the cup semi-final against Fredrikstad four days later and student Boye Skistad, a striker and son of club president Hans Skistad, was unable to join his teammates in South Wales after being refused time off by his university. "We shall return home very happy if we stop Cardiff scoring fewer goals than they did at Mjøndalen," confessed Helge Clausen, the Norwegian club's chairman. There were four changes to the Cardiff side that played in Norway. Derrett made way for Bell, Lea was sacrificed for Allan, Jones replaced Phillips and 18-year–old defender Terry Lewis deputised for Harris for the second time in four days. With Harris sidelined with a pulled muscle, Lewis had played against Rangers and won plaudits for taming Rodney Marsh, Rangers' gifted forward. A product of the club's youth system, his brilliant performance against the London side – only his third outing under Scoular – suggested the youngster from Newport had an exciting future at Ninian Park.

Terry Lewis: *If Brian was fit he would have played but as the tie was dead and Scoular wanted to make sure Brian would be OK for the Saturday game, he left me in the side. We all played well against QPR and I was lucky to be part of a good team. I remember arriving at Ninian Park on Wednesday evening for the Mjøndalen game. I was wearing a green-striped shirt, my green kipper tie and a greenish checked jacket. That was all fashionable at the time. Anyway, Scoular came into the dressing room and when he saw me he gave me a bollocking in front of the other players. 'Don't you fuckin' come in here wearing green again!' He wasn't joking, he was being deadly serious and quite nasty. I was shocked.*

> *One of the lads told me, 'He's Rangers, Terry'. Scoular supported Rangers and Celtic were green but I had no idea because I was only a kid. I didn't answer Scoular back – if I did he would have kicked me all the way down Sloper Road. That's the type of person he was.*

Mjøndalen's coach, Nilsen, blamed the heavy loss in the Nedre Eiker Stadion on his players being "too tense" and predicted a better performance at Ninian Park because they will be "more relaxed". But the second leg followed a similar pattern to the first. King opened the scoring after 15 minutes, beating Mjøndalen's second-choice goalkeeper, builder Jan-Erik Larsen, with an effort from outside the penalty box before Allan netted his hat-trick, all headers, in a seven-minute spell. As was the case in Norway, Cardiff were unable to keep a clean sheet. Egil Solberg, who worked in a paper mill, rammed home Olsen's corner just before Allan headed his second. At half-time the amateurs were 4-1 down and staring at another heavy defeat but they conceded only one goal after the break, King completing a 12-2 aggregate win just past the hour when he cleverly diverted substitute Lea's shot past Larsen with a subtle back-heel.

Peter King: *Mjøndalen put a sub on and because he was a right-sided midfielder and I was on the left wing that night, he ran over to where I was standing, which was by the Bob Bank. As he got closer and closer I realised he was wearing glasses! They were like the old-fashioned NHS specs as well. I did a double take when I saw them and I went running round to the rest of the lads saying, 'Have a look at the sub, he's got specs on!' We'd never seen anything like that before. After the game we went to Tito's nightclub and the Mjøndalen players were there. We had a drink together which didn't happen often.*

Terry Lewis: *It was an easy night. I think I spent most of it on the halfway line because I didn't have much to do. Mjøndalen were like a Welsh League side. I didn't get praise from Jimmy Scoular, ever. I'd done well against QPR and Mjøndalen so you'd think he would have said something, even just a 'well done', but he didn't say anything. Peter Jackson from the Echo came to my house in Newport, in Malpas, to interview me but nobody from the club said a word to me. Scoular would never praise you but if you made a mistake he was quick to give you a bollocking. He wasn't a nice man, that's my opinion.*

Another comfortable win for Cardiff but that European record eluded Scoular. The Bluebirds had 35 attempts on goal but scored with only five. "Desperate clearances plus the occasional fortunate save by the all-go Mjøndalen 'keeper, Jan Larsen, prevented City from scoring double figures," explained Clive Phillips in the *Western Mail*. It may have been different had the on-form Toshack not been forced off after half-an-hour with a cut eye and concussion. Before his departure the striker hit the crossbar, the post, and had a header cleared off the line. Mjøndalen's players returned to Norway with a tankard and a miner's lamp, thankful they had restricted Cardiff to five goals.

Gary Bell: *Sandy Allan came to us from Rhyl with a reputation of being a goalscorer. He scored quite a lot in the reserves but could never get into the first team because Clarky and Tosh were always in good form. But he was capable of scoring goals and he came good that night.*

After winning the first leg 7-1 we could have gone through the motions at Ninian Park but you didn't do that when Jimmy Scoular was your manager. He wouldn't stand for that, you always had to give 100 per cent.

Richie Morgan: *Scoular could have put the youth side out that night and we would have gone through. There were players like myself who would have benefited from a game and he could have rested some of his first-team regulars but he never put a weakened side out. He could have made three or four changes for the second leg and it wouldn't have made the side that inferior but it wasn't in his nature to do that. If you could train then you could play – that was Scoular's view. He didn't think it was a problem to play two games in a week. I was disappointed he didn't rest Don and give me another game in the Cup Winners' Cup – I'd like to think that change wouldn't have weakened the side that much - but he persisted in playing the strongest side available.*

Lewis was hailed as the 'next big thing' at Ninian Park following two accomplished performances in the space of four days yet the Mjøndalen game was his fourth, and final, appearance for the Bluebirds. After a disagreement with Scoular during the summer of 1970, the teenager's professional career ended just as it should have been blossoming.

Terry Lewis: *I wasn't enjoying it at Cardiff and was losing my enthusiasm for the game. Training was run until you drop and five-a-side was a matter of life and death if you were in Scoular's team. He'd make us do crazy things like carry a teammate on your shoulders and then he'd start shouting, 'Get down! Get down!' I was 10 stone and one time I had to carry Don Murray who was 15 stone. It was crazy. He'd make us run our bollocks off for two-and-a-half hours and we'd be doing this right through the season. I didn't like the football we were playing either - it was boom, boom full-back to Toshack - so I went to see Scoular not long after pre-season started. I knew there had been offers for me because different people at the club told me but Scoular just said, 'You won't play for anybody else' and I ended up walking out. He stopped me playing for another club by keeping my registration. After I left Cardiff I went into pipe fitting and then moved to Australia. I worked in pipe fitting and played semi-pro for Woollongong City although I got a bad knee injury playing for them. I came back home and went to see Cardiff to ask them to release my registration. I was on crutches at the time. Frank O' Farrell was then the manager and he kindly saw me. I told him what had gone on with Scoular and he said, 'I've never heard anything so disgusting in my life.' He called the secretary, Lance Hayward, and told him to release me. It was all done in five minutes but it was too late because of my knee. I had a series of operations on it and when I was 41, I had a complete knee replacement.*

First Round, First Leg
17 September, 1969
Nedre Eiker Stadion, Mjøndalen

Mjøndalen (1) 1   **Cardiff City (3) 7**
Olsen 44   Clark 3, 36 Toshack 42, 88
                                            Lea 71, Sutton 74, King 79

MJØNDALEN: Nilsen, Broch (Kristian), Jensrud, Loe, Svendsen, Skistad
                              Brede, Kristiansen, Solberg E, Holman (Larsen S),
                              Skistad Boye, Olsen.

CARDIFF CITY: Davies, Derrett, Carver, Sutton, Murray, Harris, Phillips
                              (Jones), Clark, Lea, Toshack, King.

First Round, Second Leg
1 October, 1969
Ninian Park, Cardiff

Cardiff City (4) 5   **Mjøndalen (1) 1**
King 16, 62 Allan 36, 39, 43 Solberg 38

CARDIFF CITY: Davies, Derrett, Carver, Sutton, Murray, Lewis, Jones,
                              Clark, Allan, Toshack (Lea), King.

MJØNDALEN: Larsen J-E, Broch, Jensrud, Loe, Svendsen, Skistad
                              Brede, Kristiansen (Larsen S), Solberg E, Holman
                              (Solberg K), Larsen E, Olsen.

(Cardiff City won 12-2 on aggregate)

11

Falling on Ash and Sand
Göztepe, 1969

'We are a strong defensive team and we will keep
out Cardiff.'

Gürsel Aksel

FROM peaceful and gentle Mjøndalen to the heat and chaos
of Turkey's third largest city. The second round draw matched
Cardiff with Göztepe, the most successful Turkish side in
Europe and one of six football clubs in Izmir. *Göz Göz*, in their
red and yellow striped shirts, had reached the last four of
the Inter-Cities Fairs Cup the previous season although they
lost heavily to Újpest Dózsa in the semi-final, the Hungarians
powering to an 8-1 aggregate win.

The Alsancak Stadium, in Izmir's elegant Alsancak suburb,
would stage the first leg on 12 November and after learning of
his latest European challenge, Jimmy Scoular pulled out a map
to discover where Izmir – on Turkey's west coast - was situated.
The draw irritated the Bluebirds chief. Not only did it require a
3,436-mile round trip but the tie was sandwiched between two
away league fixtures, at Portsmouth and Oxford United. "We

would have preferred to have played a team nearer home," he said, conscious his side would have to make their way to Oxford's Manor Ground three days after the game in Turkey. "But breaking new soil is nothing to new to us." Under the guidance of Adnan Süvari, Göztepe - conquerors of Luxembourg's Union Sportif in the first round - were enjoying the most fruitful spell of their 44-year-history. They were crammed with Turkish internationals including Ali Artuner, Turkey's best goalkeeper and nicknamed 'the Panther', midfielders Ali Ihsan and Gürsel Aksel, and strikers Fevzi Zemzem, known as 'the Bulldozer'. There was one foreigner in the side, 23-year-old Danish striker John Nielsen. Unable to speak Turkish, Nielsen conversed with Süvari in English. Göztepe also had Halil Kiraz, nicknamed 'the Bomber' and a club hero after scoring twice in the shock Inter-Cities Fairs Cup win over Atlético Madrid in 1967.

Cardiff's approach was unlikely to surprise Süvari. The amiable Turk had gained first-hand knowledge of British football following a three-year stay in Huddersfield where he was a textile student. During his time in Yorkshire he not only developed a liking for roast beef and Yorkshire pudding, he also spent much of his time watching – and studying - Leeds United, Huddersfield Town, both sides in Manchester and Sheffield as well as Division Three and Division Four games on either side of the Pennines. Before Süvari left for Turkey in 1959 he even took a Football Association course at Lilleshall and returned home to Izmir with a coaching certificate. "What my players know, I taught them – and what I know, I learnt in England," said Süvari, who could speak English, French, German and Italian.

Göztepe had not started the Turkish season well, winning only two of their first seven games and Fevzi, Turkey's top scorer in 1967-68 with 19 goals, had yet to open his account. Scoular also harboured concerns as the Bluebirds headed to

Izmir. After a fine start to the 1969-70 season, Cardiff's form had tailed off. Since the second leg against Mjøndalen they had lost four out of seven league games and flew to Turkey on the back of a 3-0 defeat at Portsmouth, a performance which infuriated Scoular. "I only hope my players are not thinking of Turkey," he rasped. "There will be trouble if they put Europe before the league." There had been two resounding Ninian Park victories – a thumping 4-0 win against Aston Villa and a 6-0 drubbing of Hull City – but they were the only high notes in a disappointing autumn run which shoved Cardiff down to 10th place, six points behind leaders Huddersfield Town. The poor results coincided with the loss of Barrie Jones, one of Scoular's most influential and creative players. Three days after starring in the 5-1 win over Mjøndalen, Jones lined up against Blackpool at Bloomfield Road and in the dying seconds of a 3-2 defeat, broke his right leg as he challenged full-back Henry Mowbray for the ball, near the halfway line. The winger, successfully converted into a midfielder, suffered a double fracture and never played for the Bluebirds again, drifting into non-league football with Yeovil Town in 1971.

The journey to Izmir, the 'Pearl of the Aegean' and birthplace of Homer, took 11 hours and was far from ideal, evoking memories of the marathon trek to Tashkent. Cardiff flew from London - the flight was delayed by a porters' strike - and arrived in Izmir via Paris and Istanbul. They stayed in a hotel overlooking the city's harbour with the Göztepe players among their fellow guests. The Turks were taking the tie seriously, Süvari pulling his players away from their families for a week so he could oversee a bonding session at the hotel. Göztepe's coach was worried about Cardiff's tackling – "there is more physical contact in British football than in Turkey" - and also the aerial ability of John Toshack, Scoular's leading marksman with 13 goals.

Steve Derrett:
I roomed with Peter King and it was quite warm in Izmir so we left the balcony doors open. Something woke us in the early hours and we accused each other of having a nightmare. Then we discovered what had woken us – it was the Adhan calling people to the mosque! It was put out over a loudspeaker so you could hear it all over the city. At the time we didn't have a clue what the sound was and we were told later it was the call to prayer. The one that woke us up was the first Adhan of the day. It must have been four or five in the morning.

Peter King:
Me and Steve Derrett went for a walk around Izmir and soon realised we were somewhere completely different. We heard the call for people to go to the mosque and it was quite spooky. We saw a lorry driver pull up, get out and put a prayer mat down by the side of his lorry. I pointed him out to Steve and he said, 'I think he's trying to get his lorry to start.' The man actually stopped to pray. We saw people praying on petrol station forecourts. They put mats down where the cars were supposed to fill up. We went into a mosque and there were all these shoes left outside. We had a peep through the door and saw people bowed down in lines.

Scoular and his players had the shock of their lives when they turned up at the Alsancak Stadium for their pre-match training routine. There was not a blade of grass on the surface which was made up of sand and grey ash. As there had been no rain in Izmir for two months, the pitch resembled a dust bowl. "It's the most unusual playing surface I've come across in my career…it would remind American astronauts of the Moon's surface," commented a bemused Scoular. After supervising a two-hour training session, the manager found himself covered in ash dust as he walked off the pitch and when he returned to his hotel room, he headed straight for the shower. "Anyone would have thought I had been working down a pit judging by the dirt left in the bath."

Fred Davies: *The pitch was diabolical. You wouldn't have thought it was suitable for a European game. When we first saw it we thought it was just a training pitch, we didn't think you could play a game on it. Jimmy Scoular made his views known and we heard he tried to do something about it and maybe appeal to UEFA, but nothing happened and we ended up playing on it. Everyone found it difficult, even the lads with good ball control. The ball wouldn't run true. It would bobble and go anywhere. It was the worst surface I ever played on.*

Steve Derrett: *When we saw the pitch nobody could believe it. I've never forgotten what Brian Harris said when he saw it - 'They've laid the grass upside down!' There were wooden stakes in the ground to mark where the penalty spots and centre circle were, and before the game and at half-time a water bowser hosed the pitch to keep the dust down. It was unbelievable. I was a substitute in Izmir and usually when you're on the bench you want the manager to put you on at some point but, being truthful, I was hoping Scoular didn't throw me on that night.*

Süvari had shown the Welsh side plenty of respect ahead of the game, saying they "seem to be an extremely fit side with skill and power". He even considered putting two defenders on Toshack who arrived in Turkey as the most prolific goalscorer in Division Two. Altan Santepe, technical director of Trabzonspor and a former Turkey goalkeeper, believed Cardiff, who had not won away from Ninian Park since August, would beat Göztepe with their small defence as long as they utilised Toshack's aerial ability and resisted the temptation to play what he called "smooth football" on the Alsancak's baked ash surface. Scoular's formation contained no surprises with Fred Davies in goal and a defence consisting of Dave Carver, Don Murray, Brian Harris and Gary Bell. In midfield, Les Lea, Mel Sutton and Peter King lined up alongside Frank Sharp, a £5,000 signing from Carlisle United and the one change to the side beaten at Fratton Park. Up front, the two Cardiff towers, Brian Clark and Toshack – with 21 goals between them – hoped to torment Göztepe's defenders.

Richie Morgan:	*Before the game the referee came into the dressing room and asked for our passports. He insisted on seeing them but we didn't have them, they were in the hotel. Why he wanted to look at our passports I don't know but he said the game wouldn't be played unless he saw them. So Scoular put me and Steve Derrett in a taxi – neither of us was in the starting line-up – and told us to go back to the hotel and get the bloody things. I remember being driven away from the ground in a taxi and seeing all the traffic going to the game and then we had to rush back but compared to the lads who had to play on that pitch, which was like red stone dust, we got the sweet end of the stick.*
Don Murray:	*When we were training we saw a spike in the centre spot. It was for the groundsman so he could paint the*

Peter King heads the second-half winner against Esbjerg in the preliminary round, second leg at Ninian Park, October 1964.

The Cardiff squad boarding their flight to Lisbon for the first leg against holders Sporting Clube de Portugal in December 1964. Left to right: Graham Coldrick, Gareth Williams, Bernard Lewis, Keith Ellis, Peter Rodrigues, Lew Clayton (trainer), Lyn Davies, Derek Tapscott, George Johnston, Bob Wilson and Greg Farrell.

Cardiff full-back Peter Rodrigues takes on Sporting's José Carlos in the second leg at Ninian Park which ended 0-0. Cardiff progressed to the last eight thanks to their remarkable 2 -1 win in Lisbon.

Derek Tapscott challenges Sporting goalkeeper Joaquim Carvalho who responds by picking up the Cardiff forward and dumping him behind the goal line.

Cardiff line up before the quarter-final, second leg against Real Zaragoza at Ninian Park. Back row, left to right: Don Murray, Barrie Hole, Bob Wilson, John Charles, Alan Harrington and Peter Rodrigues. Front row, left to right: Greg Farrell, Bernard Lewis, Derek Tapscott, Peter King and Gareth Williams.

Peter King heads at goal against Real Zaragoza but Cardiff were unable to find the net and the Spaniards marched into the semi-finals with a 1-0 win.

Lew Clayton, Cardiff's trainer, tends to the stricken Peter Rodrigues after the defender had been chopped down by Jacques Beurlet during the bad-tempered first leg against Standard Liège at Ninian Park, September 1965.

John Charles (number 9) is bundled to the ground as Cardiff and Standard Liège players clash. The Belgians returned home with a 2-1 win.

Cardiff defender Alan Harrington (centre) watches in dismay as James Storme (far left) secures a 1-0 win for Standard Liège in the first round, second leg at the Stade de Sclessin, October 1965.

Bobby Brown outjumps the Shamrock Rovers defence at Ninian Park, October 1967. The Cardiff forward scored from the penalty spot during the 2-0 win.

Cardiff defender Don Murray walks disconsolately away from his goal while NAC Breda players celebrate Jacques Visschers' early goal in the first leg in Eindhoven, November 1967. (©PA)

Barrie Jones (number 7) turns away after scoring Cardiff's second goal against NAC Breda at Ninian Park, November 1967. The Welsh side secured a 4-1 second-leg victory, progressing to the quarter-finals 5-2 on aggregate.

The Cardiff and Torpedo Moscow teams line up at Ninian Park before the first leg of their quarter-final, March 1968.

Cardiff striker John Toshack finds himself sandwiched between two Torpedo Moscow players during a closely-fought first meeting between the two sides at Ninian Park.

Barrie Jones (far right) raises his arms after watching his header beat Torpedo Moscow goalkeeper Anzor Kavazashvili. Cardiff held on to win the first leg 1-0. (©PA)

Cardiff players celebrate their first-leg victory over Torpedo Moscow in the dressing room. Left to right: Peter King, Don Murray, Barrie Jones, Ronnie Bird, Bryn Jones and John Toshack.

At Cardiff Central Station on the first stage of their mammoth journey to Tashkent, March 1968. Top, left to right: Bryn Jones, Sandy Allan, John Toshack and Malcolm Clarke. Bottom, left to right: Ronnie Bird, Norman Dean, Steve Derrett, Gary Bell, Lew Clayton (trainer), Don Murray and Brian Harris.

Sightseeing during the stopover in Moscow. Left to right: Gary Bell, Malcolm Clarke, Jimmy Scoular (manager), Barrie Jones, John Toshack and Ronnie Bird in front of the Cathedral of the Archangel.

Indoor training inside Moscow's Lenin Stadium. Front to back: Bryn Jones, Norman Dean, Ronnie Bird, Barrie Jones, Steve Derrett, Leighton Phillips, Malcolm Clarke and Gary Bell.

The Cardiff squad listen attentively to manager Jimmy Scoular during a training session inside the Pakhtakor Markaziy Stadium, Tashkent.

Cardiff players take a closer look at the Pakhtakor Markaziy's pitch before the second leg against Torpedo Moscow.

Bob Wilson (on the ground) is unable to stop Torpedo Moscow's Mikhail Gershkovich (left) wiping out Cardiff's first-leg lead.

Forced into a play-off, Cardiff players head for the dressing room after their defeat in Tashkent. Left to right: John Toshack, Don Murray, Brian Harris, Ronnie Bird and Bobby Ferguson.

At London Airport following their flight from Moscow and showing off their balalaikas purchased in the Soviet Union. Left to right: Steve Derrett, Gary Bell, Peter King, Brian Harris and Leighton Phillips.

The Cardiff team before the play-off against Torpedo Moscow inside the Rosenaustadion in Augsburg, West Germany, April 1968. Back row, left to right: Ronnie Bird, Bobby Ferguson, John Toshack, Lyn Davies, Bob Wilson, Richie Morgan and Peter King. Front row, left to right: Graham Coldrick, Norman Dean, Malcolm Clarke, Brian Harris and Barrie Jones.

Guarded by Bob Wilson, the Cardiff goal survives yet another Torpedo Moscow attack. Cardiff reached the semi-final courtesy of Norman Dean's first-half strike.

Norman Dean enjoys a drink in the dressing room after his winner eliminated Torpedo Moscow inside Augsburg's Rosenaustadion.

In high spirits on the team bus following their 1-0 triumph against the crack Soviet side. From the front, left to right: Brian Harris, Bobby Ferguson, Norman Dean, Malcolm Clarke, Graham Coldrick and Richie Morgan.

Cardiff players take part in an evening training session inside Hamburg's Volksparkstadion before the semi-final, first leg, April 1968.

Hamburg and Cardiff line up before the semi-final, first leg inside the Volksparkstadion, April 1968. (©PA)

An agitated Jimmy Scoular watches from the visitors' dugout as his Cardiff side battle Hamburg.

Norman Dean (far right) fires Cardiff ahead in Hamburg. The first leg finished 1-1. (©PA)

Cardiff duo Don Murray and John Toshack shake hands after holding Hamburg at the Volksparkstadion.

Club secretary Graham Keenor and office assistant Gloria Davies sift through ticket applications for the semi-final, second leg at Ninian Park.

Cardiff captain Brian Harris (far right) and his opposite number from Hamburg, the great Uwe Seeler, with Dutch referee Laurens van Raevens before the Ninian Park showdown, May 1968.

Norman Dean (out of picture) scores Cardiff's first goal in the semi-final, second leg at Ninian Park. Unable to hold down a regular place in league games, the versatile Dean was Cardiff's goalscoring hero during the 1967-68 European campaign. (©PA)

John Toshack takes on the Hamburg defence, watched by a Ninian Park crowd of 43,070.

Brian Harris (out of picture) heads Cardiff's equaliser beyond Hamburg goalkeeper Arkoç Özcan, watched by Norman Dean and Hamburg midfielder Hans Schulz.

Young Cardiff supporters invade the pitch following Brian Harris' dramatic equaliser. Referee Laurens van Ravens would add on the time taken to clear the youngsters, allowing Franz-Josef Hönig to snatch a dramatic winner for Hamburg.

Watched by Mel Sutton (left) and Don Murray (right), Cardiff captain Brian Harris beats Francisco Nóbrega to the ball during the 2-2 draw with FC Porto at Ninian Park, September 1968.

Cardiff board their flight to Norway for the first-round clash against Mjøndalen Idrettsforening. September 1969. From top, left to right: Jimmy Scoular (manager), Mel Sutton, Barrie Jones, Leighton Phillips, Sandy Allan, Steve Derrett, Brian Clark, John Toshack, Brian Harris, Fred Davies, Peter King, Gary Bell, Richie Morgan, Jim Eadie, Lew Clayton (trainer) and Don Murray.

Brian Clark (on the ground) leads the rout at the Nedre Eiker Stadion, scoring Cardiff's first goal in the 7-1 win over Mjøndalen Idrettsforening.

Fevzi Zemzem, nicknamed 'the Bulldozer', fires a shot past goalkeeper Fred Davies to open the scoring for Göztepe in Izmir, November 1969.

Göztepe goalkeeper Ali Artuner clears from John Toshack at Ninian Park, November 1969. Cardiff won 1-0 but the Turkish side progressed 3-1 on aggregate. (©PA)

Brian Clark (second right) outjumps the Nantes defence at Ninian Park, November 1970.

The Real Madrid players training at Ninian Park the night before facing Cardiff in the quarter-final, first leg, March 1971.

Surrounded by some of his first-team players, Jimmy Scoular (centre) reads the Real Madrid Special, published by the *South Wales Echo*, before the first leg. Left to right: Don Murray, Jim Eadie, Ian Gibson, Peter King, Mel Sutton, Bobby Woodruff and Gary Bell.

Brian Clark secures a historic victory over Real Madrid with his first-half header in front of the Canton Stand.

Ian Gibson (far right) congratulates Brian Clark after the striker had beaten José Luis Borja.

Cardiff should have travelled to Madrid with a bigger lead. Don Murray (standing, far left) misses a golden chance in the second half.

Real Madrid defender Gregorio Benito fends off Peter King as he crosses inside Cardiff's penalty area. Don Murray (far right) looks on.

Cardiff players uncork the champagne after the 1-0 win over Real Madrid at Ninian Park. Top, left to right: Richie Morgan and John Parsons. Front, left to right: Don Murray, John Parsons, Brian Clark, Freddie Pethard, Peter King, Bobby Woodruff, Alan Warboys and Jim Eadie.

Cardiff captain Don Murray (standing) shares a light moment with some of his team-mates at Rhoose Airport before boarding the flight to Madrid. Left to right: Gary Bell, Brian Harris, Peter King, Ronnie Bird and Mel Sutton.

Training inside the Estadio Santiago Bernabéu. The visitors from the Welsh capital are put through their paces before the second leg against Real Madrid.

Gary Bell (on the ground) is struck by a bottle thrown by a Real Madrid supporter. Leighton Phillips shows the offending item to referee Karol Sarka while Don Murray looks on. Cardiff lost 2-0 in Madrid and were eliminated.

The Division Two side deal with a Real Madrid attack inside the Bernabéu. Left to right: Don Murray, goalkeeper Jim Eadie and Gary Bell.

Ian Gibson (second right), watches Dynamo Berlin defender Jochen Carow head clear in front of goalkeeper Werner Lihsa at Ninian Park, September 1971. Dynamo eliminated Cardiff following a penalty shoot-out.

Cardiff captain Don Murray (far right) shakes hands with goalkeeper Vitor Damas, captain of Sporting Clube de Portugal, ahead of the first round clash at Ninian Park, September 1973. Maltese referee Anthony Briguglio (second left) looks on.

Cardiff overcome Servette at Ninian Park, August 1976. Tony Evans (centre) forces the ball over the line with Adrian Alston about to celebrate, but the effort is disallowed. Evans scored the winner two minutes from the end.

Albert Larmour clears a Servette attack in the second leg at the Stade des Charmilles in Geneva, August 1976. Cardiff lost 2-1 but progressed on the away-goal rule.(©PA)

Tony Evans controls the ball against Dinamo Tbilisi at Ninian Park, September 1976. The Cardiff forward, a free transfer from Blackpool, scored in every senior competition during the 1976-77 season.

Derek Showers heads for goal against Dinamo Tbilisi at Ninian Park, September 1976. Adrian Alston's second-half strike secured a 1-0 win.

Flowers are presented to the Cardiff players following their arrival in Tbilisi, Georgia. Left to right: Phil Dwyer, Derek Showers, Bill Irwin, Freddie Pethard, Keith Pontin and Brian Attley. The welcome at the Dinamo Stadium was not so warm. Cardiff were crushed 3-0.

The Cardiff side selected to face Derry City at Brandywell Stadium, September 1988. Top, left to right: Mark Kelly, Jason Gummer, Alan Curtis, George Wood, Nigel Stevenson and Jimmy Gilligan. Front, left to right: Phil Bater, Nicky Platnauer, Terry Boyle, Ian Walsh and Paul Wimbleton.

Jimmy Gilligan tests the Derry City defence during the 0-0 draw in Northern Ireland, September 1988.

Cardiff striker Jimmy Gilligan (centre) scores his second goal against Derry City in the return leg at Ninian Park, October 1988.

Derry City goalkeeper Tim Dalton (on the ground) and defender Paul Curran watch Jimmy Gilligan complete his hat-trick.

Cardiff's controversial equaliser against Aarhus at Ninian Park, October 1988. Jimmy Gilligan heads towards goal with Troels Rasmussen clawing his header away, but the officials rule the ball had crossed the line.

Nathan Blake tries to find a way past Admira Wacker, September 1992. The first leg at Ninian Park ended 1-1.

Tony Bird stuns Standard Liège inside the Stade de Sclessin, slotting the ball home after dispossessing André Cruz, September 1993. The Belgians roared back to win 5-2.

Damon Searle embarks on a surging run against Standard Liège at Ninian Park, September 1993. The Belgians thumped Cardiff 8-3 on aggregate.

white lines on that part of the pitch. There we were training, and in the middle of the pitch was this bloody big spike sticking out of the ground. When it came to kick-off I went to the centre spot to shake hands with the Göztepe captain, meet the officials, and all that sort of thing. When it came to tossing the coin to decide who played at which end I checked to see if the spike had been removed. Fortunately it had!

On what one member of the travelling Press corps described as "probably the worst football pitch in Europe", Cardiff soon found themselves in trouble. Fevzi set Göztepe on their way in the 14th minute with a curling free-kick over a poorly-assembled Bluebirds wall after Yugoslav referee Lado Jakše ruled Bell had handled the ball just outside the penalty area. Ertan Öznur scored the second on the half-hour mark after Fevzi's ball wrong-footed the Bluebirds defence. There was more woe for the visitors in the 32nd minute. Davies, wearing elbow pads for protection against the rough surface, dithered over Göztepe skipper Gürsel's cross, and Nielsen punished the goalkeeper's hesitation. In 18 horrible minutes, the visitors had conceded three goals.

Fred Davies: *Göztepe knew how to play on that surface – they didn't play the ball to the forwards, they hit it over the top of our defenders. They kept turning us by knocking balls behind us and that put the lads in trouble because they'd have a ball bouncing on a bad surface and a centre-forward breathing down their necks. That was hard to deal with. Even experienced players like Don Murray and Brian Harris struggled. They would go to play the ball and sometimes end up missing it completely. I remember Brian going to deal with one ball. The pitch gave him trouble and it ended up going out for a corner. On a normal grass pitch he wouldn't have had any problems.*

Les Lea: *I thought Izmir was a lovely city. When I got back home I told my wife, Maureen, how impressed I was with the place. The seafront was superb, especially at night when it was lit up, and we stayed in a lovely hotel with a beautiful pool, but the stadium wasn't pleasant. It was a good job there was fencing around the pitch because it was quite rowdy and rough. The Turkish fans gave you loads of stick when you went to take throw-ins. You didn't know exactly what they were shouting but you had a fair idea. Their fans were very volatile and close to the pitch.*

Cardiff gradually adjusted to the Alsancak's dreadful surface and offered more resistance and invention in the second half. They should have claimed a valuable away goal seven minutes after the restart when Toshack headed down Sharp's corner but Carver sliced his shot wide. Allan, who replaced the ineffective Sharp, tried to finish off a counter-attacking move but Ali preserved a clean sheet for the Turks as Cardiff slumped to their second away loss in the competition, losing 3-0. At the end, Scoular's players trudged back to the dressing room covered in bruises and grazes – "souvenirs," wrote one observer, "of the dreadful pitch." With many of his decisions, Jakše hardly endeared himself to Scoular. The Yugoslav was quick to award Göztepe free-kicks and constantly penalised Toshack when the striker challenged for high balls, but the undoubted cause of the Welsh side's heaviest Cup Winners' Cup defeat was the sand and ash pitch which was likened to the Moon's Sea of Tranquility.

Dave Carver: *The pitch influenced the result, without doubt, but we also underestimated Göztepe. They were better than we thought. When we came off at the end we had grazes and burns on the backs of our legs and the hard surface aggravated a foot injury I'd been carrying for a week or so. I probably shouldn't have played but in those days it didn't take much to prove your fitness. We wore studs in that game when really we should have worn rubber boots but Scoular didn't like us wearing rubbers because you couldn't hurt anyone with them. He wanted his defenders to wear studs and one of his favourite phrases was 'show 'em six' – that's how many studs were on each boot.*

Gary Bell: *The whole back four wore studs in Turkey and when we took off our boots in the dressing room at the end of the game we saw the studs had been completely worn away! They were flat, to the sole of the boot. A whole set of studs! That's how rock-hard the surface was. When I first saw it I thought 'What's going on here? You can't play European matches on this!' You couldn't do sliding tackles - if you did you'd rip your leg to pieces - and you couldn't help worrying you were going to twist your ankle or knee. We got used to it in the second half but by then it was too late. UEFA would never allow a game today to be played on that kind of surface. When we walked onto the pitch before kick-off there was this fella with a watering can pouring water on the white lines!*

To reach the quarter-finals, Cardiff would have to become the first British side to overturn a three-goal deficit in European competition and, to make their task even harder, Süvari admitted he would adopt a defensive strategy at Ninian Park to protect the lead. Fred Dewey, however, believed his players were capable of blitzing Göztepe. During the season, proclaimed the Bluebirds chairman, they had scored six against Hull and put four past Queens Park Rangers and Aston Villa. "Izmir may find our green grass just as strange to them as their pitch was to our players," he continued. Unbeknown to Dewey, the wily Süvari prepared for the Ninian Park game by taking his squad to Istanbul to train on a grass surface. Scoular also felt a comeback was "not beyond us", the Scot bracketing Göztepe in the same class as NAC Breda, the Dutch side Cardiff had beaten 4-1 two years earlier.

Peter King: *When we came back from Turkey some of the cocky lads in the reserves went on about the result – 'You lost 3-0!' But it was a strange game out there. It could have finished 3-3 but we didn't put our chances away. I felt we had just as much of the play. Had we scored the goals over there then that would have put the tie to bed. I didn't think Göztepe were any great shakes and I was quietly confident we would get the goals back in the second leg. I thought 'We can beat this lot.'*

To get his players used to the Welsh November cold, Süvari led his squad on a post-lunch walk along Barry's seafront. Even with a 3-0 advantage, the Turk was concerned about the return. He had seen enough of English football to know Cardiff would give it their all in the second leg. "No team coming to play a British club in Britain can feel good, even with a three-goal lead," observed the Turk. Scoular had just paid £25,000 for Crystal Palace midfielder Bobby Woodruff, a replacement for Jones, although the player with the longest throw in the

Football League was ineligible to face the Turks as he was signed after the UEFA deadline. Cardiff needed goals so the manager, unsurprisingly, went with three strikers with Sandy Allan joining Clark and Toshack up front. It was Allan who had a glorious chance inside three minutes to give the home team the perfect start but he could only find the side netting. After that, Cardiff struggled to break through the wall of Turkish defenders. Göztepe committed just two players – Fevzi and Nielsen – to attack as Süvari fulfilled his pre-match promise. Both Toshack and Clark tested Ali in the first half and King saw a 30-yard strike fly past the upright, but Göztepe, with five players constantly in front of Ali, absorbed the pressure with relative comfort.

Mel Sutton:

We didn't know anything about Göztepe, there was no dossier on their players or anything like that. They turned out to be better than we thought. We were surprised they beat us so easily in Turkey but we didn't play well over there. We thought we could get the goals back but we needed to get off to a good start. That would have put them under pressure but we just couldn't break them down and the longer it went on without us scoring, the more confident they became.

With 15 minutes left, Scoular hauled off Toshack and put on defender Graham Coldrick as a makeshift striker. "He came off because he wasn't playing well enough, it's as simple as that," replied Scoular, when asked afterwards why he substituted his most prolific goalscorer. Coldrick was involved in the only goal of the night, making a decoy run down the left flank which allowed Ronnie Bird, a replacement for the injured Lea, to come inside and beat Ali with one of his "express specials" from 25 yards out. But it was too little, too late. Göztepe progressed, 3-1 winners on aggregate. Cardiff, said Süvari afterwards, had created more chances in Izmir.

Fred Davies: *They had a three-goal cushion so they came to Ninian Park and just sat back. We had a good chance early on and if that had gone in things might have been different. Before kick-off we all agreed it would be a different ball game if we got an early goal. To be fair, they defended well at our place. They were a more organised side than people gave them credit for. They set their stall out with one man up front and plenty of width so they knew what they were doing. Looking back, the tie was won and lost in the first half in Turkey.*

Peter King: *They did surprise us at Ninian Park but after the game I was thinking 'This is the only time we've been knocked out of Europe by an inferior side.' I really believe that, even now. In the past we'd always been knocked out by a superior team – Real Zaragoza, Standard Liege, Hamburg – but I don't think Göztepe were better than us and we shouldn't have been knocked out by them. The problem was the result in the first leg.*

Göztepe's run ended in the next round where they were beaten by AS Roma. The Italians fared better on the notorious Alsancak pitch than their Welsh predecessors, claiming a 0-0 draw following a 2-0 win at the Stadio Olimpico. Without the distraction of the Cup Winners' Cup, Cardiff could concentrate on the league and after a storming run of seven consecutive wins - from 22 November to 10 January - they sat on top of Division Two. But then came a slump and after winning just one of their next eight games, the Bluebirds slid down the table, eventually finishing seventh, just four points off the second - and final - promotion spot. They reached the Welsh Cup final for the fourth consecutive year and were guaranteed another shot at Europe before a ball had been kicked since their opponents, Chester City, as an English club, could not qualify. After a failed promotion push, Scoular's charges brought some silverware to Ninian Park with an emphatic 5-0 aggregate win over the Division Four side.

Don Murray: *Göztepe wasn't one of our better experiences in Europe. The tie was dead after the first game. We were 3-0 down before we knew where we were. A lot of the lads took time to get used to the surface out there. I know I did. There was dust flying about and the surface affected the bounce of the ball. As a team, psychologically we weren't quite right, and I know Jimmy wasn't happy with the conditions but we had to play on that surface.*

Second Round, First Leg
12 November, 1969
Alsancak Stadium, Izmir

Göztepe (3) 3   **Cardiff City (0) 0**
Fevzi 14, Ertan 30
Nielsen 32

GÖZTEPE: Ali, Mehmet I, Çağlayan, Özer, Mehmet A, Ihsan,
                Mehmet F, Ertan, Neilsen, Fevzi, Gürsel.

CARDIFF CITY: Davies, Carver, Bell, Sutton, Murray, Harris, Lea, Clark,
                King, Toshack, Sharp (Allan).

Second Round, Second Leg
26 November, 1969
Ninian Park, Cardiff

Cardiff City (0) 1   **Göztepe (0) 0**
Bird 78

CARDIFF CITY: Davies, Carver, Bell, Sutton, Murray, Harris, Lea, Clark,
                King, Toshack, Allan.

GÖZTEPE: Ali, Mehmet I, Çağlayan, Özer, Mehmet A, Nevzat,
                Mehmet F, Ertan, Neilsen (Dursun), Fevzi, Gürsel.

(Göztepe won 3-1 on aggregate)

12

The Wrath of Scoular
Pezoporikos, 1970

'I believe my team could be compared to an average
English Second Division side.'

Gyula Zsengellér

FOR the second year running, Cardiff were handed a serene
first-round draw. In 1969 it was Mjøndalen. In 1970 it was
Pezoporikos, based in Larnaca on Cyprus' southern coast.
Like the Norwegians, they were an amateur side making their
debut in European competition. "I'll approach this game in the
same way I'd approach a tie against Benfica or Real Madrid,"
proclaimed Jimmy Scoular before the first leg at Ninian Park
but, in truth, his side's place in the second round was not in
doubt. The Cypriot championship was one of the weakest on
the continent, illustrated by some of their clubs' results in
UEFA club competitions. On seven occasions a side from the
Mediterranean island had conceded double figures over two
legs, the biggest defeats coming in the Cup Winners' Cup.
APOEL Nicosia were hammered 18-1 by Sporting Lisbon in
1963 and, the following year, Anorthosis Famagusta were
thumped 16-0 by Sparta Prague. And while the Cypriot season
had yet to start, Cardiff had already played seven league games

and sat proudly on top of Division Two with 10 points from a possible 14.

After losing out on the Cypriot title on goal difference to city rivals Enosis Pezoporikou Amol the previous season, Pezoporikos gained some consolation by winning the Cypriot Cup. Most of the Pezoporikos players worked as clerks for the electricity authority and trained three afternoons a week. Their 54-year-old coach, Gyula Zsengellér, was a distinguished figure in his native Hungary. A legendary forward at Újpest Dózsa, he was a key member of the Hungarian side that finished runners-up in the 1938 World Cup, scoring twice in their 5-1 drubbing of Sweden in the semi-final. As a coach, he guided Pezoporikos to the title in 1954 during his first spell in Larnaca before working in Italy with Cosenza, Salernitana and Ravenna. Because of his Italian experience, it was no surprise to hear Zsengellér say he might adopt *catennacio* – a tactical system with the emphasis on defence - at Ninian Park in an attempt to frustrate the home side and, no doubt, staunch the first-leg damage.

Cardiff had slipped up just once in their opening seven fixtures, at Bristol City where they lost 1-0, and the strike pairing of Brian Clark and John Toshack was again proving potent with eight goals between them. Scoular had fine-tuned the side since the end of the 1969-70 campaign, offloading Fred Davies to Bournemouth, Graham Coldrick to Newport County, and selling both Les Lea and Frank Sharp to Barnsley. To replace goalkeeper Davies, he brought in Frank Parsons from Crystal Palace for £15,000 but his major summer acquisition was Ian Gibson, a dynamic midfielder signed from Coventry City for £35,000, making him the most expensive buy of Scoular's six-year reign. The darling of Highfield Road, Gibson was part of the Sky Blues side that won promotion to the First Division in 1967 and left for Ninian Park after helping the

Midlands club qualify for the Inter-Cities Fairs Cup. Scoular, characteristically, picked his strongest side for the visit of the Cypriot part-timers with Parsons, Gibson and Bobby Woodruff all making their European debuts against the Larnaca club. Against the hapless and hopeless Cypriots, Cardiff had to wait 17 minutes for their opener, Mel Sutton scoring with a superb 25-yard shot. Despite Zsengellér's defensive plan, Scoular's players then scored four in 11 minutes with Gibson, Peter King, Woodruff and Clark securing a 5-0 lead at the interval. That was the end of Takis Palmiris' humiliation. The Pezoporikos goalkeeper walked off at half-time to sympathetic applause from the Cardiff public and never returned, with Michalis Kiriakidis, unenviably, taking his place for the final 45 minutes.

Peter King: *I scored in that game but I should have got another one. The ball came to me and I was right in front of the goal but I ended up putting it over the crossbar. It was one of those chances where it was more difficult to miss and I sat on the goal line, looked up at the crossbar and thought to myself 'How did I manage to miss that?' We were on a goal bonus and after the game Jimmy Scoular came up to me and said, 'You must have too much money, Kingy!' That was Scoular, he had to say something to me about that miss.*

Gary Bell: *We were a yard faster than Larnaca and we knew they were there for the taking. After about 10 minutes I could hear the manager from the dugout shouting at me. 'Gary, keep going forward! Keep overlapping!' That's what I did and a few of my crosses resulted in goals. It was a good night for the team and for me personally. The result says it all – it was one of our easiest nights in Europe, if not the easiest.*

Kiriakidis displayed "the relish of someone trying to repair the crumbing walls of Jericho" and conceded two less goals than his teammate. Toshack scored twice with Clark netting his second in between. Pezoporikos were applauded off at the end by a polite and sympathetic Ninian Park crowd of nearly 18,000. They had been thrashed 8-0 but it could have been far worse for the Cypriots. Profligacy in front of goal and some fine saves from Kiriakidis prevented Cardiff hitting double figures. "We expected six Cardiff goals but not eight," said a forlorn Zsengellér afterwards. The match statistics revealed how one-sided the game had been. Cardiff had 47 goal attempts and Pezoporikos just one, a 30-yard effort in the second-half from striker Christos Loizou which rolled straight to Parsons. Along with collecting five back-passes, that was all Parsons was required to deal with. The Cypriots also failed to win a single corner in 90 minutes. In his *South Wales Echo* report, Peter Jackson described the first leg as "the most absurd one-sided farce I've ever seen....it was a bit like putting Jack Johnson into the same ring as someone like Benny Lynch". In the *Daily Mirror*, Tom Lyons called it "the most one-sided match, or mis-match, I have seen in this competition." The Cypriot performance certainly made a mockery of Zsengellér's pre-match comment, that his side could be compared to an "average side" in the English Second Division. Pezoporikos were not the only side from Larnaca to suffer a European hammering that night. Enosis Pezoporikou Amol were crushed 6-0 at home by Borussia Mönchengladbach in the European Cup.

Dave Carver: *Larnaca were a poor team and it was a comfortable night for us. I was at Cardiff for six years and that was, without doubt, my easiest game for the club. They were bad – there were better sides in the Welsh League - and we won 8-0 without breaking sweat. Even though it was an easy win, it wasn't a game I particularly enjoyed. As a defender, you want something to do and I had nothing to do that night.*

Ian Gibson: *We slaughtered them. They weren't a great side but we did play well. I didn't think we'd win by such a big margin - I would have settled for 3-0. It was one of those nights when everything we hit seemed to go in. The Larnaca players weren't upset, they just got on with it and kept playing the same way. We didn't feel sorry for them. You can never feel sympathy for the other team. We just overran them and Jimmy Scoular was happy with us after the game.*

Cardiff flew to Cyprus from London on 26 September after a 0-0 draw at Leyton Orient, a result which saw them cede top spot to Oxford United. Instead of travelling the day before the game and returning after the match, Scoular decided to stay on the sun-drenched island - basking in temperatures well into the 80s - for nearly six days. He based his squad in Famagusta, Cyprus's busiest holiday resort. Located 23 miles outside Larnaca, Famagusta boasted some of the island's best beaches and a vibrant nightlife. "I believe a few days training in the sun will help tune up my players for their tough winter programme in the Second Division," said Scoular, explaining the September break.

Dave Carver: *On the Wednesday before the game at Leyton Orient, Scoular told all the players, 'Anyone who isn't fit won't be going to Cyprus.' I'd turned my ankle quite badly but I said nothing because I didn't want to miss the trip. It was Cyprus in September. When we got there*

203

my ankle had swollen up and Scoular knew about the problem but it didn't matter because I was in Cyprus!

Because the facilities at their GSZ Stadium were so poor, Pezoporikos offered to play their 'home' game at Ninian Park a week, rather than a fortnight, after the first leg. Scoular was not keen on their proposal, even though it might have saved the club £2,000 since it would mean four games in eight days. With promotion top of his agenda, the Bluebirds chief did not want precious points lost because of fatigue. Cardiff's board agreed to their ground staging the second leg on condition the Division Two club paid no more than £500 towards Pezoporikos's hotel bill as well as receiving 50 per cent of gate receipts, an offer the Cypriots rejected.

Gary Bell: *We arrived in Cyprus in the early hours and I remember waking up the next morning. We were in a beautiful five-star hotel, the sun was out, and tourists were walking along the beach. I thought 'This isn't bad!' It was a Sunday and we had the day off because we'd played the previous day so we did a bit of sightseeing and had a few beers in the afternoon. The night before the game a few of us went out for a meal and afterwards we took a stroll as the weather was so nice. Someone suggested we stop for a shandy. We had one, but one led to another... we had to be back at the hotel by 10 pm and by the time we got back it was 10.10 pm. The problem was, Jimmy Scoular and the directors were in the reception area so we went round the back of the hotel and got in through a door which led to the kitchens. Gibbo then says, 'I've got to have a pee' but he couldn't find a toilet so he relieved himself in a milk container. The next day we went down into the dining room for our meal and there were these American tourists sitting behind us. One of them shouted out to the waiter, 'What's the soup of the day?' And the waiter said, 'Pea soup'. Well, you can imagine the reaction to that on our table!*

Bobby Woodruff: *We had an 8-0 lead and we stopped in Famagusta for almost a week so it was a relaxing trip, really. Our hotel was more or less on the beach, we got the oil on and went sunbathing. There were no restrictions on how much sunbathing we did. Scoular wasn't bothered. Back then they didn't fuss about things like that. We also hired little speedboats. They could hold two people and created quite a wash behind them – they were pretty quick. If we'd only had a goal or two lead then that trip would have been totally different but Larnaca were not going to score nine goals.*

Before making the short journey to Larnaca, the Cardiff manager warned his players they would probably face the hardest conditions in their European experience at the GSZ Stadium. As was the case in Izmir, they would be playing on a hard surface without a blade of grass. The pitch was a couple of feet of earth laid on concrete and rolled. It was then hard-baked by the relentless Mediterranean sun. Scoular likened it to "playing on hard sand" and warned his players it would be easy to get injured. The 3.30pm kick-off time was also an issue. As well as the difficult pitch, Cardiff would have to contend with the mid-afternoon heat.

Steve Derrett: *Without putting too fine a point on it, the holiday mood did affect the performance. We were in Famagusta in*

September and it was beautiful. We were out all day Sunday and most of Monday. Some of the boys were out Tuesday as well.

Peter King: *The pitch in Larnaca was like an old cinder track. It was the worst surface I ever played on. You had to wear rubbers and no way were we going to do sliding tackles. There were a lot of British servicemen in the crowd and they'd come to see a goal-fest, but we were 8-0 up so we weren't going to flog ourselves to death. Our attitude had a lot to do with the result.*

Before the game Scoular quipped, "If Larnaca score nine I won't be coming home." Pezoporikos could not manage even one but Cardiff, too, failed to score against a side they had destroyed 8-0 a fortnight earlier. The treacherous pitch, Cypriot heat and holiday atmosphere combined to elicit a tired, disinterested performance from the Bluebirds who were held to a 0-0 draw by a Pezoporikos side desperate to salvage some pride after their Ninian Park mauling. Afterwards, Scoular made excuses for the dreadful performance – the wind coming off the Mediterranean "blew the ball about a fair bit", the referee made "confusing" decisions, and it was "never easy for British players to show their skills on a pitch without grass" – but inside the 'Iron Man' was seething, and he tore into his players behind closed doors.

Don Murray: *We were well-supported that day because the British Forces were in Cyprus and they came in their droves to watch us play but we didn't serve up a good performance. We were poor out there. Jimmy had a way with words and he laid into us after the game. We'd struggled against a team we'd put eight past at Ninian Park and he was mad. He said we should be ashamed of ourselves, that we had let ourselves and Cardiff City down. He was angry and rightly so because it was a bad performance. We were through after the first leg but Jimmy still wanted us to win out in Larnaca.*

Dave Carver: *We were embarrassed by the result. A lot of servicemen came to the game and we could only draw 0-0. We really did feel we had let them down. We should have given them a refund, that's how bad it was. It was hot and the pitch was rock hard. I wore rubbers for that game and I'm sure that's the only time I wore them. The ground was like a public park but there was no excuse for our performance over there. We treated that trip as a holiday - the weather was gorgeous, our hotel was right by the beach, and we had an 8-0 lead. The morning after the game we were round the pool and getting ready to while away a few hours. We always had the day after a game off. We were all looking forward to a nice morning by the pool but then Lew Clayton turned up and said, 'There's been a change of plan – you're training today.' It was Scoular's way of punishing us and he ran us to death that day.*

The pitch was a significant factor in the limp display, particularly after Toshack fell on its hard surface after 20 minutes and picked up an injury which forced him off. His concerned teammates gathered around their stricken teammate as he clutched his gashed leg. "What they saw," wrote JBG Thomas in the *Western Mail*, "made them trip through the next 70 minutes like ballet dancers. City held back in the tackle and rarely went flat out in attack." Pezoporikos went close to claiming a famous victory

20 minutes from the end but Parsons saved from Giannis Stavrinos after the midfielder cut through a defence tiring in the heat. Despite delivering a turgid performance on the Mediterranean island, Scoular's players were each rewarded with a £12.50 windfall, the agreed bonus for a draw.

Ian Gibson: *We never tried in Larnaca, we treated it as a holiday. During the game nobody wanted the ball. If someone went to give me the ball I'd say, 'I don't want it, pass to someone else'. It was steaming hot and the pitch was atrocious. It was like the Sahara Desert - camels should have been on it, not footballers. We were also 8-0 up and it's hard to get up for a game when you've already got an 8-0 lead. Jimmy expected us to give 100 per cent all the time but we just weren't interested. He was raging after the game, he went bonkers, and made us train the day after. He trained the daylights out of us. We just ran and ran and while we were running he was shouting, 'I'll show you, you bastards!'*

First Round, First Leg
16 September, 1970
Ninian Park, Cardiff

Cardiff City (5) 8   **Pezoporikos (0) 0**
Sutton 18, Gibson 23
King 30, Woodruff 42
Clark 44, 70
Toshack 55, 79

CARDIFF CITY: Parsons, Carver, Bell, Sutton, Murray, Harris, Gibson, Clark, King, Toshack, Woodruff.

PEZOPORIKOS: Palmiris (Kiriakides), Petrou, Paridis, Constantinou, Kyriacou, Hatzistillis, Kounnidis, Karapittas, Loizou, Filiastides, Konstantinou.

First Round, Second Leg
30 September, 1970
GSZ Stadium, Larnaca

Pezoporikos (0) 0   **Cardiff City (0) 0**

PEZOPORIKOS: Palmiris, Petrou, Paridis, Constantinou, Kyriacou, Hatzistillis, Kounnidis, Karapittas, Loizou, Filiastides, Konstantinou.

CARDIFF CITY: Parsons, Carver, Bell, Sutton, Murray, Harris, Gibson, Clark, King, Toshack (Phillips), Woodruff.

(Cardiff City won 8-0 on aggregate)

13

Bluebirds versus Canaries
Nantes, 1970

'The linesman was waving so much, I thought the
Queen must have been in the crowd.'

Brian Harris

IN 1963, Cardiff, the capital of Wales, was twinned with
Nantes. Seven years later, and the cities' football clubs were
twinned in the Cup Winners' Cup. Cardiff and Nantes, the
culturally Breton city and capital of the Pay de la Loire region
in France. The second-round tie was also an intriguing clash
of football philosophies; the direct, no-nonsense approach
favoured by Scoular against the technical, short passing game
preached by Nantes' Spanish coach, José Arribas.

The Ligue 1 side had comfortably beaten Norway's
Strømsgodset Idrettsforening in the first round and, on
paper, represented a serious threat to Cardiff's European
ambitions. Nantes, hammered 5-0 in the French Cup final
by all-conquering Saint-Étienne, boasted six internationals,
among them one of the most exciting talents in French football.
Full-backs Roger Lemerre and Gabriel de Michèle as well as

winger Bernard Blanchet and striker Philippe Gondet were all French internationals. Gondet played for his country at the 1966 World Cup and was voted French Player of the Year in both 1965 and 1966 after helping *les Canaris* (the Canaries) win back-to-back titles. The one foreigner in the Nantes side, Allan Michaelsen, had played for Denmark and was named Danish Player of the Year in 1969 while at Boldklubben 1903. However, the shining light in the *Canaris* line-up was Henri Michel, a midfielder who had made his France debut three years earlier. Nantes' sporting director and former player, Robert Budzynski, claimed the stylish 23-year-old "has the lot" and rated him "the best player in France".

For the first time since arriving at Cardiff in 1964, Jimmy Scoular personally scouted his next opponents in the Cup Winners' Cup. A week before the first leg at Ninian Park, he made the trip to Nantes' Stade Marcel-Saupin, their 25,000-capacity home on the banks of the Loire river, to watch them draw 0-0 with Metz. Gondet was left out as Arribas wanted to keep his main goalscorer fresh for the game in South Wales. "I believe we're in for a very hard game," said Scoular, after returning home from western France. Nantes may not have won any silverware since their Ligue 1 triumph in 1966 but they had built a reputation for playing beautiful football. Arribas demanded speed, movement, intelligence and technique from his players, advocating a brand of football the French later dubbed *jeu à la nantaise* (the play of Nantes). Bilbao-born Arribas – who moved to France when he was 14 to escape the Spanish Civil War - also did his homework before the game in Cardiff. He was among the 25,968 crowd at Ninian Park which watched the Bluebirds draw 2-2 with Leicester City four days before the first leg. They were impressive in the first half, less so after the interval, but Arribas feared their physical strength and aerial power would prove too much for his side. "Cardiff look a very good team and should beat us," he remarked. Scoular, though, dismissed the Spaniard's comments as "a con game to lull us into a false sense of security. I've seen Nantes play and believe me they are a fair side".

For Cardiff's 26th Cup Winners' Cup game – a new record in the competition, eclipsing Rangers' total - Scoular named the same side that played in Larnaca apart from goalkeeper Frank Parsons who was replaced by Jim Eadie, following a series of costly mistakes in the league. The 4-3 home defeat against Middlesbrough, where Parsons was at fault for three goals, proved the final straw for Scoular who relegated the 23-year-old Londoner to the reserves. For the Nantes game, Parsons could not even make the bench due to a broken finger so 18-year-old John Williams was promoted to back-up goalkeeper just a week after making his Football Combination debut.

Eadie's Cup Winners' Cup baptism began in nightmarish fashion with Gondet beating the strapping Scotsman after just 90 seconds. Nantes, third in the French top flight, floored the Bluebirds with a dose of *jeu à la nantaise*, an incisive move involving four players. Michaelsen fed de Michèle who made an overlapping run down the left. He then passed to Patrice Kervarrec. Kervarrec then flicked the ball to Gondet – the man known as *la Foudre* (the Lightning) - who smashed it past Eadie. It was a goal which epitomised the Nantes ethos under Arribas. The French side were in a different class in the opening minutes but Cardiff, driven on by the clever Ian Gibson in midfield, soon exposed Nantes' defensive frailties and John Toshack levelled in the eighth minute with a classic British goal. The striker was fouled by Jean-Claude Osman, and Brian Clark headed on Gary Bell's subsequent free-kick to the far post where his teammate was waiting.

BLUEBIRDS VERSUS CANARIES

Leighton Phillips: *Jimmy went to watch Nantes and when he came back he told us, 'Right from the start they go at 100 miles per hour'. I was a sub on the bench for the first leg and I was sitting near Jimmy. When they scored after 90 seconds he went berserk and he was shouting, 'I bloody told them! I bloody told them!' Nantes did start very quickly, it was unbelievable. They were impressive but they didn't have the stamina to keep playing that way for the whole game.*

Steve Derrett: *Nantes wore yellow and green and they were like bees at the beginning, flying about the pitch. They looked brilliant, they did start fantastically well. They were a good side but then we scored. Our equaliser took the sting out of them. At the time I was in Scoular's bad books for some reason. I'd be in the squad but never play. In two seasons I probably played a dozen games. I don't think I did anything wrong but I was out of favour with Scoular. Gary Bell and Dave Carver were the full-backs and Leighton Phillips started to push through. He was converted from midfield to defence which didn't help my cause.*

Nantes capitulated after the equaliser and a mistake by Jean-Michel Fouché gifted the Bluebirds a second just two minutes later. The goalkeeper cleared Bobby Woodruff's long throw straight to Gibson who lobbed the ball into the empty net. Toshack then claimed his second of the night eight minutes before half-time after dispossessing Osman. Before that, Nantes had a fortunate escape when Patrice Rio handled Bell's cross. Cardiff appealed for a penalty but the East German referee, Wolfgang Riedel, ignored the protests.

Gary Bell: *I remember this match well. For the first few minutes we couldn't get a kick. Nantes knocked it about so well we were chasing shadows. We couldn't get near them, it was all one-touch and two-touch. We hardly got a kick! They played well in the opening minutes but then we scored and that seemed to knock the stuffing out of them. They buckled when we got the equaliser. That goal completely changed the game.*

Cardiff scored twice in the final 14 minutes, after Scoular had replaced Clark with Leighton Phillips and moved Woodruff up front, a role he sometimes – and successfully - filled at Crystal Palace. Toshack forced an error from centre-back Rio and then released Peter King who netted a fourth. Phillips then made it 5-1, finishing off a move involving Gibson and Mel Sutton. The substitute should have made it six, slicing through the French defence by playing a double one-two, only to shoot just wide.

Dave Carver: *We were superb in the first game. When they went 1-0 up very early on I thought we were in for a hard night. When the lad scored, my first thought was Scoular. I remember thinking 'Who's he going to blame for this?' Nantes were a skilful side and they started impressively but we came back ever so well. We were a better team than we thought we were. We weren't an up 'n' under team. We had good players like Ian Gibson, Peter King, Brian Clark, Leighton Phillips and Gary Bell.*

Ian Gibson: *Nantes looked a useful side and when they scored so early I thought we were going to struggle. I would have taken a 2-1 win and then try and get a result in France after they went 1-0 up but we were strong at*

home and we played well that night. At the end the
Nantes manager said he couldn't believe it. He didn't
think we were as good as that. Teams would come to
Cardiff and think we were nothing because we played
in Division Two but we were a decent side and we had
a good defence. We had two excellent full-backs in Dave
Carver and Gary Bell, and Don Murray was a tough
centre-half.

Scoular hailed his side's performance as "terrific" and compared it to the display that eliminated Torpedo Moscow in 1968. Cardiff flew to France with one foot firmly in the quarter-finals and their league form suggested a collapse in Nantes was unlikely. Since the first leg they had played three Division Two games, drawing 1-1 at Carlisle United before beating both Portsmouth and Hull City at Ninian Park. Ominously for the French side, Toshack was in superb form. The Wales international scored the only goal against Pompey and then struck a hat-trick in the 5-1 demolition of a Hull side leading Division Two when they arrived at Ninian Park. Anxious to exorcise any complacency in his camp, Scoular dismissed talk Cardiff were already in the last eight and made one change to the side that swept Nantes aside in the Welsh capital, with Phillips drafted into midfield and Woodruff moved up front at Clark's expense. There was a scare over Brian Harris, not because the veteran defender was injured or ill, but because thieves had broken into his car and stolen a number of personal belongings, including his passport. Fortunately for Cardiff and Harris, a replacement arrived in time. Nantes' hopes of staging a dramatic comeback suffered a severe setback when Gondet was ruled out after picking up an injury in the 3-0 win over Stade de Reims. Bernard Gardon, an 18-year-old defender who did not feature at Ninian Park, was assigned the unenviable job of marking Toshack.

Peter King: *Before the second game I thought we were going to be the first team to win the first leg 5-1 and then get knocked out in the second. I thought Nantes were that good. I really thought we'd get turned over in France and I was thinking about the shame of going out after winning the first leg 5-1. We scored five at Ninian Park but it was one of those nights when everything we tried came off. I thought Nantes were a good side and I was apprehensive before the game over there.*

Nantes needed an early goal and, just as they did in Cardiff, *les Canaris* started brightly. Michel blew a wonderful chance in the first minute, blasting wide after collecting Joel Audiger's through ball. Soon after, Gibson's error gifted possession to Audiger but he shot straight at Eadie. French interest in the competition was effectively ended in the 13th minute when Toshack claimed his 100th career goal, and what proved to be his last for his home club. King's free-kick smacked the crossbar and the striker - making his 203rd appearance for the Bluebirds - knocked home the rebound. Nantes thought they had equalised when Michael Pech's shot went in off the post but the Greek referee, Timoleon Latsios, had spotted a foul by Kervarrec. With 14 minutes left – and after Latsios had disallowed a Pech strike - substitute Clark made it 2-0 when he headed Bell's cross past Fouché. Nantes did score a consolation goal five minutes from time. Following a short corner and from the edge of the 18-yard box, Blanchet chipped the ball over Eadie and Bell, the left-back trying to head clear at the far post. Arribas' men had been well beaten over both legs, losing 7-2 on aggregate.

Ian Gibson: *We played just as well in Nantes as we did in Cardiff. We all remembered what happened after the game in*

*Larnaca so before the Nantes second leg Don Murray,
who was our captain, got us together and said, 'Look,
we don't want that again.' None of us fancied an
extra training session like the one Scoular made us do
in Cyprus, so we gave 100 per cent in Nantes even
though we were 5-1 up. As long as you gave your
all – in training and in matches – Scoular was happy.
I thought we were fantastic in France and the result
was no fluke, we played really well. We looked like a
First Division side. I have to say I enjoyed both games
against Nantes.*

Gary Bell: *In my opinion, that performance in Nantes was one
of our best in Europe. We were great that night. They
had a good pedigree and they started quickly but we
knew what to expect after the first game. Right from
the kick-off everyone played well and in the end we
got a super result. We really performed and to go over
there and win the game when we were already 5-1
up was pretty impressive. Scoular was happy with us
afterwards.*

The display inside the Stade Marcel-Saupin drew praise from
the Press. Nantes "were at times completely outplayed and
outclassed," enthused the *Western Mail*'s Clive Phillips while
the *South Wales Echo*'s Peter Jackson described Cardiff's victory
as "probably their most serene night in Europe". For the third
time in their history, the Bluebirds were in the last eight of
the Cup Winners' Cup where they were joined by Real Madrid,
Chelsea, Manchester City, Club Brugge, PSV Eindhoven, Górnik
Zabrze and Vorwärts Berlin.

Peter King: *If Nantes scored first we would have been in trouble but, thankfully, we got the first goal. We got a free-kick and I whacked it. The goalkeeper dived for it, the ball hit the underside of the crossbar, and Tosh stuck it in the back of the net while the goalkeeper was still on the floor. That away goal set us up because Nantes now had to score six to go through. We beat them 7-2 on aggregate yet in my view they were a better team than Göztepe who beat us the year before. Scoular had a right go at me in the second leg just because I jogged to the corner flag to take a corner when we were 2-1 up. He said, 'With all your experience you run over to take a corner – you should have slowed it down!' We won 2-1 and he still had a go!*

Mel Sutton: *We had a good team in 1970-71. We were strong at the back and we could always rely on Clarky and Tosh to score. We used to joke about those two, that we'd get the ball in the middle and they would play head tennis before scoring. They were two good strikers. They were both strong in the air and they could play too. They had a knack of knowing which way the 'keeper was moving and Nantes just couldn't cope with them.*

Cardiff, though, would have to contest their quarter-final tie without Toshack. His goalscoring exploits in Division Two and the Cup Winners' Cup had caught the attention of Liverpool's manager, Bill Shankly, and a week after hitting the century mark in Nantes, and with Scoular's side two points behind leaders Leicester City, the 21-year-old Wales international signed for the Merseyside club in a £110,000 deal - a record sale for Cardiff and a record signing for Liverpool. "He'd be cheap at a million," was Shankly's assessment of a deal which sparked controversy and outrage in South Wales. Some Cardiff supporters even threatened to boycott matches. Toshack had turned down Fulham in 1968 but, two years later, he was unable to resist the lure of Anfield. "Liverpool are among the half-dozen best clubs in Britain and I feel, without any disrespect to Cardiff, the move can make me a better player," he explained.

Second Round, First Leg
21 October, 1970
Ninian Park, Cardiff

Cardiff City (3) 5   **FC Nantes (1) 1**
Toshack 8, 38 Gibson 10   Gondet 2
King 76, Phillips 80

CARDIFF CITY: Eadie, Carver, Bell, Sutton, Murray, Harris, Gibson, Clark (Phillips), Woodruff, Toshack, King.

FC NANTES: Fouché, Lemerre, de Michele, Osman, Rio, Michaelsen, Blanchet, Michel, Kervarrrec, Gondet, Pech (Audiger).

Second Round, First Leg
4 November, 1970
Stade Marcel-Saupin

FC Nantes (0) 1   **Cardiff City (1) 2**
Blanchet 85   Toshack 13, Clark 76

FC NANTES: Fouché, Lemerre, Rio, Gardon, de Michele, Michel, Michaelsen, Blanchet, Kervarrec, Pech (Albalajedo), Audiger.

CARDIFF CITY: Eadie, Carver, Bell, Sutton, Murray, Harris, Gibson, Phillips (Clark), Woodruff, Toshack, King.

(Cardiff City won 7-2 on aggregate)

14

Three Minutes of Madness
Real Madrid, 1971

'We've got nothing to be afraid of.'

Don Murray

JIMMY Scoular made no secret of his desire to face Real Madrid. After beating Pezoporikos in the first round, the Cardiff manager said he hoped the second-round draw would twin his side with the most decorated club in Spanish – and European - football. He repeated the comments after his side had steamrollered Nantes. "Real Madrid is a name famous throughout the world," said Scoular, as he prepared to leave western France. "That is as good a reason as any for wanting them next." On 18 November, at the quarter-final draw in Paris, the French singer, Mireille Mathieu, granted Scoular his wish as the *Piaf d'Avignon* (Sparrow from Avignon) paired Cardiff with the football aristocrats from the Estadio Santiago Bernabéu. The first leg – on 10 March - should have been played in Madrid since Real came out of the draw first but it was switched to Ninian Park as Atlético Madrid were playing Legia Warsaw in the Spanish capital on the same night.

For the Division Two club it was the dream tie. Real, Europe's most glamorous and successful football club, were champions of Spain a record 14 times and kings of Europe on six occasions. But Scoular had every right to fancy his side's chances against the current crop. While they were thumping Nantes, Real were scraping past Wacker Innsbruck. The *Madridistes* had suffered a shock 1-0 defeat in the first leg at the Bernabéu before winning 2-0 in Austria, winger Manuel Bueno scoring the decisive goal seven minutes from the end. Real were also having a difficult time in La Liga. When the draw was made, Real were a lowly ninth in the 16-team division, winning just three of their first nine games. Miguel Muñoz, who had won three European Cups with the club as a player and two as their coach, was a man under considerable pressure. The glory days, when Real made the European Cup their own and the likes of Alfredo Di Stefano, Raymond Kopa and Ferenc Puskás wore the famous all-white strip, had passed, but *los Merengues* (the Meringues) were still a huge box-office draw, evidenced by Cardiff's decision to start selling tickets for Ninian Park's Enclosure at the end of November. The club, explained secretary Graham Keenor, was responding to public demand as the Ninian Park offices had received "countless inquiries" from people wanting to buy a ticket as a Christmas present. To whet Welsh appetites, 12 days before the first leg the Bluebirds Club organised a Grand Film Show for its members, screening Real's remarkable 7-3 victory over Eintracht Frankfurt in the 1960 European Cup final at Hampden Park.

Peter King: *When we drew Real Madrid in the last eight, I remembered something Tosh had said to me before we played Nantes. He pointed towards the dressing room at Ninian Park, which the away side used, and said, 'If we beat this lot, Real Madrid will be sat in that*

221

dressing room next.' He actually said that. Well, we beat Nantes and look who came out of the hat! Tosh got that one right. But of course he'd left the club and gone to Liverpool by the time the draw was made.

Gary Bell: *From the day of the draw right up to the game, it was fantastic. My dad told me we'd drawn Real Madrid. I drove home after training and when I got in my wife said, 'Your dad's been on. He wants you to call him back.' So I rang and he said, 'Have you heard the draw?' I told him I hadn't and asked who we'd got. He said, 'Real Madrid!' and mentioned all my uncles and cousins had been on and that he needed 10 tickets. So I went to see Scoular in his office and told him my relatives in the Midlands wanted to come down and see the game. I asked him how many tickets we were allowed. He said, 'How many tickets do you want?' I told him 10 and he just said, 'Yes, no problem.' I suppose some of the other lads went in and asked for a ridiculous amount. On the day, the relatives drove down in three or four cars. They came to the house – on top of St Fagans hill – just after lunchtime for a cup of tea and a bite to eat, but I had to leave early as Scoular wanted us at the ground by 5pm, before it got mad outside Ninian Park. He was worried we'd get caught up in the traffic if we left it any later.*

Real had last won the European Cup in 1966 when an all-Spanish side containing Ignacio Zoco, Manuel Sanchis, Pirri, Amancio, Pedro de Felipe, José Araquistáin, Pachin, Fernando Serena, Ramón Grosso, Manuel Velazquez and Francisco Gento came from behind to defeat Partizan Belgrade 2-1 in the final. They were christened the *Ye-Ye* side - from the yeah-yeah-yeah chorus in the Beatles song *She Loves You* - after four players posed in the *Marca* newspaper wearing Beatles-style wigs and clothes. But in 1971 the *Ye-Ye* era was drawing to a close. Several members of the side who had helped Real to a sixth European title – such as Zoco, Pirri, Amancio, Grosso and Velazquez – were still at the club, so too was veteran winger Gento, the only survivor from the glory days of Di Stefano and Puskás, and coach Muñoz. However, the class of 1970-71 was hardly vintage Real Madrid. After winning three consecutive La Liga titles, they had been dethroned as Spanish champions by neighbours Atlético and for the first time since the European Cup's inception in 1955, they were not involved in UEFA's premier club competition. Instead, they were competing in the inferior Cup Winners' Cup courtesy of their Copa del Rey triumph.

Despite an opening-day win over a Valencia side that would go on to win the title, the domestic campaign had started poorly. The next eight fixtures brought three defeats, among them a 1-0 loss against bitter rivals Barcelona in the Bernabéu, but a 5-0 win at Real Zaragoza marked a turning point for *los Merengues* and they prepared for the Ninian Park game on the back of three consecutive 1-0 wins – Barcelona in the Nou Camp, the Madrid derby in the Bernabéu, and Athletic Bilbao in the San Mamés. It was a run that lifted them to third in the table, a point behind Valencia and Atlético Madrid. Scoular had flown out to Spain to cast his eye over Muñoz's side on 14 February, visiting the Nou Camp where he saw José Antonio Grande settle *El Clásico* in favour of the capital club with his 67th-minute winner. Real defended well and the two players who caught Scoular's attention were defender Zoco, their captain, and Pirri, a player he hailed as "world class". Still, the Cardiff manager saw nothing to frighten his players who had returned to the Division Two summit after a thumping 4-0 win over Carlisle United at Ninian Park. "I came home impressed with them but not in a trance," he remarked. "I believe we can beat them." His present side, he continued, was better than the one which had reached the semi-finals in 1968.

Scoular was unable to pick Alan Warboys, his £42,000 record signing from Sheffield Wednesday and the striker who scored all four goals against Carlisle. Remembering how well Warboys had played against his side at Hillsborough the previous August, he identified the Yorkshireman as John Toshack's replacement as soon as the Wales international finalised his switch to Liverpool on 11 November, yet the deal to bring the abrasive forward to Ninian Park was not completed until Christmas Eve – eight days past the UEFA deadline. Warboys, who had already struck nine goals for his new club, would be a spectator for both games with Brian Clark taking his place. Clark was going through a lean spell having scored just one league goal all year. Nevertheless, Scoular believed the fair-haired forward could make an impact in the quarter-final. "He's our top scorer with 16 league and cup goals and I see no reason why he can't continue on the goal trail." The club had demonstrated its faith in the player by rejecting a £30,000 bid from Preston North End for the marksman.

Alan Warboys: *When I joined Cardiff I knew they were playing Real Madrid but I didn't know I was going to be ineligible. I signed and just thought about getting on with my career. When I got down to Cardiff it all came to light, that I was signed a few days too late to play in the game. I was really disappointed, especially as my career at Cardiff was going so well. I settled quickly and started scoring straight away. My record was unbelievable. We played my old club, Sheffield Wednesday, on my debut and I scored two, and I also*

scored four in the first half against Carlisle. Even
though I couldn't play in the game, Scoular took me to
Madrid for the experience. I got a Real Madrid watch
and shirt out of it.

Apart from Clark deputising for Warboys, Scoular planned to field the same line-up which blitzed Carlisle but, unbelievably, the Football Association of Wales threatened to tear up his Real battleplan. The previous month Nigel Rees, a promising 17-year-old winger who had recently forced his way into the Bluebirds first team, had been called up to play for Wales in a UEFA Youth Tournament qualifier against Scotland at Wrexham's Racecourse Ground. The game was on the same night Cardiff faced Real at Ninian Park.

Scoular wanted to play Rees in the first leg, and six days before Real's visit, Cardiff formally requested his release from the youth qualifier, but this was rejected, triggering a bitter war of words between the club and the Football Association of Wales. "I'm disgusted with the Welsh FA," snarled Scoular. "They are depriving me of one of my first-team players for a minor competition. It's unbelievable." His chairman, Fred Dewey, went ever further, saying, "The Welsh FA must be anti-Cardiff City." Mike Smith, the Welsh FA's director of coaching and in charge of Wales' youth teams, had called up four other Cardiff youngsters for the qualifier - goalkeeper John Williams, defender Phil Dwyer, midfielder Alan Couch, and striker Derek Showers - so Scoular felt it was not unreasonable to spare Rees.

Bridgend-born Rees could defy his country's orders and play against Real but, by doing that, he risked a misconduct charge and the likely termination of his international career. "It is the worst decision I have ever known," continued Dewey. "In fact, I think it stinks. I can't think of another football association in the world doing such a thing." Cardiff's forceful – and public - protests achieved the desired result. Two days before the game, Trevor Morris, secretary of Welsh football's governing body and a former Cardiff manager, told the club if Rees failed to report for international duty the following day at Wrexham "it will not affect his international future". Rees, unsurprisingly, decided to pit his wits against Real in the Cup Winners' Cup rather than Scotland's youth team in an Under-18s qualifier. Wales went on to qualify for the UEFA Under-19 tournament which was staged in Czechoslovakia in May. Rees was not included in the squad.

Nigel Rees: *I had a letter from the Welsh FA telling me to report for this game in Wrexham and it was a UEFA qualifier so the country had first call. I had to report on the Sunday before the Real game but Scoular told me not to go to Wrexham until the next day and to just say I was staying in Cardiff to get treatment for an injury. Anyway, on the Monday I trained with City and as you can imagine the place was absolutely buzzing because the Real game was on the Wednesday night. Scoular had me taking corners and making decoy runs with free-kicks and throw-ins. That's when I first realised I might not be going to Wrexham. When I was in the shower, Harry Parsons, the kit man, came in and said the gaffer wanted to see me. I went to his office and he told me Trevor Morris had been on about the Wales game and he also said he had me down to start against Real Madrid. He had to give the Welsh FA an answer by 1pm and he said to me, 'The decision is yours.' I've never forgotten what he said as I was about to leave his office. 'Nigel, don't forget who pays your wages.' There was no choice really, it had to be*

Real Madrid. If I'd told him I wanted to play for Wales he would have had me in the corner and gone face-to-face with me, I'm sure about that. He was a hard man and he got what he wanted. One or two of the young players were scared of Scoular. They'd rather have fought the Apaches than have played for him. As for the Welsh FA, to have put me in that position showed their mentality.

Real, who included their 75-year-old president, Santiago Bernabéu, in their party, had a difficult trip to the Welsh capital. A freak blizzard in Madrid delayed the flight for six hours and they did not arrive at their Cardiff hotel until the early hours of Tuesday morning. Unbeaten since 17 January when they lost at Granada, their resurgence was built on a formidable defence. Real had kept clean sheets in six of their nine La Liga fixtures since Christmas and their defensive work in the Nou Camp impressed Scoular who was convinced Muñoz's side would pull down the shutters on Cardiff's patchy surface.

A crowd of 47,500 flooded through Ninian Park's turnstiles to watch what Dewey described as "the biggest club match played in Wales" and a game that netted the club a cool £25,000 in ticket sales. Brian Harris had recovered from a hamstring injury picked up the previous month but Scoular preferred Leighton Phillips alongside Don Murray in defence while Rees was on the left wing. The rest of the team picked itself; Jim Eadie in goal, Gary Bell and Dave Carver the full-backs, Mel Sutton and Ian Gibson in central midfield, Peter King on the right, with Bobby Woodruff supporting Clark in attack. Gibson was the player who most concerned Real's coach. Muñoz had watched the Division Two side play 18 days earlier, in the 1-1 home draw with Charlton Athletic, and the busy midfielder - who scored Cardiff's goal from the penalty spot - impressed the Spaniard. "He was almost in two places at one time," said the Real coach.

Gary Bell: *Ninian Park was full an hour before kick-off, I'd never known anything like it. The official attendance was 47,500 but to me it looked nearer 50,000. Back then it was easy to sneak into the Bob Bank round the back. When we came out of the tunnel, I looked at the Bob Bank in front of me and all I saw was a mass of faces. Everybody was jammed in. It was the same in the Grange End.*

Leighton Phillips: *I was living in Neath and travelled to Cardiff by train. I then picked up a taxi at the station but we couldn't get to Ninian Park because there was such a big crowd about. In the end I had to jump out and walk. There were so many people on the pavement that I slipped on the kerb and went over on my ankle. Luckily it was OK but I could so easily have missed the Real Madrid game because of a kerb outside the ground.*

Real's line-up contained six players, all Spanish internationals, who had starred in their European Cup success in Brussels five years earlier – defenders Sanchis and Zoco, midfielders Pirri and Velazquez, right-winger Amancio and striker Grosso. Amancio, nicknamed *el Brujo* (the Wizard) because of his dribbling ability, scored his side's equaliser in the 2-1 win over Partizan and, along with Zoco, was in the Spain side crowned European champions at the Bernabéu seven years earlier. Zoco had played at Ninian Park before, in April 1961, when he made his first appearance for Spain in their 2-1 World Cup qualifying win over Wales. Pirri – real name José Martínez Sánchez - was regarded as one of the finest Spanish players of his generation, a born leader with an eye for goal and tremendous stamina.

Nigel Rees:	*It was a cold night. I was a young pro at the time so I knew the apprentices at the club and they told me the first thing Scoular got them to do was to turn off the central heating in the away dressing room so it was freezing for those warm-blooded Spaniards – and when those dressing rooms got cold, they were cold! It must have upset the Real players, especially when you think of the facilities they were used to back home but there was nothing they could do about it because the boiler systems back then weren't like the ones today. You couldn't just turn on the heating and the room would start to warm up straight away, it would probably have taken a couple of hours. The away dressing room was small as well, you couldn't swing a cat in it! I would imagine Real were affected by those conditions.*
Dave Carver:	*Scoular named the team the day before the game. We were on top of Division Two and doing well so the side picked itself although the selection of Nigel Rees was a bit of a shock. It was a brave decision. Scoular must have seen something about Real that Nigel could exploit. Ronnie Bird was hoping to play in the game. He was a big Real fan but the gaffer went for Nigel. Ronnie never got over being left out of that one.*
Leighton Phillips:	*I watched Real Madrid beat Eintracht Frankfurt 7-3 in the European Cup final on TV when I was a kid and you dreamed about playing them. We were expecting them to wear their famous all-white strip at Ninian*

229

Park. We were the first to go out onto the pitch before kick-off and Real kept us waiting for a couple of minutes - while we were on the pitch they were still in their dressing room. When they finally came out we discovered they were wearing all red. It was so disappointing because we thought they would be in the the white kit for which Real was famous throughout the world. We had no idea they would be wearing red for our game.

Cardiff began nervously and Eadie was forced into making an excellent early save after Carver's careless back-pass let in Miguel Pérez. The winger from Buenos Aires was given another sniff soon after when Phillips' header to Eadie fell slightly short but, fortunately for the midfielder-turned-defender, it was still too far for Perez who guided the ball into the net with his hand. Velazquez, the most dangerous Real player in the first half, then hit a first-time shot wide from the edge of the penalty area after a sweeping move involving Grosso and Pirri.

When the Division Two leaders settled down, they began to apply pressure on a Real side that had come to Cardiff to defend. After Clark headed a Gibson free-kick wide, Ninian Park erupted with joy precisely 31 minutes and 15 seconds in when the striker placed Rees' cross beyond the reach of José Luis Borja. Bell began the move well inside his own half, knocking the ball to Woodruff on the left side who, after fooling Grosso, passed it to Rees. The youngster then wriggled past sweeper Zoco and right-back Sanchis, with a blend of skill and good fortune, before delivering a pinpoint cross to Clark who, from eight yards out and in front of a packed Canton Stand, headed the ball into Borja's net. Recalling the most famous goal of his 19-year career, Clark, who died in 2010, aged 67, said, "I was making a run but then I saw what Nigel was doing so I came back out and made another run. I'd lost my marker because I'd moved back out so I was unmarked as I moved back into the box. Nigel's cross couldn't have been better. When it was coming towards me I thought to myself 'I can't miss this' and just headed it into the net. We were confident we could beat Real - it was a cold night, the pitch wasn't great and we had nearly 50,000 people behind us so the conditions were in our favour. The Real players didn't put themselves about and we absolutely battered them."

Nigel Rees: *I had two players with me and one of them was the sweeper (Zoco) who was out of position so I looked to go between them. There was a little gap and none of the Real players were quicker than me. When I went to go past the second defender (Sanchis) the ball came off his shin – in cricket it would have been LBW – but it went the way I wanted it to go so I had a bit of luck. I took one touch and looked up because I had time. I saw Clarky on the half-moon outside the box so I aimed for the penalty spot because strikers want the ball knocked into space. Clarky had an uninterrupted run, there wasn't a Real player near him when he headed the ball into the net. We scored in front of the Canton Stand but if it had been the Grange End I would probably have been pulled off the pitch because that's where all my mates were. I think half of Port Talbot was in the Grange End that night!*

The second half belonged to Scoular's men but, despite their domination, they were unable to beat Borja again. Clark headed Bell's cross wide and Sutton shot straight at the goalkeeper after charging his way into the penalty box. Bluebirds skipper Murray squandered the best opportunity of all. Bell's free-kick

231

fell to the big centre-half who was eight yards out but he was unable to make a firm connection, allowing Gregorio Benito to clear his effort. "A striker would surely have punished Real," wrote Peter Jackson. Cardiff had beaten the mighty *Madridistes* 1-0 and afterwards champagne flowed in the jubilant Bluebirds dressing room although the margin of victory could – and perhaps should - have been greater. Real had showed little ambition, particularly in the second half, and Eadie was never tested after the interval.

Don Murray: *We had a right go at Real at Ninian and we should have scored more than one goal. We had two or three good chances but didn't take them and it was disappointing we didn't finish them off. If we'd put them away then we would have gone to the Bernabéu with a nice cushion but it was always going to be difficult in Madrid with just a one-goal lead. I had a great chance in the second half but fluffed it completely. I was shocked to find myself in a position I wasn't usually in, to be honest! It was a super night and I often wonder what the Real manager said to his players about the goal because their marking was awful, it was shocking. Brian took his goal brilliantly but he was all on his own when he headed the ball. I couldn't believe top-class defenders like that would give a forward so much room. I know Jimmy wouldn't have been happy with us if we'd given away a goal like that.*

Peter King: *Leighton Phillips had a blinder at the back and Real gave Ian Gibson space so he shone as well but I had a stinker. Scoular put me on the right and I detested playing there. I was used to playing on the left and felt more comfortable on that side. I didn't play well and was disappointed with my performance. I got booked as well, it was one of only two bookings I got in my career. The first one was against Plymouth – it's not often you mention Plymouth and Real Madrid in the same sentence! Against Real, the bloke (Fernando Zunzunegui) fouled me and while we were tangled up on the floor he didn't half kick me with the bottom of his boot so I kicked him back, which was unlike me really, and the ref showed me a yellow card. It sounds silly but it didn't seem like we were playing Real Madrid because they were wearing all red. If they were in white you'd think 'This is Real Madrid' but because they were in red it didn't seem like the real McCoy. It took the edge off them.*

Gary Bell: *We walked onto the pitch to a crescendo of noise and the only thing that beat it was the roar when Clarky's header hit the back of the net. Now that was a noise. I'd never heard anything like it. We could have scored three or four that night, we created that many chances. At the final whistle the Madrid players trooped off without acknowledging us.*

Cardiff were the only British success story in the competition that night with holders Manchester City losing in Poland against Górnik Zabrze and Chelsea tasting defeat in Belgium against Club Brugge. Scoular paid tribute to his players. They were "great, just great" and deserved to have won by "at least two clear goals" instead of just one. Murray agreed, saying they could have won 3-0. According to Clive Phillips in the *Western Mail*, City "ran themselves to a standstill...their non-stop powerwork bothered a normally well-drilled and cool defence." Clark had sent Real packing but as the 28-year-old sipped champagne in the dressing room, he was unsure if Scoular would pick him for Saturday's game at Blackburn. "No goal has ever given me greater pleasure," Clark told journalists afterwards, "and I don't suppose I'll ever get one to please me as much again...to score the goal in any match is pleasing. To score it against Real Madrid, that is something I only dreamed about." Clark had guided the ball to the goalkeeper's left but admitted "it went a bit closer to him (Borja) than I intended but I knew before I fell over that he couldn't get to it". Cardiff's show surprised Muñoz. "Cardiff played well – a lot better than they did when I watched then in a league match last month," said the 49-year-old. "We played a defensive game. We did so because I considered it best for us. But at the Bernabéu we shall attack."

Ian Gibson: *Real gave us room to play, that's what good teams did. They would let you play up to a certain point and then they would close you down. But the Real players didn't pick us up because they thought they were miles better than us. They could have scored early on when Dave Carver made a mistake but after that we got on top of them and they began to panic. It was all one-way and Jim Eadie didn't have much to do. At the end you could tell the Real players were relieved to lose just 1-0. They were chuffed with that. We were happy with the result but we should've scored more. After the game we went upstairs to celebrate and Fred Dewey was in the boardroom counting the money.*

Leighton Phillips: *A few of my mates in Briton Ferry came to watch the game. They came down in a bus and I met up with them afterwards and we went to a club in Ely for a few beers before we popped into the Chinese take-away*

across the road to get something to eat. Then they gave
me a lift back home. That's how I celebrated the result.
Most of the players went to the Electricity Club in
Pontcanna.

Nigel Rees: *After the game I didn't stick about. I didn't do any*
interviews or drink champagne and milk the result like
the other lads. I wanted to get away from it all and
get back home. I was a young kid and my father was
waiting for me outside so as soon as I'd had a shower
and changed, I was gone.

The following Saturday, at Ewood Park, the Blackburn Rovers'
players acknowledged Cardiff's achievement against Real by
giving Scoular's men a guard of honour as they walked onto
the pitch although a 1-1 draw meant Leicester City replaced
the Bluebirds at the Division Two summit. But when they flew
out to Madrid, they were back on top courtesy of a 1-0 home
win over Queens Park Rangers – Warboys the scorer - which
extended their unbeaten league run to 10 matches. Real had
recovered from their Ninian Park loss to beat Real Zaragoza
at home but, three days before the European rematch, they
suffered their first La Liga defeat in nearly two months, going
down 2-0 at Celta Vigo. Scoular knew Pirri and his teammates would pose a bigger threat inside the 125,000-capacity
Bernabéu, but he was in bullish mood ahead of the second leg.
"I am confident," he declared, "and so are my players." Murray
was equally upbeat, telling his teammates they had "nothing
to be afraid of".

Dave Carver: *Over in Madrid we were like one of those little clubs*
that get to play Manchester United at Old Trafford
in the FA Cup. We were just pleased to be there. We

had a look at their trophy room and had a tour of the Bernabéu. We did a training session at the stadium and some of the stuff Scoular got us doing was really antiquated. He made us do squats while carrying another player on your shoulders. We looked more like commandos than footballers and we were aware the Real players were watching us – they must have wondered what kind of preparation is that! When we were walking off the pitch I remember Clarky saying he felt embarrassed.

Nigel Rees: *When we trained at the Bernabéu on the Tuesday evening there were thousands of people there watching us – and I mean thousands. The boss lost his head. He got us doing everything – corners, 5-a-side, this thing he introduced where you put another player on your shoulders and they dropped off, crawled between your legs and then you got on their shoulders. At the time we thought Scoular was putting on a show for the crowd, a pantomime! He was just milking it. Normally a session would last so long but in the Bernabéu it went on and on, it was just stupid. I think the training session started at around 7pm and it was well past 10pm before we got back to our hotel.*

Scoular had thought about the second leg for a whole week, what team to pick and what strategy to adopt, and decided his starting XI and tactics the night before the game. The Cardiff chief chose to stick with the side that won at Ninian Park and said the key to success was keeping Real out in the first 60 minutes, what he called "the hot hour". Scoular expected an early Spanish assault but if his players could contain Real for an hour the Spaniards would, he believed, become frustrated and then vulnerable. For the first 50 minutes the players heeded their manager's advice. The score was 0-0, they were comfortable – Real threatened just once in the opening 45 minutes when Eadie saved from Amancio - and an unimpressed Madrid public was turning on its team, hurling seat cushions at Muñoz's players as they walked off the pitch at half-time. They also vented their frustration at the visitors, throwing bottles and beer cans at the men in blue, a broken bottle hitting Bell.

Gary Bell: *I tackled one of their players and the ball went out for a corner. As I turned to get up I could see something coming out of the crowd and it hit me on the thigh. It was an empty bottle. Don Murray and Leighton Phillips came over to see if I was OK. I called the ref over, he just looked at me, dropped the bottle behind the goal and said, 'Play on.' We got nothing from the ref over there. Every time one of the Real players went down, they'd get a free-kick and there were some bad decisions against us in the second half. We held Real without too much difficulty in the first half. They created hardly anything and their fans started to turn. I remember Scoular saying at half-time – 'Just keep it as it is. Keep playing as you are and we'll be all right.'*

Muñoz introduced Sebastián Fleitas for the ineffective Marañón during the break, in an attempt to ignite an attack that proved disappointing. Fleitas made little impression when he came on at Ninian Park, although he was not helped by his side's negative approach, but inside a Bernabéu which was nearly half empty, the Paraguayan forward etched his name on the second leg. After a trouble-free 45 minutes, Cardiff lost their solidity at the start of the second period and conceded twice inside three crazy minutes, both goals stemming from errors.

In the 50th minute, Amancio delivered a high ball deep into the penalty box but Murray's poor headed clearance forced Eadie to intervene. The goalkeeper punched the ball straight to Velazquez who volleyed home from 15 yards out. With the visitors still reeling from Velazquez's strike, Pirri headed on Andrés Junquera's goal kick and a moment's hesitation by Carver allowed Fleitas to reach the ball and flick it past Eadie with his right boot.

Peter King: *Real didn't look like scoring in the first half. It was 0-0 and we had cancelled each other out. For the neutral, it was a boring game. Then they brought on this little left-winger (Fleitas) at half-time and the whole atmosphere changed. There was a big fuss when he appeared, with photographers on the pitch taking pictures of him, and everybody wanted him to play. He seemed to be a crowd favourite – he was certainly a popular guy – and there was a new enthusiasm about Real Madrid after half-time. They were a different team in the second half and that winger ended up getting the goal which put them through.*

Cardiff would still progress with an away goal but, with Gibson and Clark both closely marked, they struggled to create the opportunities they carved out in the first leg. In a bad-tempered second period, Real used their nous to wind the clock down, retaining possession and wasting time. Lew Clayton clashed with Junquera after he ran down the touchline to retrieve the ball which had gone out of play. The goalkeeper, deputising for the injured Borja, came way out of his goal to try and knock the ball out of Clayton's hands. And when a Pirri shot ended up in the Bernabéu stands, the Real supporters refused to return the ball. For the final 15 minutes Scoular replaced

Rees with Harris and moved Phillips into midfield. He hoped the former Everton defender's experience might influence the game but Real held out, winning 2-0 and booking their place in the last four.

Dave Carver: *Scoular gave me a bollocking about the second goal. He was having a go at me during the game! I knew I was responsible. It wasn't a bad blunder but I could've done better. I was by the touchline and he was giving me a load of abuse, he just wouldn't let it drop. Scoular would go on and on. I was trying to get on with the game and there he was having a go at me from the dugout. We were really cut up about losing because Real didn't have to work hard for the goals. We were comfortable at half-time. We weren't under any pressure and Jim Eadie didn't have much to do. I was so pissed off because we'd lost and I was being blamed for the second goal that I didn't notice the lads swapping shirts at the end. I was in the dressing room and I saw them walk in holding Real Madrid shirts. I thought 'I want one of those!' so I knocked on their dressing room door and swapped shirts with Perez who was one of the subs.*

Leighton Phillips: *I went into Real's dressing room at the end to swap shirts with their number 10, Velazquez. They knew they'd been in a hell of a game, you could sense it. They were all lying flat out, they were knackered. Real gave us a watch each and what did we give Real? A small Cardiff City pennant! The ref was diabolical. He didn't give us a thing all night. You knew Real were going to get a lot of decisions their way because they were at home but it was ridiculous. The Spanish smashed*

239

bottles and threw them onto the pitch – one of them hit Gary Bell. He was lucky because it was the neck of the bottle that hit him. If it had been the jagged end it would have ripped his leg open.

After the game Scoular – who doubted the Spaniards would go on to win the trophy - said his side were out of the Cup Winners' Cup "because of two stupid defensive errors" but slammed the Czechoslovakian referee, Karol Sarka, describing his performance as "the worst I've ever seen in all my years in the game". The official from Bratislava awarded Real 35 free-kicks and Cardiff just six. He booked only one player - Bell for a foul on Amancio - and played no stoppage time. "This isn't sour grapes because we lost but some of his decisions were baffling," said Scoular, who was also upset the Real crowd had thrown bottles and cans at his players. "Real did most of the fouling yet they seemed to get all the free-kicks." His opposite number, Muñoz, admitted his side played badly in the first half but then improved after the restart. "We did enough to deserve our victory," remarked the relieved Real coach.

Richie Morgan:	*After the game everyone, including the subs, decided to swap shirts with the Real players but the manager wasn't happy and said the cost of the shirts would be docked from our wages. He said to us, 'Each one of you bastards will pay for that shirt!' It was typical Jimmy Scoular. He wasn't happy because we hadn't asked his permission to swap shirts but he didn't dock our wages in the end. He was just disappointed about the result and that's the way he reacted to it.*
Ian Gibson:	*The wives and girlfriends came over for this game – it was the first time my wife, Joan, had been on a plane*

- and we thought we had a chance. We were hoping for a bit of luck on the night but the ref denied us a penalty. A shot beat the 'keeper and one of their full-backs dived full-length to turn it behind the post. The ref said the 'keeper saved it but afterwards we watched the highlights on TV and it clearly showed the 'keeper didn't get near it, it was the defender who touched the ball. The ref gave Real everything. They dived and rolled about as if they'd been shot by a machine gun and he gave them free-kicks. I was getting kicked, obstructed and pulled by my shirt, and he never gave me a free-kick. But we made two mistakes and good teams punish your mistakes. I was glad we chose the right bonus. Before the first game the club gave us two choices - a £100 bonus for beating them at home or £300 for knocking them out altogether. We went for the £100 bonus because we felt we could beat them at Ninian but it would be difficult to beat them over two legs.

Real beat PSV Eindhoven to reach the final but failed to win a seventh European title, losing 2-1 to Chelsea in a replay in Piraeus, Greece. However, the *Ye-Ye* side mustered one more league title the following year before breaking up. For Cardiff, there would be more heartbreak on the domestic front as they missed out on promotion. With five fixtures remaining, they were second in the table, ahead of Sheffield United – who had played one game more - on goal difference. But a shock 1-0 home defeat by lowly Watford and a crushing 5-1 loss against United at Bramall Lane handed the initiative to the Yorkshire side with their 3-0 home win over Watford on May Day condemning Cardiff – and Scoular - to yet another year in Division Two.

Mel Sutton: *We tried to play the same way in Madrid as we did at Ninian Park. Jimmy always thought we could beat the opposition. He had it ingrained in him as a player and he passed that on to us. We played quite well and tried to hold out. Even when it was 2-0 we were still having a go and right up until the final whistle we were in with a shout. Everyone thought we'd done well because we were playing Real Madrid but all of us were disappointed at the end. We'd had a real chance of reaching the semi-finals.*

Quarter-final, First Leg
10 March, 1971
Ninian Park, Cardiff

Cardiff City (1) 1   **Real Madrid (0) 0**
Clark 32

CARDIFF CITY: Eadie, Carver, Bell, Sutton, Murray, Phillips, King, Gibson, Clark, Woodruff, Rees.

REAL MADRID: Borja, Zunzunegui (José Luis), Sanchis (de Felipe), Grande, Benito, Zoco, Amancio, Pirri, Grosso (Fleitas), Velasquez, Perez.

Quarter-final, Second Leg
24 March, 1971
Estadio Santiago Bernabéu, Madrid

Real Madrid (0) 2   **Cardiff City (0) 0**
Velasquez 50, Fleitas 52

REAL MADRID: Junquera, Zunzunegui, Sanchis, Grande, Benito, Zoco, Amancio (Perez), Pirri, Grosso, Velasquez, Maranon (Fleitas).

CARDIFF CITY: Eadie, Carver, Bell, Sutton, Murray, Phillips, King, Gibson, Clark, Woodruff, Rees (Harris).

(Real Madrid won 2-1 on aggregate)

15

Behind the Wall
Dynamo Berlin, 1971

'We know nothing about Dynamo.'

Jimmy Scoular

CHECKPOINT Charlie and one of the world's most extraordinary – and frightening - journeys awaited Cardiff in September 1971. The first-round draw sent them to East Germany to face Dynamo Berlin, the club which represented East Germany's security forces and whose honorary chairman was Erich Mielke, head of the *Staatssicherheit* - commonly known as the Stasi – the German Democrat Republic's secret police agency.

Cardiff prepared for their second trip behind the Iron Curtain following a poor start to the 1971-72 campaign, losing three and winning just one of their first seven league matches. They had the worst defensive record in Division Two and their only victory, a 3-2 home win over Sheffield Wednesday which lifted them to 16th place, came at the seventh attempt. Not only were they leaking goals, their main goalscorer, Alan Warboys, was struggling for form at the other end, netting only three goals – two of them coming in the win over former club Wednesday. Brian Clark had scored four while the only other goalscorer was young John Parsons, the son of kit man Harry.

Alan Warboys: *I had a lot of success in my first season at Cardiff but the goals didn't happen for me in my second. I was married in the summer and Jimmy Scoular blamed it on that. He said I wasn't the same after I got married – it was the wife's fault! – in one of the papers and I wasn't pleased with those comments. We just didn't seem to gel as a team that season. The goals dried up for me – but a lot of things dried up for us that year.*

There had been few changes since the previous season's promotion heartbreak. Brian Harris and Ronnie Bird had both moved to Newport County with three new faces arriving at Ninian Park. Jimmy Scoular paid Southampton £6,000 for full-back Ken Jones, £20,000 to Newcastle United for midfielder Alan Foggon, and another £20,000 to Luton Town for midfielder Roger Hoy although the latter's transfer was completed after the UEFA deadline, making him ineligible for the Dynamo tie. Coached by Hans Geitel, Dynamo contained three East German internationals – defender Dieter Stumpf, midfielder Peter Rohde and striker Harald Schütze while forward Dietmar Labes played for the Under-23 side. Not for the first time in his managerial career, Jimmy Scoular boarded the aeroplane "not knowing the slightest thing" about the opposition. He was, however, pleased the second leg was at Ninian Park. "I don't dislike playing the first leg away as we'll know exactly what we have to do when Dynamo come to Cardiff." Despite their Stasi connections, Dynamo had yet to taste sustained success. Their one piece of silverware, the Free German Trade Union Federation Cup, was claimed in 1959. In 1970-71 they finished ninth out of 14 in the Oberliga and were beaten by East German champions Dynamo Dresden in the cup final. Cardiff's form had been unimpressive but they were expected to conquer Mielke's favourite club.

BEHIND THE WALL

A delay at Düsseldorf International Airport, where Cardiff caught a flight to West Berlin, meant the journey to East Berlin took nine hours. After landing in the western side of the city, Scoular and his squad were taken to Checkpoint Charlie – a crossing point in the 96-mile Berlin Wall for the Allied armed forces, at Freidrichstrasse, in the centre of the city. In the darkness of night, they passed the infamous 'YOU ARE LEAVING THE AMERICAN SECTOR' sign and entered Soviet territory. After being searched by armed guards, they changed buses and were then driven to their East Berlin base, a sparsely-decorated sports hotel.

Peter King: *Our coach had to drive past huge concrete blocks which were put up to make a series of chicanes to stop people bursting through the checkpoint in vehicles and we saw 'no man's land' which was on the eastern side of the wall and about the size of a cricket pitch. There were two huge platforms, one on the east side and one on the west, with people standing on them and waving at each other. They must have been families split up by the wall and it was a sad and moving sight. When we got to the east side we had to change buses so we stepped off our beautiful and luxurious West Berlin coach and got onto this khaki-coloured boneshaker of a bus which had clearly seen better days. There was barbed wire everywhere, and Achtung signs, and while West Berlin was all done up, in East Berlin you could still see the remnants of war. Many buildings had bomb damage with big chunks missing from walls.*

Mel Sutton: *When we crossed into the eastern side our bus stopped in a courtyard and we had to get off. I looked around and there were four towers, one in each corner, with machine guns on them! Then we were driven into East Berlin and I noticed a lot of buildings had the East German flag hanging outside a window. It was a dull place and our hotel wasn't that good, it was bland. The fruit we were given was always bruised and that's stuck in my memory.*

The wall was a barrier between two different worlds. West Berlin was a typically capitalist city, cosmopolitan and colourful with smart shops, five-star hotels, restaurants, casinos, street cafés and a vibrant nightlife. In contrast, East Berlin was grey and drab. Its streets, lined with dreary Russian-style terraced houses and ugly apartment blocks, were lifeless and often eerily empty. There were few shops and little traffic. Many buildings - some half-destroyed - still bore the devastating scars of the Second World War and walls were covered with propaganda posters and pockmarks caused by bullets. While West Berlin glittered at night, the eastern half was virtually in darkness.

Ian Gibson: *West Berlin was full of cars, motorbikes, lights and people. Then we went into East Berlin and didn't see a soul. There was a street light maybe every 100 yards and you couldn't see down the side streets because it was so dark. It was very eerie. It was as if everyone was in prison, I couldn't believe it. The locals scurried about in big coats. If we tried to talk to them they didn't want to know because they were nervous. They thought the police might be watching and would assume they wanted to escape to the West. Our hotel was like a hostel. We had just a bed and a wardrobe, that was it. The food was awful, everything was rubbery and stuck together. We heard that when*

246

the Dynamo players came to Cardiff they stole towels and other stuff from their hotel to take back home. That showed what it was like living in East Germany at that time.

Don Murray:
I woke up early one morning and I could hear this noise. It must have been four or five o'clock. I got out of bed and looked out of the hotel window. I saw thousands of East Germans going to work on their bikes. That was the noise I could hear. It was dark outside but when I looked over to West Berlin all I could see were lights. The difference between east and west was incredible. It was two different worlds. East Berlin was bleak and the people looked miserable. All the Iron Curtain places were the same.

Dynamo moved the game from their newly-built but modest Dynamo-Stadion to the larger Friedrich-Ludwig-Jahn-Sportpark, a sports complex close to the wall and its infamous 'death strip' – a sandy, mined and heavily-guarded no man's land between the East side's inner wall and the larger outer wall on the West side. With its futuristic floodlights and changing rooms 100 yards outside the stadium, the venue could hold 20,000 spectators which was double the Dynamo-Stadion's capacity but Cardiff's visit attracted a crowd of just under 12,000. Officials attributed the disappointing attendance to Dynamo Dresden's European Cup clash against Ajax being shown live on television.

Revealing before kick-off he would be happy to return to the West with a goalless draw, Scoular bolstered his midfield by sacrificing a left-winger, Foggon, for a fourth midfielder with Peter King being handed his first start of the season. Foggon's exclusion came as no surprise. A member of the Newcastle

United side that defeated Újpest Dózsa to lift the Inter-Cities Fairs Cup two years earlier – he notched the winner in their 3-2 second leg win in Hungary - the long-haired and portly Foggon had failed to make an impact since moving to the Welsh capital. A disappointing performance against Wednesday the previous weekend ended with Scoular hauling him off. Dave Carver was another absentee with Jones keeping the right-back shirt. Ever-present in the side for more than three years, Carver had hit what his manager called "a bad patch" and was axed for the fixture against Wednesday. Jones and Warboys were the two changes to the side that had lost in the Bernabéu six months earlier.

The Welsh side looked to have won the first leg with 12 minutes left when Ian Gibson – Cardiff's best player that night – swept the ball past Werner Lisha after Berndt Brillat, Dynamo's sweeper, misjudged the bounce of Gary Bell's long clearance. It was City's 51st goal in the Cup Winners' Cup, equalling Atlético Madrid's record. But with the final whistle approaching, police mechanic Schütze - wearing a bandage over his head following an earlier collision - threw the Bluebirds defence off balance with a sharp turn and, from 20 yards out, beat Jim Eadie with virtually the last kick of the game. By then Dynamo should have been down and out. King and Clark wasted two chances in the first half, Mel Sutton and Gibson squandered another two after the break. Until Schütze's equaliser, Dynamo had been restricted to shooting from 40 yards out, so impressive was the visitors' defensive display. Günter Schröter, Dynamo's assistant coach, said his players "froze almost with awe and respect" in the first 45 minutes. Scoular, meanwhile, claimed his side had been "robbed of victory". Nevertheless, he was in an upbeat mood afterwards. "The players should not be too disappointed. They were great. They did a tremendous job and I'm very pleased with the result even though we could have won." Before he left the Freidrich-Ludwig-Jahn-Sportpark, Scoular told the Press he was confident his Bluebirds would win at Ninian Park "without too much difficulty".

Leighton Phillips: *After the game me and a few of the other lads went to a bar for a drink. West Berlin was all lights and razzmatazz but in East Berlin nobody was about. It was a foggy night and all you could hear was the sound of our footsteps on the cobbled streets. We had a couple of beers and then went back to the hotel. Thank God we were going the next day! It was an unbelievable place. We saw what looked like beautiful houses but then when we went past them, we discovered they were just frontages. There was nothing at the back, they were being held up by partitions.*

Bobby Woodruff: *East Berlin reminded me of Beirut, it was like a bomb site. A few of us changed money in West Berlin. We got East German marks so we could go out and have a drink while we were in East Berlin. When we got back to West Berlin we went to change the East German marks we didn't use but nobody would accept them. You could get East German currency in the West but you couldn't take them back, so we ended up losing all that money.*

As they exited the Soviet sector, the bus carrying the Cardiff squad received the same treatment as any other vehicle crossing to West Berlin, with armed guards rigorously searching the coach to check no East Germans were trying to escape through this gateway to the West. Wide mirrors were slid under the coach to inspect its underside and passport photographs were carefully matched with faces.

Gary Bell: *On the way back, guards wearing trench coats, fur hats and jackboots, and carrying machine guns, searched our bus. They were very strict and serious. They put mirrors underneath the bus to check we weren't taking any East Germans back with us. These mirrors were about three feet wide and on wheels so they could be moved around. They wanted to see if anyone was trying to escape by hanging onto the axle. They searched the whole bus, the boot and even the skip in which our kit was stored. We were kept waiting quite a while. We saw hardly anyone in East Berlin. We didn't see people shopping, walking in the park, or anything like that.*

Alan Warboys: *Armed guards came onto the bus and checked everything and we were stationary for ages. It was quite frightening. East Berlin was an intimidating place and I couldn't cope with it. I just wanted to play the game and get out, but we ended up staying the night over there! After the game a few of the lads went to a bar near the hotel for a drink and they said it was OK but I stayed in the hotel. I didn't sleep much that night. I just wanted to get on the bus and go home.*

Richie Morgan: *There was a lot of laughter and joking on the bus as we left our hotel, but when we got to the checkpoint it turned to silence. We had a few pranksters in the squad but they went quiet, which was unusual for them. Armed guards checked our passports and looked at our photos three or four times. Nobody on the bus spoke out of turn. It wasn't the time or the place to be cracking silly jokes. We all felt pretty uncomfortable.*

250

Cardiff were favourites for the second leg despite losing both league games – against Middlesbrough and Swindon Town - since returning from East Berlin. Gibson had injured his instep during the 1-0 home loss against Swindon but passed a late fitness test after taking sea salt baths which healed the bruising. Gibson's recovery was a real fillip for Scoular who knew the intelligent midfielder was the player the East Germans most feared. But the concern was not one way. Schütze, the man who netted Dynamo's late equaliser in the first leg, worried Scoular, who told his players to make sure they contained the 22-year-old at Ninian Park. "He is strong, has good control and is not afraid to shoot," he warned, clearly remembering the player's strike inside the Freidrich-Ludwig-Jahn-Sportpark.

As expected, Cardiff created a number of glorious chances. Clark, set up by Gibson's astute pass, put the home side in front after 58 minutes, calmly slipping the ball past Lihsa. But just as they did in East Berlin, Cardiff allowed Dynamo back into the tie. Just minutes after Clark's opener, Eadie failed to hold Stumpf's cross-shot and Labes knocked home the easiest of equalisers. Cardiff bombarded the Dynamo goal in extra-time but a second goal eluded the Division Two side. Lihsa tipped a Sutton shot over the target, King - who had struck the post before Clark's opener - hit the crossbar, Gibson saw his effort cleared off the line by Joachim Hall, Clark watched his header bounce twice on the crossbar and Lihsa produced another superb save to deny the forward. Dynamo held on and forced a penalty shoot-out. With Gibson, Don Murray, King, Bell and Bobby Woodruff volunteering to take Cardiff's spot-kicks, Clark, the main striker, declined to take one of the penalties telling Scoular he "did not feel confident enough". Murray's previous attempt from the spot had been unsuccessful with Reg Matthews saving the defender's penalty during the Bluebirds' 4-3 win at Derby in February 1968.

Bobby Woodruff: *We were standing in the centre circle and Scoular came over and said, 'Who wants to take a penalty?' I took penalties when I was at Crystal Palace so I volunteered, so did Belly, Kingy, Gibbo and Don. We were all amazed Clarky didn't volunteer because he was a goalscorer. He never used to take penalties which was strange as he was a striker.*

Peter King: *The game went to penalties but beforehand nothing had been said about who was going to take our penalties if it got to that stage. So Jimmy comes onto the pitch with a vacant expression on his face and says, 'Who's going to take a penalty?' I said I'd take one, so did Bobby and Gary. Don also said he'd take one because he was captain but I told Jimmy, 'Don't let Don take one. Make Clarky take one.' I did have reservations about Don taking a penalty. I remembered him taking one at Derby and missing. Jimmy turns to Clarky and says, 'You take one.' But Clarky said he didn't want to, so Jimmy said Don could take one. I felt taking a penalty should be second nature to Clarky so I piped up again. I said to the boss, 'Make Clarky take one, he's a striker.' Clarky then said he didn't feel confident so Don was picked. Usually strikers are up for taking penalties because they want to score goals. Tosh had regularly stepped up but not Clarky.*

Cardiff's wretched luck continued in the penalty shoot-out which took place in front of the Grange End. Gibson opened the scoring with Norbert Johannsen replying for Dynamo. Murray, making his 300th appearance for Cardiff, took the second penalty and, to the delight of the Dynamo players standing in the centre-circle, blasted it high over the crossbar. Frank

Terletzki then put Dynamo in front. King scored for Cardiff before Jochen Carow restored the East German advantage. Bell and Woodruff both converted their kicks but so did Manfred Becker and Labes, meaning Dynamo triumphed 5-4 on penalties. Scoular accepted "total responsibility" for the defeat as he allowed Murray to take one of the five spot-kicks. "Don didn't say a word when he came into the dressing room," said the Bluebirds manager afterwards. "He was pretty cut up about it but he is big enough to take it."

Gary Bell:	*Don's penalty went way over the bar — I think it landed up in the bus depot further down Sloper Road! When Jimmy asked who wanted to take a penalty, we got four players but needed a fifth so Don said he'd take one because he was captain. You'd have expected the strikers to take one but they didn't want to know. Clarky didn't fancy penalties — I never saw him take one. After the game we were in the bar upstairs for a pint and I said to Don, 'Never mind, it was good of you to step forward.' I've never forgotten what he said to me. 'Gary, let me tell you something now. Only great players miss penalties because only great players take them.' He had his lines ready.*
Don Murray:	*There weren't many volunteers to take a penalty. There was a lot at stake and maybe players didn't want to be blamed if we didn't go through. As captain you've got to lead by example so I put myself forward. I felt confident but unfortunately I missed. I decided to blast it but got underneath the ball and it ended up in Grangetown somewhere! The lads were brilliant about it. They were very understanding. Alan Ball had recently missed a penalty for Arsenal and his comment*

was only great players miss penalties because only great players take them. That's what I said to the boys and it got them laughing. Jimmy said it wasn't the best penalty he'd ever seen but he was fine about it although I never took another penalty again.

Dynamo enjoyed so much luck in Cardiff, remarked Peter Jackson in the *South Wales Echo*, the cup "could conceivably end up in East Berlin". Indeed, Geitel's side went on to reach the last four but there, in the semi-finals, good fortune deserted them as they lost on penalties to Dynamo Moscow after both legs ended 1-1. As for Cardiff, they had gone from promotion contenders to also-rans, finishing the season in 19th spot. A mediocre season ended without even the Welsh Cup as Wrexham defeated Scoular's side in the final. For the first time in six years, European football would not be gracing Ninian Park.

Ian Gibson: *I couldn't believe we lost to Dynamo Berlin. We were miles better than them and I wondered how they'd gone through and not us, but we were starting to go downhill. We were selling our best players instead of keeping them and bringing new players in. Had we kept Tosh in 1970 we would have gone up that season. Selling him was the turning point.*

First Round, First Leg
15 September, 1971
Friedrich-Ludwig-Jahn-Sportpark, East Berlin

Dynamo Berlin (0) 1   **Cardiff City (0) 1**
Schütze 90   Gibson 78

DYNAMO BERLIN: Lihsa, Stumpf, Brillat, Filohn, Halle, Rohde, Terletzki, Becker, Schütze, Labes, Johanssen.

CARDIFF CITY: Eadie, Jones, Bell, Sutton, Murray, Phillips, King, Clark, Woodruff, Warboys, Gibson.

First Round, Second Leg
29 September, 1971
Ninian Park, Cardiff

Cardiff City (0) 1   **Dynamo Berlin (0) 1**
Clark 58   Labes 62

CARDIFF CITY: Eadie, Jones, Bell, Sutton, Murray, Harris, King, Clark, Woodruff, Warboys (Foggon), Gibson.

DYNAMO BERLIN: Lihsa, Stumpf (Hubner), Carow, Trümpler, Halle, Rohde, Terletzki, Becker, Schütze (Schulenberg), Labes, Johanssen.

(2-2 on aggregate, Dynamo Berlin won 5-4 on penalties)

16

Return to the Alvalade
Sporting Lisbon, 1973

'I am convinced we will get through.'

Mário Lino

NEARLY a decade after their remarkable victory over Sporting Clube de Portugal, Cardiff were once again paired with the Portuguese giants in the first-round draw of the 1973-74 competition. Following a year-long exile from European football, the Bluebirds were back in the Cup Winners' Cup after defeating Bangor City in the Welsh Cup final. Scoular's 10th season in charge at Ninian Park had started with real promise as six points from the first five league games left Cardiff three points adrift of Division Two leaders Bristol City. Sporting, though, represented formidable opposition. Their squad shimmered with quality with coach Mário Lino able to call on 13 international players - a dozen from Portugal and one, striker Héctor Yazalde, from Argentina. And unlike 1964, when they were eliminated by two gallant Cardiff performances, Sporting were not a team in disarray – the *Verde-e-Brancos* (Green and Whites) would be crowned Portuguese champions at the end of the season – and travelled to the Welsh capital for the first leg looking to avenge their Christmas exit nine years earlier.

Lino's side had played only two domestic fixtures before the trip to Cardiff, losing 1-0 at Vitória Setúbal before beating Boavista 3-1 in the Alvalade. Yazalde, who would finish the campaign as Europe's top goalscorer and claim *L'Equipe* magazine's coveted Golden Boot with 46 goals, delivered his own warning to the Bluebirds, scoring twice in front of Cardiff scout Jack Foxton, sent to Lisbon by Jimmy Scoular who wanted information on Lino's side. Sporting, noted Foxton, "have a lot of good individual players who are very clever on the ball" but Scoular was buoyant about his side's chances due to their fine Division Two form. A 1-0 win at Ninian Park would satisfy the Scot since he felt his defenders were playing well enough to protect that lead in Lisbon.

Scoular also remembered Sporting's disastrous capitulation at the hands of Hibernian in the Cup Winners' Cup the previous year. They had arrived at Easter Road clutching a 2-1 lead but were crushed 6-1 in the second leg, their heaviest defeat in Europe. Hibernian's wingers, Alex Edwards and Arthur Duncan, tore the Portuguese defence apart and Vitor Damas, Sporting's goalkeeper, looked vulnerable whenever the ball was pumped into his penalty area. Ronnie Allen, the Walsall manager who was in charge of Sporting that night in Edinburgh, told Scoular that Damas, Portugal's first choice, was "poor" dealing with crosses.

Lino had watched his opponents twice, his second viewing the 5-0 demolition of Oxford United at Ninian Park, a contest dominated by striker Andy McCulloch, a £42,000 signing from Queens Park Rangers the previous year, who scored a hat-trick. Cardiff had done enough to concern Sporting's 36-year-old coach who identified McCulloch, midfielders Johnny Vincent and Tony Villars, and winger Willie Anderson as the Welsh side's key men. Villars was signed from Welsh League side Panteg in 1971, Vincent was a £35,000 signing from Middlesbrough, and Anderson, a former Manchester United apprentice, came from Aston Villa in a £60,000 deal.

After a complicated journey which saw them arrive in Cardiff via Paris and Bournemouth, Lino's players trained in the grounds of Cardiff Castle and then at Ninian Park. The night before the first leg, Newport County invited the Portuguese visitors to Somerton Park to watch their Division Four clash against Crewe Alexandra but Lino turned down the offer, using the time to hold a tactical talk with his players. "We have come here to try and beat Cardiff City," he explained, "not to watch other teams play football." Cardiff's squad contained two survivors from the 1964 tie, Don Murray and Peter King. Murray, still the Bluebirds' skipper, started against Sporting while King was named as a substitute. Six players were making their European baptism – goalkeeper Bill Irwin, defender Phil Dwyer, a local boy and product of the Ninian Park youth system, midfield trio Villars, Vincent and George Smith, and McCulloch. Anderson had played in the European Cup in 1966, during his time at Old Trafford. It was certainly a new-look Cardiff side. Brian Clark and Ian Gibson had been sold to Bournemouth in a £100,000 deal, Mel Sutton had moved to Wrexham for £15,000, Dave Carver left for Hereford United on a free transfer, Jim Eadie packed his bags for Bristol Rovers, and Alan Warboys was transferred to Sheffield United in exchange for striker Gil Reece and midfielder Dave Powell.

As for Sporting, their starting line-up contained seven internationals; Damas, José Carlos – the only member of the side that faced the Bluebirds nine years earlier - Carlos Alhinho, Nélson Fernandes, Fernando Tomé, Joaquim Dinis and Yazalde. Despite their quality, Sporting were content to defend in numbers while Cardiff's creative players failed to make an impact. Villars was anonymous, Vincent was ineffective, Anderson was marked out of the game by full-back

Carlos Pereira while McCulloch and Bobby Woodruff were closely watched by João Laranjeira and Alhinho. Damas, seen as a potential weakness before the game, was in excellent form, denying McCulloch on three occasions. His finest moment came inside the first quarter-of-an-hour, a twisting save to deflect McCulloch's 10-yard shot over the crossbar after the striker played a sweet one-two with Woodruff. After the game, McCulloch complimented Damas on his performance, describing him as "brilliant...one of the best goalkeepers I've played against" and there was also praise from the Press. "His full name is Vitor Manuel Afonso Damas de Oliveira and at times it seemed that Sporting had all five of them in goal," wrote Clive Phillips in the *Western Mail*.

George Smith: *We weren't the favourites and we did as well as we could. Jimmy Scoular wanted us to get stuck in and that's what we did. This was the priority because that was the type of manager he was. The emphasis was to stop Sporting playing and to win the battle early on. They were defensive in the first leg and we had to break them down but we didn't have the quality needed to win the game. We were a team of good pros and we had some good players, people like Don Murray, Leighton Phillips, Johnny Vincent, Phil Dwyer and Willie Anderson. But we didn't have that match-winner, that someone who could turn the game for us.*

Despite his side's negative approach and the close attentions of Murray, Yazalde had one chance to score a precious away goal, just before half-time when Dinis – a 6ft 4ins winger from Angola - crossed into the penalty box, and it needed a brilliant save by Irwin to deny the former Independiente player. Cardiff had a strong penalty claim 17 minutes from the end when Dinis pushed McCulloch, but the home side's protests were ignored by Maltese referee Anthony Briguglio. An anti-climactic first leg, watched by a disappointing 13,330 crowd, ended 0-0.

Andy Mcculloch: *We were unlucky at home. I had a few chances in the first half but their 'keeper made some really good saves. A few of my friends came down from London to watch that game and they thought we were unfortunate not to win but we were quite happy with the way we played. We did well and stopped Sporting playing. Even though it finished 0-0, we had a bit of a celebration after the game. Sporting had this name in Europe and they had some top players like Yazalde, so we saw 0-0 as a good result.*

It was advantage Sporting although in his post-match briefing Scoular insisted the tie was "far from over". His optimism was based on a defence which had leaked just three goals in seven games, but by the time his players landed in Lisbon nearly a fortnight later, that defensive solidity had evaporated. Six goals had been conceded in their two league games since the first leg, a 3-3 draw at Crystal Palace followed by a 3-1 home defeat against Hull City. Scoular was also without Anderson, sidelined with a groin injury, while Smith was struggling with a bruised chest muscle, an injury which would rule the £40,000 signing from Birmingham City out of the second leg.

Having arranged for Cardiff-based newspapers to be posted to him in Lisbon, the meticulous Lino was well aware of Cardiff's recent problems. His charges, meanwhile, were playing like champions-elect, winning 3-0 at Leixões and then beating Belenenses 4-1 at the Alvalade. Sporting, second in the Primeira Liga behind Vitoria Setubal, were confident they would claim *vingança* (revenge) for their 1964 elimination, with Damas epitomising their confidence. "I don't expect to be nearly as busy as I was in Cardiff," the goalkeeper confidently told journalists before the game. Cardiff stayed 16 miles outside the Portuguese capital, in a hotel owned by businessman and Fulham chairman Ernie Clay. Scoular banned his players from sunbathing and using the hotel swimming pool. However, if they progressed to the second round they would each receive a £200 bonus. Scoular believed the second game would be "completely different" to the first. Sporting had been content to sit back at Ninian Park but now they would have to attack. "Their eagerness to go for goals should be to our advantage," he remarked, emphasising a 1-1 draw would send the Division Two side through. There were two changes to the side held at home. Derek Showers replaced Anderson and King deputised for Smith, with Woodruff dropping back into midfield.

Bobby Woodruff: *I wasn't selected for the game in Lisbon but George Smith couldn't play so the team changed and I was in. It happened quite late as I didn't know I was playing until we were in the dressing room! Harry Parsons, our kit man, came over and told me. The problem was I hadn't brought my boots to the stadium because I didn't think I was going to play. They were back in my hotel room. Scoular didn't know I didn't have my boots – he would have gone mad – so I told Harry and he sorted it out. Harry, or someone else, went back to the hotel to get them. I was actually more worried about getting my boots than I was about playing Sporting Lisbon!*

Yazalde opened the scoring with a superb half-volley following Samuel Fraguito's 40-yard run down the right wing, but five minutes before half-time Villars, a former electrician who had been playing in the Welsh League two years earlier, stunned the 50,000 crowd with a well-taken equaliser, his second goal for the Bluebirds. Gary Bell's cross eluded Alhinho and fell to the midfielder who swept past Pereira and then placed the ball over Damas who had come off his line.

Tony Villars: *I made a run from deep and the ball came to me. I was just inside the box and pretty central. I hit it with my right foot and it went into the corner. It was a lovely feeling seeing the ball go in. We did well out in Lisbon and I had a decent game. Sporting were a hell of a side but we did OK in the first leg and we put up a good show out there. We didn't think we'd win, we just went out and tried to do the best we could. We ended up doing really well. It's fair to say we played better in those two games against Sporting than we did in the league.*

Sporting's lead was restored early in the second half when Fraguito beat Irwin with a powerful shot from 15 yards out. Cardiff, though, refused to surrender and Showers almost netted a second goal for Scoular's men, Damas pushing his angled effort behind the post, a save that kept his side in the competition. Sporting lost Dinis in the 76th minute when the winger was sent off for throwing a punch at Dwyer, but the Welsh side were unable to make the extra man count. Just as they did in December 1964, Cardiff had produced a stirring display inside the Alvalade, but this time, Sporting prevailed.

Andy McCulloch: *What has stuck with me about that game in Lisbon was the walk onto the pitch before kick-off. We had to go through a tunnel, then up stairs. It was totally different to the grounds back home. Then we went onto the pitch and heard this huge roar from the crowd. There were 50,000 Sporting fans at the game. It was like the Christians being thrown to the lions, it was quite frightening. We did well and a few people said we were unlucky not to get a result. After the game, the Sporting players came up and congratulated us on the way we played. They thought it would be a walkover but in the end they were lucky to get the win.*

Derek Showers: *We played well in Lisbon. We were up for that game and we rattled them. They didn't like it and they had a go at us. I remember that. Someone caught me as well. I got punched. They were a very technical side but they didn't like the physical aspect of the game. If you caught them, they would put on a show in front of the referee. Then, when nobody was looking, they would have a go back at you. That way they didn't get into any trouble. When we returned home I read a few reports of that game and they all said we'd done well. I've never forgotten the stadium - a big oval bowl.*

Bill Irwin: *My memory of Lisbon was the kick-off time. It was so late. The game didn't start until 10pm which was common in countries like Portugal. Back home the game would have finished by then because we kicked off at 7.30pm so it felt a bit strange to be starting so late. It meant we we had loads of time to kill on the day and there was a lot of hanging around before we were taken to the stadium. We weren't used to that but we did well on the night. We must have done OK because Jimmy Scoular didn't give us a bollocking afterwards even though we'd lost – and Scoular was a manager who could really give out a bollocking.*

For Villars, the misery continued well after the final whistle. The Cwmbran-born midfielder had suffered a bang on the jaw late in the game and was replaced by Reece two minutes from the end. The coach taking the Bluebirds squad back to their hotel had to stop on the side of the road so Villars, unable to talk because of the severe pain, could vomit. On arriving at the hotel, the 21-year-old was given a sleeping tablet and then helped to bed by his teammates. He was taken to hospital as soon as Cardiff landed in Rhoose and an X-ray showed his jaw was broken, ruling him out of Saturday's 5-0 drubbing at Aston Villa.

Tony Villars: *I got tackled when I was running with the ball, and as I was falling, my jaw caught the knee of a Sporting player who was coming towards me. I came off because I was in such pain. It was near the end of the game. My jaw was swollen and I felt a bit rough. I was given painkillers and they worked for a bit but on the way back to the hotel I started to feel ill. I thought I was going to be sick and I needed some fresh air. I said to one of the boys, 'I need to get off. I'm gonna be sick' so the bus stopped and I went for a little walk. Lew Clayton, our trainer, came with me. While I was walking, the lads on the bus were giving me stick, shouting, 'Get in! Get in!' They wanted to get back to the hotel and I was slowing the journey down. When we did arrive, there was this lovely buffet put out for us but I went straight to bed because I was feeling so ill. All the lads were tucking into this great food and there was me in bed with a swollen jaw. When we got off the plane at Cardiff I was taken to the Royal Infirmary for an X-ray. I went with my wife, Scoular, and the club doctor. We were told the jaw wasn't broken but the next day it was still swollen and I was still in pain. I couldn't eat and I could hardly talk, so my wife rang the club and said I was still in a bad way. This time I was taken to the hospital in Heath, Cardiff, and the X-ray showed the jaw was broken in two places!*

Leighton Phillips: *I remember it was a beautiful day when we played over there and we did well but they were a good side. They were technically better than us. We were staying in a lovely hotel but it was outside Lisbon and it took us a while to get back there after the game. The journey was about an hour. There was a big buffet waiting for us when we got back with hundreds of prawns on display. To me, and all the other lads, it was unbelievable. We'd never seen anything like it before. That's what Jimmy Scoular liked, prawns and Mateus Rosé. He wasn't one for a pint of beer. He loved Mateus Rosé.*

The defeat in Lisbon proved to be the last European game for both Scoular and the club's longest-serving player, King. Cardiff's decline continued after the Cup Winners' Cup exit and in November, with his side floundering in the bottom three after five defeats in seven games, Scoular was sacked by chairman David Goldstone, a property developer who had replaced Fred Dewey at the helm the previous year. Scoular's reign had lasted nine years and five months, the Scot overseeing 509 matches. There were many memorable European nights under Scoular's tenure, but promotion to the top flight – his brief when hired in the summer of 1964 – eluded the 'Iron Man'. He was dismissed following a 1-0 home defeat against West Bromwich Albion.

Gary Bell: *For a long time under Jimmy we were one big, happy family. Everybody got on, there was no bickering or*

265

backstabbing. Nobody talked about other players. They were great days and we were fortunate to be at the club at that time. But then the old side started to break up and we began to drop away. We were no longer a side challenging for promotion. The new players brought in to replace the old guard weren't up to the mark and results went the wrong way. In the end it cost Jimmy his job.

George Smith: *We were all upset when Jimmy got the sack. I certainly was. He was a Jekyll and Hyde character. He was a hard man when it came to football. In a five-a-side he was so competitive he would think nothing of nailing one of his first-team players - and he'd do it on a Friday morning, the day before a game! But away from football Jimmy was a lovely guy. He would do anything for you. You could speak to him about anything, he was very understanding. When I was down about things I went to his house many times for a chat. I remember going there and asking him if he felt I'd justified the fee he had paid for me. If the club had stuck with him, I don't think they would have gone down in 1975.*

King, a survivor of the club's Cup Winners' Cup baptism in Esbjerg, was unable to shake off an Achilles tendon injury and retired the following year after making 465 outings for the Welsh side and scoring more than a century of goals, among them Cardiff's first in Europe.

Peter King: *In 1972, I started having problems with my Achilles tendon. I did my tendon at Torquay during pre-season training. A specialist said I needed an operation, which*

I had, and came back playing but I was still having problems. I wore boots with extra layers on the heels – about an inch thick – to try and stop me stretching the tendons too much and I also had cortisone injections, but it wasn't curing the problem and I was in and out of the side with injury. In my last game, it was at home against Sheffield Wednesday (20 October, 1973), I was shuffling about like a penguin! I thought I was going to cripple myself if I carried on so I gave up football and took a job with the Prison Service as a physical education instructor.

Sporting advanced to the semi-finals where they were beaten 3-2 on aggregate by eventual winners FC Magdeburg of East Germany, but the *Verde-e-Brancos* dominated their championship, clinching their 14th Primeira Liga title and the Portuguese Cup. As for Cardiff, a turbulent season saw them successfully defend the Welsh Cup and avoid relegation on the final day of the season. Scoular's successor, Frank O'Farrell, quit the club in April 1974 after just 158 days in the job, the Irishman accepting the offer to coach Iran. His assistant, 46-year-old Jimmy Andrews, was appointed caretaker-manager for the remaining four league games and the quietly-spoken Scot preserved the Bluebirds' Division Two status. Cardiff beat the drop in the last league fixture with a 1-1 draw against fellow strugglers Crystal Palace at Ninian Park, a result which relegated the London side. Andrews' reward was to be given the job on a permanent basis.

First Round, First Leg
19 September, 1973
Ninian Park, Cardiff

Cardiff City (0) 0   **Sporting Clube de Portugal (0) 0**

CARDIFF CITY: Irwin, Dwyer, Bell, Smith, Murray, Phillips, Villars (King), Woodruff, McCulloch, Vincent, Anderson.

SPORTING CLUBE: Damas, Manaca, Alhinho, José Carlos, Pereira, Nélson, Wagner, Peres, Tomé, Yazalde, Dinis.

First Round, Second Leg
3 October, 1973
Estádio José Alvalade, Lisbon

Sporting Clube de Portugal (1) 2   **Cardiff City (1) 1**

Yazalde 24, Fraguito 51   Villars 40

SPORTING CLUBE: Damas, Manaca, Laranjeira, Alhinho, Pereira, Fraguito, Nélson, Marinho, Tomé (Chico), Yazalde, Dinis.

CARDIFF CITY: Irwin, Dwyer, Bell, King, Murray, Phillips, Villars (Reece), Woodruff, McCulloch, Showers, Vincent.

(Sporting Clube won 2-1 on aggregate)

17

Hard Times
Ferencváros, 1974

'We are too good a side to defend.'

Jenő Dalnoki

FOR the first round of the 1974-75 competition, Cardiff would meet another famous name in European football, Ferencváros of Budapest. Hungary's most successful club with 23 league titles and 12 Hungarian Cup victories, *Fradi* had also appeared in two European finals, winning the Inter-Cities Fairs Cup in 1965 before losing the same trophy to Leeds United three years later. With four Hungarian internationals in the side – goalkeeper István Géczi, centre-back László Bálint, midfielder István Juhász and forward János Máté – as well as two of the most exciting young talents in Hungarian football, strikers Tibor Nyilasi, 19, and 18-year-old Ferenc Szabó, Ferencváros were expected to dispatch a Cardiff side in deep crisis. Before flying to Budapest for the first leg, Cardiff were bottom of Division Two after losing five of their first seven league fixtures and scoring just three goals. The club was haemorrhaging £2,000 a week and to offset most of the previous season's £100,000 loss, Andy McCulloch was sold to Oxford United for £70,000 with chairman David Goldstone admitting the club would have to sell players before new faces could be brought in.

As if the task in Hungary was not hard enough, it was made even tougher by the departure of Leighton Phillips. The talented Wales defender had been seeking a move out of Ninian Park for the last two years and was finally granted his wish, signing for Aston Villa in a £100,000 deal the night before the Bluebirds flew to Hungary. So with the game at the Stadion Üllői úti just 48 hours away, manager Jimmy Andrews – already without Phil Dwyer and George Smith, both suspended, and the injured Gil Reece – had lost one of his most important players. To bolster a depleted squad, Andrews added long-serving defender Richie Morgan and transfer-listed midfielder Dave Powell.

Leighton Phillips: *I knew a month before the deal was done that I was going to Villa. The club was on its arse at the time and Jimmy Andrews told me Villa were interested. He said I could go but he wanted to keep me for a few more weeks for a couple of games. I couldn't wait to get out of Cardiff. I'd been there since I was 15 and travelled the world with them – Australia, New Zealand, East Africa and much of Europe – but since missing out on promotion in 1971 we had struggled. I'd put in a few transfer requests in my last couple of years there but, when he was still at the club, Jimmy Scoular kept telling me to stay, saying he was going to build a good team.*

Andrews' side contained a number of European debutants – goalkeeper Ron Healey, defenders Albert Larmour, Freddie Pethard and Clive Charles, Powell, forward Jimmy McInch and former Wolverhampton Wanderers and Leicester City winger

John Farrington, Cardiff's record £62,000 acquisition. Don Murray, making his 32nd appearance in the Cup Winners' Cup, provided much-needed experience at the back while Tony Villars, Johnny Vincent, Derek Showers and Willie Anderson had all faced Sporting Lisbon the previous year. Despite a dreadful start to the season, Andrews felt his patched-up side had an outside chance of claiming a positive result in Budapest's ninth district. Ferencváros, coached by their former defender Jenő Dalnoki, had not enjoyed a good start to the season, winning only two of their first five games. Dalnoki was also without two key players, Juhász, his midfield leader, and right-back Győző Martos. Furthermore, their technical director, Flórián Albert, a former Hungary forward and European Footballer of the Year, admitted the Hungarians knew nothing about their Welsh opponents. "We are playing a great club, an international-class team, and on our current form nobody would give us a chance," said Andrews. "But Ferencváros have their problems this season and they're not scoring goals."

Tony Villars: *I remember coming out of the airport in Budapest and there were women pushing wheelbarrows of cement about. I was totally gobsmacked. I looked at them and thought 'What the hell's going on here?' None of us had seen anything like it. I think they were doing building work at the airport, I assume it was some sort of an extension, and women were wheeling wet cement to the building area. There were quite a few of them doing it too. Obviously that was the sort of job women were expected to do in Eastern Europe. Our hotel was OK, it wasn't great. Everything in the bedrooms was old, all the furniture. There was nothing modern.*

FROM TASHKENT WITH LOVE

Willie Anderson: *Budapest was a beautiful city but trips behind the Iron Curtain were a grind. They would take forever. The hotels weren't great, the food was terrible, and the people were dowdy. We were pretty worn out when we got there and we didn't eat properly either. There wasn't much choice when it came to the food. With all that in the background, it was hard to then go out and play in a big game. When the Iron Curtain teams came to Cardiff they would stay in a hotel where there was bread and butter ready for them on the table and they wouldn't be able to believe what they were seeing. Butter was a luxury for them back home. The Hungarians didn't have much and someone in our group – I think it was the trainer (Ron Durham) – took over 20 pairs of jeans to sell on the black market, and he sold all of them. We went to look at this big church on a hill and the locals were coming up to us offering to buy our English money. You could have sold them the clothes you were wearing.*

Albert Larmour: *As we were driven through Budapest we could see reminders of the Hungarians' war against the Soviet Union. A number of buildings had bullet holes in their walls. I'm from Belfast so I was used to things like that but it was still interesting to see. It was quite an intimidating atmosphere at the stadium. There were plenty of policemen holding dogs and their fans were making a lot of noise while we had hardly any support out there. It was pretty tense. I remember coming out of our dressing room and hearing all this shouting. The Ferencváros fans were trying to gee up their side and at the same time they wanted to give us, the Westerners, a hard time. It was a frenzied atmosphere*

272

and intimidating. It wasn't a huge stadium and there was a decent crowd at the game. Because of the atmosphere and the fact Ferencváros were a good team, we had a tough time.

Andrews, looking for a valuable away goal, went for a bold 4-3-3 formation with two wingers, Farrington and Vincent, supporting centre-forward Showers. On a warm afternoon – the match kicked-off at 3.15 pm with the temperature well over 21°C – Nyilasi side-footed the Hungarians into a deserved 15th-minute lead. Farrington then sliced wide from just five yards out after goalkeeper Géczi had pushed Anderson's centre against the crossbar. Ferencváros scored a late and controversial second with Szabó, standing virtually on the goal line, turning home Nyilasi's header. "He must have been offside," remarked a bemused Murray afterwards. Ferencváros pressed for a third but the Bluebirds defence, which included the outstanding Murray and Powell, held out. Cardiff had their moments. Aside from Farrington's miss, Géczi made a spectacular save to deny Villars, and McInch and Showers both went close during a promising 20-minute period after the interval.

Freddie Pethard: *I'm not sure why the kick-off was in the afternoon. There was a massive military parade in the city that day with soldiers marching through Budapest and all these weapons being shown off, so maybe that was the reason we played early. Ferencváros were slick and skilful. They were just too good for us. I remember Budapest. It was a stunning city despite the oppression at the time. We went to this place after the game for the reception and it looked down onto the Danube. The view was absolutely fantastic.*

Andrews felt his players were "beginning to put it together" before Ferencváros scored their controversial second goal. Before the game, he told the Press that a 1-0 defeat "would be a moral victory" so Ferencváros's late and controversial second incensed the Cardiff manager who described some of referee Jose Bucek's decisions as "atrocious" but, in truth, the scoreline flattered Andrews' side. As Dalnoki remarked afterwards, "We missed a lot of chances. We could have won by four or five goals."

John Farrington: *It was very warm out there and after the game I had to take salt tablets because I felt so terrible, but we couldn't use the weather as an excuse – Ferencváros were a different class. They were a cracking side, the way they kept the ball and passed it about. We were chasing shadows throughout, we just couldn't get near them. We thought we'd done quite well to lose 2-0 because they were on a different level to us. The trip wasn't that great. We didn't get out much and our hotel wasn't clever. It was a basic three-star place and I couldn't eat the food. I remember the reception after the game – they served us goulash. It was horrible. I didn't eat much out there. I was a Geordie boy who loved his steak and chips. You'd think we'd have stayed in a top hotel. I don't know, maybe it was one of the best in the city at that time.*

Derek Showers: *They murdered us, really. It was a 2-0 hammering. They were a very good side and they had a few Hungary internationals. We just couldn't get anywhere near them. Everything about them was better. They were far superior to us. The one player who really shone was Nyilasi. Personally, what stood out for me in*

Budapest were the guards who were all armed. We'd go into a café and there'd be police inside with guns in their holsters. That was something new to me. I didn't see that sort of thing back home in Merthyr!

Andrews insisted the tie was "not all over by any means", pointing to Ferencváros' uncertain defending on the few occasions his forwards did attack, but such was the Hungarian side's superiority that a Ninian Park comeback appeared unlikely, particularly as Cardiff's league form continued to disintegrate. An encouraging 2-2 draw at Portsmouth was followed by a 4-0 thrashing at Blackpool and a 2-1 home defeat against Hull City. No wonder the confident Dalnoki arrived in South Wales sniffing blood, warning his opposite number he had the forward power to score more goals in the second leg.

Richie Morgan: *We were a side in decline at that time. There was very little spirit in and around the place and it wasn't a happy club. Jimmy Andrews was trying to make changes and there were players coming and going. He was a great coach – the best I worked with – but man-management wasn't his forte. We were at a low ebb and you can see that from the result and the crowd. We had less than 5,000 for the game yet three years earlier we'd seen nearly 50,000 for the Real Madrid game. The side had been thrown together and there was apathy around the place. Losing had become a habit. You'd expect a battling display at home but we just didn't have the spirit anymore.*

The first half was goalless and during the interval Andrews, in an attempt to keep his Bluebirds in the competition, decided to make a bold tactical change. Farrington and John Impey came on, replacing Gil Reece and Villars. Dwyer, playing at right-back, was moved up front to replace Reece with Impey slotting into defence. Andrews felt Ferencváros were vulnerable at crosses and that Dwyer was the man to exploit that weakness. But the plan backfired badly. His reshaped side fell apart with Ferencváros scoring three in a devastating 11-minute spell. László Takács opened the scoring in the 53rd minute after strolling through the Cardiff defence. The 19-year-old clerk, who controlled the midfield in the second half, then turned provider, setting up both Szabó and László Pusztai.

George Smith: *They had a different style. With us it was blood and thunder, get the ball forward quickly, but they had another mentality. They played from the back, they were more patient and they opened us up whenever they wanted to. We tried to play our way and hoped to get that bit of luck to win the game. The manager moved Phil Dwyer up front to be a sort of battering ram but that was the last resort. We just didn't have the quality to trouble a side as good as them. We went for a more direct approach with Phil up front but that changed the shape of our side and they took advantage. They were more gifted. Between the two sides, there was a real gulf in technical ability.*

Dwyer did pull a goal back for the Bluebirds, heading Anderson's cross past Géczi, but it was the impressive Hungarians who had the final say with Máté scoring in the dying seconds to seal a 4-1 win on the night and a comprehensive 6-1 victory on aggregate. "The second-half surrender," wrote Karl Woodward in the *South Wales Echo*, "was so alarming as to raise serious doubts about morale within the club." A crowd of just 4,229 - the lowest Ninian Park crowd for a first-team game, apart from Welsh Cup fixtures, since 1945 – watched *Fradi* condemn the Bluebirds to their heaviest defeat in the Cup Winners' Cup. At the final whistle a disillusioned Cardiff public chanted 'We want a new team!' although given the club's dire finances, there was little chance of a dressing room revolution. Cardiff's chairman was also the target of abuse as cries of 'Goldstone Out!' emanated from the Enclosure, directly below the director's box.

Phil Dwyer: *Jimmy sometimes moved me up front if we were struggling to score, and he wanted someone who could reach crosses and bring the midfield players into the game. I played in a few positions for him. I didn't mind, I was just glad to be involved. He moved me up front for the second half against Ferencváros but it didn't work. They were a really good side while we were struggling. We'd not started the season too well and that showed with the crowds – just over 4,000 came to watch Ferencváros and I very much doubt 4,000 were still inside Ninian Park at the final whistle. Our league results hadn't been good for a while so we weren't getting the big crowds anymore. We couldn't blame the supporters for staying away. We gave 100 per cent and we did our best but things were bad at the time.*

Willie Anderson: *Ferencvaros were on a different level to us. Technically they were great but they were also fit, strong and aggressive. They were way ahead of us while we were a side heading for relegation. Looking back, I should never have gone to Cardiff. I'd lost my place at Villa and Jimmy Scoular came in for me. I thought 'Someone wants me'. I didn't care who it was. I didn't even think about it. I just signed for Jimmy. Then I discovered the training facilities at Cardiff were absolutely terrible. There was no training ground and coming from Villa, which had its own training ground, that was a culture shock. Everything at Cardiff was run down and the club was on its way down. It was a move I shouldn't have made.*

John Farrington: *I thought we had a bit of a chance in the second leg but they were just too good for us and they showed their class at our place. We were 0-0 at half-time and doing quite well but then we pushed forward to try and get goals and they just took over. It didn't matter how hard we worked, we couldn't get the ball off them. I thought they were brilliant. I'd never played against a team like that and it was a big shock for me. We were playing long balls and they were playing one-twos. They played a different type of football altogether. They were definitely the best team I played against in my entire career.*

Somewhat inevitably, Cardiff's season ended in relegation as Andrews' charges won only two of their last 17 league fixtures. This time there would be no final-day escape. They even failed to retain the Welsh Cup, losing to Wrexham in the final. Ferencváros marched all the way to the Cup Winners' Cup final in Basel, defeating Liverpool, Malmö and Red Star Belgrade along the way, but a Dynamo Kiev side inspired by Oleg Blokhin proved too strong and *Fradi* were soundly beaten 3-0. For the transfer-listed Murray, who made his 33rd appearance in the competition, the second-leg defeat was a sad final chapter in his eventful Cup Winners' Cup story which began a decade earlier with Cardiff's first venture into European football, against

Esbjerg. After 529 first-team appearances for the Bluebirds, the defender would return to his native Scotland in December 1974 to sign for Heart of Midlothian, although he eventually returned to South Wales, to join Newport County where he was reunited with his old boss, Jimmy Scoular.

Don Murray: *Ferencváros played well at Ninian Park and we took a hammering. They were a strong side while we were having a difficult time. The good days under Scoular were well and truly over. There were less than 5,000 people for the second leg which was terrible really, especially when you think of the crowds we got for European games in the past. Jimmy Andrews had come in and wanted to change things. He wanted to bring in new faces and I knew my time was up when I was loaned out to Swansea (in October 1974). I felt I left Cardiff sooner than I should've done, but Jimmy was determined to change the playing side. The way I left the club was disappointing. I thought I would be given a free transfer after all the years I'd been at Cardiff but instead they asked Hearts for a £15,000 fee.*

First Round, First Leg
18 September, 1974
Stadion Üllői úti, Budapest

Ferencváros (1) 2　　　　**Cardiff City (0) 0**
Nyilasi 15, Szabó 80

FERENCVÁROS:　Géczi, Viczkó, Balint, Mucha, Megyesi, Takács, Nyilasi, Szabó, Pusztai, Kelemen (Ebedli), Máté.

CARDIFF CITY:　Healey, Larmour (Impey), Murray, Powell, Pethard, Charles, Villars, McInch, Farrington, Showers, Anderson.

First Round, Second Leg
2 October, 1974
Ninian Park, Cardiff

Cardiff City (0) 1　　　　**Ferencváros (0) 4**
Dwyer 81　　　　　　　　　Takács 53, Szabó 60, Pusztai 64
　　　　　　　　　　　　　Máté 89

CARDIFF CITY:　Healey, Dwyer, Murray, Powell, Pethard, Smith, Villars (Impey), Vincent, Reece (Farrington), Showers, Anderson.

FERENCVÁROS:　Géczi, Eipel, Balint, Megyesi, Takács, Mucha, Szabó, Pusztai, Kelemen, Ebedli (Onhausz), Máté.

(Ferencváros won 6-1 on aggregate)

18

A Geneva Convention
Servette, 1976

'It was like the Alamo.'

Freddie Pethard

TWO years after their blackest night in Europe, the Bluebirds were back in the Cup Winners' Cup and paired with Servette, of Switzerland, in the preliminary round. Jimmy Andrews was still at the helm and had guided Cardiff back into Division Two at the first attempt, building a talented and attractive side spearheaded by the prolific forward partnership of Tony Evans, a free transfer from Blackpool, and Australian international Adrian Alston, a £20,000 signing from Luton Town. Born in Preston, Alston had moved to Australia in 1968 to join South Coast United and became an Australian citizen, making his international debut against Greece the following year. He played for his adopted country at the 1974 World Cup in West Germany and the tall striker was the one Australian player who concerned the great Helmut Schoen, whose West Germany side faced the Socceroos in the first-round group stage. "We have nothing to fear from Australia – apart from Adrian Alston," said Schoen in a television interview before the game. Australia were beaten 3-0 in Hamburg, but Alston left his mark, delighting the watching Australian nation by audaciously dribbling around the legendary West German sweeper and captain, Franz Beckenbauer.

Optimism certainly pervaded Ninian Park during that hot, dry summer of 1976. The grim Goldstone era had ended the previous year, the property developer selling his interest to a consortium headed by Stefan Terlezki, the Ukrainian hotel owner and politician who had acted as Cardiff's interpreter for Torpedo Moscow's visit. Andrews' side had won both promotion and the Welsh Cup in considerable style and – with the exception of former Wales defender Mike England, who crossed the Atlantic to play for the New England Teamen – the quiet Scot could call on the same players for the 1976-77 campaign with Willie Anderson, Alan Campbell and John Buchanan expected to provide the ammunition for Alston and Evans.

An ambitious club based in Geneva and champions of Switzerland on 13 occasions, Servette were keen to make an impression on the European stage, evidenced by the recent £80,000 acquisition of Martin Chivers from Tottenham Hotspur. Andrews knew the 31-year-old striker well having worked with 'Big Chiv' when he was on the coaching staff at White Hart Lane. Chivers, scorer of 174 goals in his eight-year spell in north London, quickly began repaying the fee, netting half of Servette's 10 goals as they lifted the Alps Cup, a minor tournament involving French and Swiss clubs. Andrews dispatched youth coach Alan Sealey to watch the final in Geneva which saw Servette face French outfit Nimes. Chivers scored the winner.

John Buchanan: *The good thing about the Cup Winners' Cup was that it broke up the fixture list. It gave us a break from the league. We were lucky because winning the Welsh*

Cup meant we qualified for Europe. Very few clubs in Britain qualified for Europe but we had an opportunity through the Welsh Cup. We also seemed to be under pressure all the time. While I was at Cardiff it felt as though we were always struggling, apart from 1975-76 when we won promotion. Europe was a nice change, it was something different. We were happy with the draw although Servette turned out to be quite useful. They were one of the best teams in Switzerland at that time and they weren't bad at all. To get past them, we had to play well.

Coached by Hungarian Péter Pázmándy, who had been a fixture in Servette's defence for more than a decade, Cardiff's opponents contained a number of Swiss internationals, notably the central-defensive pairing of Gilbert Guyot and Lucio Bizzini, and the creative forward Hans-Jörg Pfister, reputed to have the hardest shot in Swiss football. Sealey was impressed with what he saw, noting how swiftly Servette broke from defence and how well they used both flanks. "I think we're in for a hard early-season test," he told Andrews after returning from his scouting mission. There was a further concern for the Cardiff manager. His players would face Switzerland's second most successful club without having played any competitive football, the only preparation being two pre-season friendlies, against Pwllheli and Bangor. He would also be without defensive lynchpin Phil Dwyer and winger Anderson, both ruled out with ankle injuries.

Phil Dwyer: *I told Jimmy Andrews I'd done in my ankle at home, carrying furniture up the stairs. The truth was I did it playing baseball. I didn't tell Jimmy that because he wouldn't have been too pleased. I used to play baseball*

*for a Grangetown Catholic club in the summer. It
helped keep me fit during pre-season. We had a game
in Newport two days before the Servette match. I hit
the ball and fell over as I was running around the
bases. I must have stepped into a hole or something. At
first I thought I'd just twisted my ankle but I went to
hospital and came out with the ankle in plaster, which
was a bit of a shock. I'd broken a bone and ended up
being out for six weeks. That turned out to be my last
competitive baseball game!*

Servette landed at Heathrow without Chivers who was already
in the country and training with his old Tottenham teammates. The former England player, capped 24 times, made his
own way to South Wales the day before the first leg, missing
Servette's two-hour training session at Ninian Park and a trip
to a city centre cinema where Pázmándy and his squad took
their minds off the first leg by watching *All The President's
Men*. Andrews fielded an adventurous side with three forwards
– Alston, who could drop into midfield, Evans, and the transfer-
listed Derek Showers. With Dwyer out, the job of marking
Servette's expensive purchase was assigned to Richie Morgan
whose last taste of European action was the remarkable play-
off victory over Torpedo Moscow in Augsburg eight years
earlier. That night, Morgan was asked to contain Torpedo's
most gifted player, Eduard Streltsov. Now the long-serving
defender, described by his manager as "a great battler", had
to shackle Servette's star man.

Morgan won the battle, just as he did in Augsburg. Chivers
threatened only once when his chipped shot deflected off
his marker and went over the crossbar. As well as snuffing
out the Chivers threat, Morgan set up Cardiff's late winner,
scored by Evans two minutes from the end. Andrews had

resigned himself to a 0-0 draw when Morgan beat Chivers to Clive Charles' free-kick. He then turned the ball to Evans who smashed it past Karl Engel from six yards out. It secured the Welsh club's first European triumph since the win over Real Madrid in 1971.

Richie Morgan: *It was a bit of a struggle at home. Servette had played a lot in Europe and they must have been a decent side for Chivers to have gone there, so it was a reasonable scalp for us. He was in the twilight of his career – in his 30s at the time - but he was still a good player. I remember he had big, piercing eyes and didn't say much on the pitch. When you tried to wind up the guy you were marking, usually you'd get a bit of banter going but I got nothing back from Chivers.*

Cardiff understandably looked a side lacking fitness and rhythm but the slender victory was deserved. They almost scored in the first minute, Engel turning a Charles shot around the post. The Swiss B international then produced a spectacular save to stop Buchanan's stinging drive. He also prevented a Bizzini own-goal and denied Showers who was deputising for Anderson. "I would have been extremely concerned if we had been forced to go to Switzerland on level terms," remarked a satisfied Andrews afterwards. "Although Servette are not a great team, they have some fine individuals with plenty of European experience."

Freddie Pethard: *Servette weren't in the same league as the Ferencvaros side we played in 1974 but they had Martin Chivers up front. He was coming to the end of his career but he was an England international and still a top-class player. He was a strong, bustling centre-forward – a real handful - but Richie did well against him that night. Chivers was a nice character as well. After the game he came up and spoke to all the lads. He had played for England and Tottenham and achieved a lot in the game, but he was a pretty down-to-earth person. He didn't seem to be a big-time Charlie at all.*

Tony Evans: *It was great to score the winner, especially near the end. Richie gave me the ball and I wasn't that far out. When I was playing I used to say I was dangerous from a yard out! I scored some spectacular goals during my career but most of them were inside the box. That season I scored in every competition – the league, the FA Cup, the League Cup, the Cup Winners' Cup and the Welsh Cup. No Cardiff player had done that before so I'm very proud of that record. Something comical happened to me before the game. I used to do this thing before kick-off where I'd flick up a ball on the halfway line, then keep it off the ground as I moved towards the edge of the box before volleying it into the net. Doing that used to make me feel good. I was going to do it before the Servette game but then all these balls were rolled out onto the pitch. I think the ball boys just put them all out and they came my way. I rolled across them and ended up sliding over. Everyone burst out laughing. I didn't think it was a good idea to do my trick after that.*

Chivers declined to comment on his side's first-leg reverse but he was certainly vocal ahead of the second leg, telling Swiss journalists that Cardiff "have no star players, except perhaps Tony Evans who scored a lot of goals in Division Three last season, but even he isn't a big name in British football". He also upset his former coach by accusing the Division Two side of using strong-arm tactics at Ninian Park and that Cardiff "will be physical again in the return". Andrews responded, claiming Chivers "never relished the robust side of the game". Pázmándy added further spice to the second leg by telling journalists, "We have got the measure of Cardiff. I am confident we will beat them and qualify." The welcome in rain-soaked Geneva was also lukewarm. Andrews and his squad were refused permission to train at the Swiss club's stadium, the Stade des Charmilles, by Servette officials worried an intense training session would damage a surface softened by 24 hours of steady rain. They tried to persuade the visitors to use a nearby training ground and there were even rumours, later rubbished by the Cardiff manager, the Servette groundstaff were ready to turn their hoses on the Cardiff players if they refused to move. Andrews, keen for his players to practise on a pitch that was four yards narrower than Ninian Park's, won the argument. He reminded the Swiss club that Cardiff were entitled to train at the stadium under UEFA rules and that Servette had trained for two hours at Ninian Park before the first leg, although he agreed to a compromise by keeping his players away from the two goalmouths.

Andrews made one change to the side that won a week earlier, replacing Buchanan with Peter Sayer whose pace had unsettled the Servette defenders when he came on as a substitute at Ninian Park. Anderson was now fit but Showers, impressive in the first game, kept his place and justified his selection with a crucial away goal in the 34th minute. Engel was unable to hold Sayer's cross, Showers and Evans both went for the rebound with Showers, feeling he was in a better position, shouting 'Let it go!' Evans obliged and the Wales international – who had shed more than a stone during the summer thanks to running six miles every morning for a fortnight – stroked the ball home.

Derek Showers: *It was great to score an away goal. They put us under a lot of pressure in the second half. At the reception after the game, Servette gave us these lovely Swiss watches. I think we gave them Welsh flags! We stayed in a great hotel right by Lake Geneva and we could see the fountain coming out of the lake (the Jet d'Eau). We always stayed in nice places when we went abroad, we never slummed it. Credit to the club, they never skimped when it came to the hotel.*

Peter Sayer: *I was 21 when we went to Geneva and it was massive to go away. It was unusual to go abroad in those days and there I was, flying to Switzerland for nothing! For someone who usually went on family holidays to Yarmouth, it was a big thing. It was only my third trip abroad. I'd been to France for a youth tournament and I was in the squad that went to Budapest to play Ferencvaros. I always found there was a different smell and atmosphere in other countries. I know it sounds strange but Budapest smelt of cigarettes. Geneva was expensive – coffee, lager and things like that cost far more than they did back home. The atmosphere at the stadium was spine-tingling. It was a European game and the floodlights added to the drama. I liked playing at night. I had a decent game and I made the goal. I cut in from the left and had a shot which the 'keeper saved but the ball fell to Derek who tucked it away. Servette weren't a bad side. They had eight Swiss internationals and they had a right go at us after we scored.*

Unbeaten at home for more than a year and now needing to score three to progress, Servette heaped tremendous pressure on Cardiff in the second half and were awarded a penalty seven minutes after the break, West German referee Heinz Aldinger pointing to the spot after Charles handled Kurt Müller's shot on the goal line. "Now it's going to be tough," Sayer told Healey. "Don't worry," replied the goalkeeper. "I'll save it." Healey, who had saved three out of four penalties the previous season, normally moved to his left when it came to penalties but, during the first leg, he noticed Pfister pulled his shots to his right so decided to dive that way. The former Manchester City apprentice kept his promise, pushing away Pfister's spot-kick.

Ron Healey: *Servette were awarded a penalty and I remember one of our lads (Sayer) having a moan about it to me so I said I would save it. I had to show I was confident! I did end up saving it and it was a great feeling. I looked at Pfister's run-up to see where he was going to put it. It looked as if he was going to my right and that's where he tended to aim for in the first game against us, so I dived that way. He did strike the ball well but I got my hand to it. I didn't have a bad record with penalties. I did save quite a few during my career and that was one of the most vital ones. I always looked at the penalty-taker's run-up to decide which way to go. Servette put us under a lot of pressure in the second half. They were a good team and they moved the ball well. We came up with a typical Cardiff City backs-to-the-wall display.*

Servette continued to pour forward – Freddie Pethard likened the second half to the Alamo - and the Bluebirds defence finally buckled in the 63rd minute, Bizzini's header beating Healey after Marc Schnyder's cross was flicked on by substitute Jean Thouvenel. Four minutes later, Cardiff lost Morgan with a cracked rib, allowing 20-year-old Keith Pontin to make his first-team debut. Andrews tried to tighten up his creaking side by taking off a striker, Showers, and putting on a midfielder, Anderson. But still the Swiss storm raged and Evans, who cleared Alfred Hussner's header off the line just before the break, produced a second rescue act, this time preventing Franco Marchi from putting Servette in front.

Keith Pontin: *Richie had to come off so the manager put me on. I had to mark Martin Chivers because that's who Richie had been marking. I was a young lad and it was my debut but there were no nerves. I never got nervous when I was playing football. Whoever I came up against, I was confident I could get the better of him. That's how I felt playing against Chivers. It was a big leap for me, especially facing someone of his stature, but I did what I had to do and stopped him from scoring. It was a hard game. They needed to score and they did put us under a lot of pressure in the second half.*

Adrian Alston: *Servette were the favourites but we fancied our chances of getting a result and it was wonderful to do that. We were playing decent football at the time, we had good players like Doug Livermore and Willie Anderson, and we were well-coached by Jimmy Andrews. Servette were a good side. You had to do something to qualify for the Cup Winners' Cup, you didn't get into that competition for nothing. They also had Martin Chivers up front. Looking back at the tie, keeping a clean sheet in the first leg at home was very important.*

The home side did score a second, four minutes from the end when Pfister – a player, according to the Cardiff manager, "who could command a place in any side" - netted a fine individual effort, but Servette were unable to stop the Welsh side marching into the next round where they would play the winners of the Soviet Cup final, either Dinamo Tbilisi, of Georgia, or Armenia's Ararat Yerevan. A long and wearisome trip to the Soviet Union was hardly ideal. "From a time-consuming point of view," moaned Terlezki, "it's a terrible draw."

Alan Campbell: *I thought over the two games we deserved to go through. After the game in Switzerland we were sitting down for a meal and got chatting to the waiters and waitresses. We found out they were earning more money than us! No wonder, because Geneva was so expensive. It was shocking. We couldn't afford anything. A few of the lads went to a club for a drink and it was something like £5 for a bottle of beer – and this was in the 1970s.*

Preliminary Round, First Leg
4 August, 1976
Ninian Park, Cardiff

Cardiff City (0) 1   **Servette (0) 0**
Evans 88

CARDIFF CITY: Healey, Charles, Morgan, Larmour, Pethard, Buchanan, Livermore, Campbell (Giles), Evans, Alston, Showers.

SERVETTE: Engel, Schnyder, Guyot, Bizzini, Valentini, Barberis, Hussner, Marchi, Pfister, Chivers, Müller (Thouvenel).

Preliminary Round, Second Leg
11 August, 1976
Stade des Charmilles, Geneva

Servette (0) 2   **Cardiff City (1) 1**
Bizzini 63, Pfister 86   Showers 34

SERVETTE: Engel, Schnyder (Barriquand), Guyot, Bizzini, Valentini, Barberis, Hussner (Thouvenel), Marchi, Pfister, Chivers, Müller.

CARDIFF CITY: Healey, Charles, Morgan (Pontin), Larmour, Pethard, Sayer, Livermore, Campbell, Evans, Alston, Showers (Anderson).

(2-2 on aggregate, Cardiff City won on the away-goal rule)

19

Back in the USSR
Dinamo Tbilisi, 1976

'Peter Sayer is the fastest player we have. They have
five or six as quick as him.'

Jimmy Andrews

DINAMO TBILISI, the pride of Georgia, awaited Jimmy
Andrews' side in the first round following their emphatic 3-0
Soviet Cup final victory over holders Ararat Yerevan. The win
not only broke the Kiev-Ararat monopoly in Soviet football,
it cemented Dinamo's emergence as a genuine football force
in that vast country. The side revolved around David Kipiani,
their creative number 10 and a member of the Soviet side
which won bronze at the Montreal Olympics that same year.
Kipiani was a pivotal figure in Dinamo's cup success, scoring in
every round and heading their first goal in the final, although
forwards Vladimir Gutsaev and Revaz Chelebadze were also in
excellent form.

Andrews was preparing his side for a league fixture at
Oldham Athletic when Dinamo confirmed their place in
the Cup Winners' Cup. He was given a rundown of the
Georgian side by Tottenham Hotspur manager and friend
Bill Nicholson who, after learning of Cardiff's first-round

opponents, telephoned the Bluebirds manager at the squad's Lancashire hotel. Nicholson had travelled to the Georgian capital in 1973 when his Tottenham side tackled Dinamo in the UEFA Cup. But the current line-up was stronger than the side which had crumbled 5-1 at White Hart Lane. Their first Soviet Cup triumph marked the beginning of what the Tbilisi public would call 'the Great Team', a label which stemmed from the mobile and technical football preached by Dinamo's progressive coach, Nodar Akhalkatsi.

The Georgians were facing the Second Division side at an ideal time. Cardiff had lost their previous two league games – against Oldham and Notts County - and conceded six goals in the process. Andrews admitted he had given his players "a roasting" following the 3-2 reverse against County, a performance their manager described as "shocking". A repeat against Dinamo would surely end in a heavier loss and certain elimination from the competition with the second leg still to play. Looking to take a two-goal lead to the Soviet Union, Andrews was unable to select his strongest side. He was without his first-choice goalkeeper, Ron Healey, who had undergone an ankle operation and had not played since the League Cup tie at Bristol Rovers on 17 August, so Bill Irwin kept his place. Another absentee from the starting line-up was the in-form Derek Showers, called up by Wales for the October friendly against world champions West Germany after hitting five goals in six appearances. The Merthyr-born striker had picked up a groin injury on the weekend and so started on the bench but Adrian Alston, who had missed the previous two games with a toe injury, was back to resume his partnership with Tony Evans.

In the opening 45 minutes, Dinamo lived up to their reputation, their quick and intelligent football impressing the thoughtful Andrews, a disciple of West Ham's 'Academy of

Football' during the 1950s and an advocate of the passing game. Yet it was the home side which created the best opportunity of the first half, after 34 minutes. Willie Anderson seized on Shota Khinchagashvili's dreadful back-pass and squared to Alston, who was completely unmarked near the penalty spot, only for the striker to miskick. It was Cardiff's turn to enjoy a fortunate escape just before half-time when Chelebadze's header hit the crossbar.

Dinamo, with Manur Machaidze outstanding in midfield, Kipiani skilfully cutting through the Cardiff defence and Chelebadze and Gutsaev both causing problems with their movement and flicks, continued to probe for an away goal in the second half and it required a brilliant goal-line clearance in the 69th minute by Freddie Pethard to preserve parity. Gutsaev rounded Irwin after being put through by Chelebadze's pass and Dinamo's clever striker stroked the ball towards the empty net but full-back Pethard, realising he had no chance of tackling Gutsaev, sprinted towards his goal and somehow reached the striker's shot, the ball spinning off his outstretched right boot and over the crossbar. "I stuck out my right leg and hoped for the best," was how Pethard recalled his clearance, which the *South Wales Echo*'s Karl Woodward called "miraculous".

The introduction of Showers on the hour - the forward replaced midfielder Alan Campbell – turned the game in Cardiff's favour, his aggression and aerial ability unsettling the Dinamo defence which was unlocked 17 minutes from the end by Alston's superb winner, the Australian atoning for his earlier miss. Doug Livermore, the Bluebirds' captain, sent his free-kick into a crowded goalmouth. The ball eventually fell to John Buchanan who picked out Alston with a quick return pass. Alston then showed why he had been courted by so many West German clubs - including Hamburg, Hertha Berlin and

Eintracht Frankfurt - after the World Cup, chesting the ball down before firing it past David Gogia from 12 yards out. It was his 23rd goal for the Welsh club and the first scored with his left foot. More significantly, Alston's goal also secured a 1-0 advantage for the Bluebirds.

Adrian Alston: *Tbilisi were a fantastic side so it was a fabulous feeling to beat them. I scored with a volley. I could hit the ball with both feet and I always fancied my chances when it came to shooting. The ball fell nicely to me and I hit it well but I stretched so far to reach it that I got cramp in my calf and could hardly move, which meant the last quarter of an hour or so wasn't comfortable for me. My match fitness wasn't up to standard. I noticed I was getting cramp during the World Cup and it was because I'd come back too soon after being injured. I scored a few nice goals during my career and the Tbilisi one is high on the list. I was proud to score that goal – I'm proud of all the goals I scored for Cardiff City. The most enjoyable time of my career was at Cardiff. I had a wonderful two years there.*

John Buchanan: *We did well in the home game. They were an excellent side and their players were really fit so it was great to beat them. We didn't know much about them because they came from another world. We just went out and tried to do our best. No matter who we were playing, we always had a chance at home with our supporters behind us. I almost scored in that game. I was quite useful shooting from long-range and I hit one from 25-30 yards with my right foot. Their 'keeper saved it, he flicked it over the bar. There was a photo of that save on the front cover of our next programme.*

Alston's volley settled the first leg which saw Cardiff's strength and determination triumph over Dinamo's elegance and artistry. Andrews was "delighted" with the result, particularly as Dinamo were blessed with Kipiani, a player he described as "world class". But Andrews acknowledged his players would have to score in Tbilisi if they were to have any chance of progressing. As for Terlezki, his joy was tempered by the knowledge the club would lose money on the trip to Georgia, which cost around £8,000. A gate of 15,000 was needed to cover the costs but just over 11,000 turned up to watch the first leg. Dinamo had paid the price for failing to make their first-half superiority count. Kipiani conceded the Soviet Cup winners had not been at their best, blaming the way they faded towards the end on a gruelling two-day journey to Cardiff, via Moscow and Paris. His coach believed European inexperience was also a factor. "Some of my team," remarked Akhalkatsi, "were playing abroad for the first time."

Albert Larmour: *I don't think some of the Tbilisi players had travelled that much and we had a right crack at them. From my, experience, if you're expected to beat somebody and you're not in the right frame of mind then it's going to be difficult and it's ridiculously hard to be in that position and then try and turn a game. I think that's what happened with Tbilisi. Also, they had quite a long and tiring trip. They landed in London and then had to travel to Cardiff. That's a whole day travelling and it would have been laborious so they were fatigued, both mentally and physically. We were up for the game, there was a fantastic atmosphere inside Ninian Park, and we had a real go. Adrian scored a good goal and he was capable of doing that. He was a clever and confident guy, and he'd have a go from anywhere if he thought there was a chance of scoring. In the end, maybe the Tbilisi players felt OK about losing 1-0.*

Derek Showers: *The Tbilisi players weren't too happy with me after the game because I'd knocked a few of them about. I'm not sure what they were calling me in their language, I think it was 'the bull'. We needed to shake them up and that's what I tried to do after Jimmy put me on. I was quite an aggressive player and I used to charge about, that was my game. I went on and got stuck into them. You could do that sort of thing back then. Mind you, they got me back in the second leg. They didn't hold back over there. They remembered me from the first game and they knocked me about. They kicked me from pillar to post.*

The 2,324-mile trip to Tbilisi, with a stopover in Moscow, echoed the club's remarkable journey to Tashkent in 1968. Andrews and his squad flew to the Soviet Union from London after the 0-0 draw with Millwall at Ninian Park, taking with them a chef, an interpreter and their own food which included steaks, lamb chops, eggs and cereal. "Why do you bring your own food? We will not poison you," a bemused airport customs officer told kit man Harry Parsons, as he inspected the squad's portable larder following their arrival in Moscow. Andrews had taken 16 players behind the Iron Curtain but there was no Richie Morgan, the centre-half suffering a hamstring injury against Millwall.

Bill Irwin: *Everywhere we went, we were followed by the KGB. We'd cross a road and these guys would be behind us. Then we'd cross back over and they'd cross back as well! We were given a bus tour of Moscow and our guide, a woman who could speak English, was telling us everything the Party had done, all the good things. Then we saw this little old lady digging a ditch on the side of the road. One of the lads – I can't remember who – shouted out, 'What's the Party done for her?' The guide didn't answer. She didn't say anything, she just ignored the question.*

Adrian Alston: *I'd been to Vietnam, I think it was in 1969, to play in Saigon when the war was going on. It was a peace trip, to entertain troops. I'd rather have been back in Saigon than have been in Moscow and in that hotel we stayed in. That's how bad it was. I remember going into my room and the mattress was rolled up on the bed. I had to roll it out flat – and this was supposed to be one of the best hotels in the city. I've been to 43 different countries and Moscow was the worst place I've visited. The place was dead, it felt very strange. A big city like that and the streets were empty, and the people we did see were petrified. They walked about scared stiff. In Saigon there was a war going on and people were struggling but at least there was cooking on the streets and people would come up to you and try and sell you stuff. There was life in Saigon. Moscow, when we were there, was a dead hole. I was glad to leave the place.*

Alan Campbell: *When we landed in Moscow we were greeted by soldiers carrying machine guns. The Russians were also slicing our luggage open and when we were having our passports checked, we just hoped everything was OK. I remember sightseeing in Red Square. There was this line you weren't supposed to cross. When you*

299

> *did, you'd hear a whistle which came from an armed*
> *soldier. Our hotel in Moscow was terrible and the food*
> *was horrible.*

Following an overnight stay in the freezing capital, where they were detained at the airport for two hours so passports and visas could be checked "and double-checked", they made the three-hour flight to Tbilisi, the in-flight meal consisting of two boiled sweets. The players hardly ate at their Moscow hotel, the Ukraina, a striking 34-storey, neoclassical Stalinist construction overlooking the Moskva River, with 2,000 rooms and which had just relinquished its status as the world's tallest hotel to a new building in the United States, the Westin Peachtree Plaza Hotel in Atlanta. With no time to prepare their own food, the guests from Wales had to rely on the Ukraina's kitchen, but a meal of cold meat, cold chips and cake with a caramel topping hardly proved appetising and some players ate just the dessert and bread brought over from Cardiff.

Albert Larmour: *The Moscow hotel was a fabulous building but the food was basic. The starter was some sort of coleslaw. The main course was meat, chips and the coleslaw again and then we had a piece of cake. To drink, we were given a bottle of orange juice. One of the lads - I do believe it was Phil Dwyer – called the waitress over and asked for another bottle. She waved her finger at him and said, 'No. One.' We were only allowed one bottle each. Anyway, Phil got up, walked over to where the bottles were kept and took another one. The waitress ran after Phil and actually snatched the bottle off him! We were given a packed lunch to take with us to Tbilisi. It consisted of a hard-boiled egg, an apple, a piece of meat and a slice of the cake we'd eaten the night before. The meat – and for all we knew it was horsemeat - was bloody and the apple was sour so they didn't go down very well and the only thing they gave us on the plane, which was like a caravan inside, was a couple of sweets.*

Freddie Pethard: When we arrived in Moscow it was snowing. The reception we received was just as cold - the Muscovites weren't sociable and the hotel staff weren't friendly. It was totally different in Tbilisi. The weather was warmer and so was the welcome. When we got off the plane we were greeted by girls who gave each of us a rose. The Tbilisi people were different to the Muscovites. A few of us were walking around the city and an old man approached, asking to clean our shoes so we let him and he did a fantastic job. Anyway, we gave him a few roubles, it wasn't much, and he broke down in tears right in front of us. Apparently we had given him seven times more than he earned a week. It was a humbling experience. There was also a big difference in the two flights. We flew to Moscow with Japan Airlines. The hostesses were stunning, the service was fantastic, really professional, and we were given caviar as part of our meal. We then flew to Georgia with the Soviet airline, Aeroflot. What a contrast. The inside of the plane was like an old bus and the hostesses were big, fierce-looking Russian women. I remember them giving us sweets. That was the meal.

Willie Anderson: We flew to Moscow with a Japanese airline and were served sake. We'd never drunk it before and I think a few of us were a bit tipsy by the time we got to Moscow.

301

We had to go through about five checkpoints before we got out of the airport. The Russians were checking this and searching that. We had a female minder with us on that trip. She came with us everywhere. We would see old ladies – and they must have been in their 80s – sweeping streets and I'd ask her, 'Why is that allowed?' She replied, 'They are doing it for the country.' She was totally indoctrinated. We flew to Georgia with Aeroflot and the flight was terrible. The plane was falling apart and the stewardesses looked as if they'd just come out of the army. If anyone stepped out of line they would have had no problem throwing them off the plane.

Tony Evans: *The flight to Moscow was the best I'd ever been on. It was with Japan Airlines and the food was to die for. We were served giant king prawns, and they gave us slippers to wear, and a hot towel to wipe our faces. It was so impressive. Then we got to Moscow and every 100 yards we saw a huge billboard showing Stalin. Each floor in our hotel was in the shape of a cross with four corridors and at the central point was a desk where a man and woman were always sitting. If we wanted to go to our rooms we had to report to them and get the key, then they would get up and follow us to our rooms. I roomed with Doug Livermore and one morning we were both having a lie-in. A tour of the city had been arranged but I was someone who preferred to have a rest. Anyway, the guy on the desk came into our room, slapped my foot, which was sticking out of the bed, and told us to wake up. Then he left! It was unbelievable, he just came into our room and told us to get up. Then we flew to Tbilisi with Aeroflot. The trays you were supposed to eat on were wooden shelves and we were given a warm, sweet drink which was like Ribena in colour. It came in semi-porous cups so you had to get it down quick before the cup disintegrated. I remember one of the stewardesses pulling the curtains on the plane and there was a big hole in one of them.*

Situated in the southern corner of the Soviet Union, and bordering Turkey, Armenia and Azerbaijan, Georgia's September climate was far more comfortable than that of Moscow. The temperature in Tbilisi – which means "warm location" - was 20 degrees higher. Like many Soviet cities, Tbilisi had developed an impressive professional sports infrastructure, housing around 250 separate facilities. The jewel in the crown was its latest construction, and the venue of the second leg, the Dinamo Stadium. Capable of holding more than 100,000 people, Gia Kurdiani's creation – which took 10 years to build - was the fifth largest stadium in the Soviet Union. The Cardiff players would share centre stage in its grand opening.

Bill Irwin: *I remember going downstairs for breakfast in our hotel. We saw boiled eggs in eggcups ready for us on the table but they were cold and when we sliced them open we found they weren't cooked so we had to send them back. Nobody would take roubles, they all wanted foreign currency like dollars, sterling or francs. I went into a barber shop in Tbilisi because I'd always fancied a shave with a straight razor, like the one Sweeney Todd used. I had a shave and then paid the barber in roubles. I handed him the lot because I couldn't spend them. I've no idea how much I gave the guy but he was very, very happy! From his reaction, I must have given him a week's wages. When we went out for a walk, people would come up to us wanting to buy our clothes. It was a great experience going to the Soviet Union at that time, but in the end I couldn't wait to leave.*

Alan Campbell: *The night before the return leg we were taken to a nightclub to watch a show. It was an unusual thing to do just before a game but Jimmy Andrews was happy to go. We went down the stairs and into a room which was packed with people and as we walked in, everyone started clapping which none of us expected. We weren't allowed to drink although the manager had a few. Tbilisi was completely different to Moscow. The sun was out, our hotel was unbelievable, and the food was great. We knew it would be different as soon as we arrived at the airport. As we approached the entrance, girls came up to us and put garlands around our necks.*

Derek Showers: *Moscow was dark and not very inviting. It looked like all the houses there had gas lights. The trip to Red Square was an experience. We had to stay between two red lines and armed guards were watching, to make sure you didn't cross the line. Nobody strayed. Tbilisi was totally different – what a change! It was a nice city and the locals were friendly. There were people keeping an eye on us. The club doctor, Doc Hamilton, was being followed by strange men in black coats. The doc was Jewish and, at the time, Jews were being persecuted in the Soviet Union. The authorities obviously identified he was Jewish so they kept an eye on him. When we were out there, somebody told us he was going to see Jewish people in Tbilisi. The doc would ask us if we wanted to go into Tbilisi with him but, because he was being followed by men in black coats, we always said, 'No thanks, you go on your own!'*

Peter Sayer: *When we were walking around Tbilisi, people would come up to us wanting to buy what we were wearing. They were after our jeans. They were desperate to buy them. Had I taken a sackful with me, I would've made a lot of money. They wanted to look like us. They couldn't buy jeans in their country so they tried to buy the ones we were wearing but I don't think any of the lads sold theirs. Compared to what the locals were wearing, we did stand out. We looked unusual. It was obvious we were from the West. I preferred Tbilisi to Moscow. Tbilisi was warmer and friendlier. Moscow was very communist and we stayed in this grand hotel with big, studded doors. It was almost frightening.*

Tony Evans: *My mum collected national dolls so I went looking for one from Tbilisi. I went into the centre of the city and found a department store. There was hardly anything on the shelves. I went upstairs – I think it was the third floor - and saw this big, metal gate. It was like the back of a lorry. There were loads of people about and they were all queuing to buy second-hand clothes. It was a communist country where everyone was supposed to be equal but we saw a lot of poverty, beggars in the street and things like that. I did a find a doll for my mum in the end, in a small shop.*

Andrews and his Bluebirds were warned to expect a hot reception inside Tbilisi's new concrete coliseum. Alexei 'Tiger' Khomich, the goalkeeper in the Moscow Dynamo side which crushed Cardiff 10-1 at Ninian Park in 1946 and who was now working as a photographer for the *Soviet Sports* newspaper, said the Welsh Cup holders "will not survive in our arena". Akhalkatsi promised an attacking performance. "We shall be going for goals from the kick-off." Interest in the second leg was extraordinary. Dinamo had received 300,000 ticket applications – almost half of the city's population – while around a thousand curious locals watched Cardiff's two-hour workout the night before the game.

Albert Larmour: *The Georgians really looked after us. The night before the game we had quite an extensive meal in the hotel. We had steaks, which we had brought over with us, but they gave us other things to eat, like big pots of caviar. Tbilisi is near the Caspian Sea so it was the best black caviar you could get. There were all different things for us to eat. It was top-notch food and we tucked in. We ate well – too well probably. They gave us too much and you do wonder if they were trying to bloat us up before the game. Maybe they were being generous so as to give their football side an advantage the next night. They didn't need it. Tbilisi were a lot better than us in most aspects. They were stronger, fitter and more skilful. They would definitely have held their own in what was then our First Division. We tried not to give them time on the ball and we worked hard to try and reduce their skill level but they were just better than us. Kipiani, their number 10, was a fabulous player. He was tall and lean, very skilful, and hard to knock off the ball.*

Freddie Pethard: *The second leg was the first-ever game at Tbilisi's new stadium and everyone was telling us there would be a crowd of about 100,000 to watch it. We all thought*

'No way!' I've never forgotten what we saw on the evening of the game, it's my most vivid memory of that trip. There were people hanging off the edges of buses because they were so packed. It really was an amazing spectacle. We were on our coach and we all looked at one another and said, 'Surely they're not all going to the game?' But they were! Inside the stadium there were also hundreds, if not thousands, of soldiers around the perimeter.

Andrews made two changes to the side that started the first leg, dropping Campbell and Anderson, and drafting in Showers, who was rewarded for his impressive first-leg cameo, and Brian Attley. Anderson had missed the Millwall game with a groin injury and the Cardiff manager claimed he was "not convinced" of his fitness despite being declared fit to play and naming the winger in his original team to tackle Dinamo. But in between midday and 6pm, when he finally decided on the line-up that would face the Georgians, Andrews had changed his mind and opted for a more defensive approach with Attley in midfield. His U-turn incensed Anderson. "I've been messed about by Cardiff City for too long...I've had enough," snapped the former Manchester United trainee after the game. Apart from dropping Anderson and Campbell, the Scot made another bold move by asking full-back Pethard to play as a sweeper.

Willie Anderson: *I had a big fight with Jimmy Andrews because he left me out of the side in Tbilisi. He told me an hour before kick-off that I was on the bench and I went off on one in the dressing room. I had a real go at him saying, "Why bring me all the way over here and not pick me?" That was bad. I shouldn't have done that but as a player, you've got an ego. You think you're the best,*

307

that you're better than anyone else. I was young at the time. I was 29 and I thought I knew it all but I didn't. Jimmy was a good guy and he made all his decisions for the right reasons. He obviously wanted to play a more defensive side and he picked Brian to try and lock up the midfield. I wasn't a happy camper because I was dying to play. It was a big European game in a huge stadium packed with 100,000 people. I really thought I was going to play and I was shocked when Jimmy told me I was a substitute when we got to the stadium. He could have told me in the morning, either in the hotel or after our practice session. That would have given me time to get over it and cool down but Jimmy wasn't a brave manager. He didn't like confrontation which is probably why he didn't tell me until an hour before kick-off.

Andrews dubbed the clash "a game for fighters that will require 100 per cent effort from every member of my team". The visitors found themselves under siege from the start and the impressive Irwin kept the home side out by denying Gutsaev and Vakhtang Kopaleyshvili. Dinamo levelled the tie in the 22nd minute when Gutsaev, who ran the Cardiff defence ragged until injury forced his departure at half-time, beat Irwin at the near post after meeting Machaidze's beautifully-timed pass. Irwin, who made a stunning reflex save to foil Kipiani, then raced off his line in the second half to stop Zorbegi Ebralidze scoring a second. The busy Ulsterman also prevented a Charles own-goal, pushing the defender's back-header over the target as he tried to clear from Chelebadze. Before that Pethard, in a sweeper role, produced another goal-saving clearance to block Kipiani's drive.

Cardiff rarely ventured forward. Their first serious raid

came just past the hour when Buchanan's 18-yard drive flashed wide. To procure a crucial away goal, Andrews made a double substitution, replacing Alston and Showers with Sayer and Anderson, but within eight minutes of the switch, Dinamo built up an unassailable 3-0 lead. Their crucial second goal came 18 minutes from time and in controversial circumstances. Zsurab Tsereteli, who replaced Gutsaev, crossed for Kipiani who headed the ball past Irwin. The Cardiff defence, however, stopped, believing referee Werner Spiegl had blown his whistle and the linesman raised his flag, after Dwyer handled the ball before Tsereteli's cross. To their dismay, the Austrian allowed the goal to stand after consulting his linesman. "Even Kipiani, who speaks English well, said he stopped because he thought Tbilisi had been given a free-kick," moaned Dwyer afterwards.

Phil Dwyer: *The second goal shouldn't have been allowed. The whistle definitely went. Everybody heard it. You play to the whistle so we stopped. They carried on, the guy puts the ball into the net, and the referee lets the goal stand. It was 1-0 at the time and if we'd got an equaliser then we would have gone through but that second goal turned the tie. They were a good side and on the night they fully deserved the win but that decision didn't help us. It left a sour taste and it's not nice, feeling you've been cheated. We were all angry afterwards. But they had some excellent players and were a strong side. We did well to beat them at home.*

Dinamo ensured their progress eight minutes later when Piruz Kanteladze scored from the spot after Pethard was ruled to have fouled Tsereteli. "I played the ball, he (Tsereteli) took a dive and the referee fell for it," said Pethard. Spiegl further incensed the visitors in the 82nd minute when he waved away Cardiff's own claim for a penalty after Anderson was pulled back by Khizavishvili. The second leg ended in a 3-0 triumph for Dinamo who progressed 3-1 on aggregate. Akhalkatsi's men had made up for their disappointing display in South Wales.

Freddie Pethard: *Until late in the second half, we were still in the game. The tie was level on aggregate. Then they got two controversial goals although Dinamo did seem to move up a gear. I was disappointed with the penalty decision because I didn't catch the guy. Jimmy played me as a sweeper that night and I was pleased with my performance. He put me in that position a few times because I was quick and I'd played there for Celtic reserves. Even though we lost 3-0, the game in Tbilisi is one of my favourite memories. The stadium and atmosphere really inspired me. The only thing that spoiled it was the penalty decision because it wasn't a foul.*

Adrian Alston: *There was a massive crowd at the game, we were told it was about 100,000, yet it was deathly quiet until the game started. All these people inside the stadium and they were as quiet as anything. It was eerie. Then when the match kicked off they went into a frenzy. It was strange, it was really amazing. Tbilisi smashed us over there. They took control early on. They were a fantastic side, awesome. They had a few internationals and they were very impressive on the night. We did well to beat them at Ninian Park.*

Tony Evans: *After the first game, we felt we had a chance in Tbilisi. Dinamo were OK at Ninian Park, nothing special, and we deserved the win. But at their place, they absolutely flew about. We couldn't get near them. We couldn't get the ball. It was as if we were playing a totally different side. We were up for the game. We lost purely and simply because of the improvement in fitness of the Dinamo players. Mo Farah would have had trouble keeping up with them that night. They were running non-stop and flying about right, left and centre. That's why they wiped the floor with us.*

In Tbilisi, class had prevailed over strength. Cardiff were comfortably swept aside in the 'City of Warmth' and in front of around 100,000 ecstatic Georgians. "They (Dinamo) outplayed Cardiff City in every department," wrote Clive Phillips in the *Western Mail*. "There was never any doubt about the result." Andrews blamed Spiegl for his side's exit. Dinamo's two second-half goals, he claimed, should not have been allowed. "They are a fine side but we had no chance. You can't play against that sort of control. We were never given a chance to play because the referee kept pulling us up for trivial fouls yet he let Dinamo get away with their infringements." Akhalkatsi was scathing of Cardiff's performance, scoffing at their "heavy style" and describing them as "yesterday's men".

John Buchanan: *We had a right tonking out there. They were a better side than us and a lot fitter. At that time they were one of the top teams in the Soviet Union. We didn't create much that night. We'd travelled quite a distance – we'd been on the move more or less for two days and it had been freezing in Moscow. That didn't help and we found it quite hard going in Tbilisi. We could get a kip here and there but it's not the same. I remember the crowd at the game, it was unbelievable. We heard there were 100,000 people inside the stadium. They were all blokes, no women, with soldiers around the perimeter. Afterwards we were taken to a place up in the mountains for the post-match reception. There was all this drink and food, it was incredible. It was after a game and it was a Wednesday night so we could have a few beers but the Tbilisi players weren't allowed to drink. We were at Chelsea on the weekend and, considering all we'd been through that week, we didn't do too badly. We only lost 2-1.*

Albert Larmour: *Kipiani, who I'd marked, came up to me after the game and wanted to swap shirts. He said I'd played well and wanted my shirt as a souvenir. We only had two shirts for the whole season, one with long sleeves and one with short sleeves, and Harry Parsons, our kit man, would have had my guts for garters if I gave my shirt away, so I told Kipiani I couldn't swap. He had a confused look on his face and shrugged his shoulders. A few of their players could speak English and we had a chat at the reception after the game. They were telling us about their diet and that's when we heard about carbohydrate-loading. Back home footballers ate steak. Ours was a protein diet and you were frowned upon if you didn't eat steak. But the Tbilisi players ate carbohydrates – pasta, things like that. They were taught that a carbohydrate diet ensured peak performance on match day, that it helped your fitness. We were quite surprised when they told us. We'd never heard about this in the UK and it showed how far ahead of us Tbilisi were. What their players told us stuck with me and not long after that trip I became a vegetarian.*

Surprisingly, Dinamo's interest in the Cup Winners' Cup ended in the next round where they were crushed by MTK Budapest, losing 4-1 in Hungary and 1-0 in Tbilisi. The glory days, however, were not far away. Akhalkatsi guided the talented Georgians to the league title two years later before lifting the Cup Winners' Cup in 1981, his side overcoming Carl Zeiss Jena in the final in Dusseldorf. Cardiff spent the remainder of the 1976-77 campaign fighting to stay in the second tier and Andrews' Bluebirds only clinched safety on the final day of the season, grabbing the point they needed against Carlisle United inside a tense and nervous Ninian Park. They enjoyed success in the FA Cup, reaching the fifth round after dramatic home victories over Tottenham and Wrexham but Everton ended the cup dream on the Bluebirds' own turf. Andrews' players secured European football for 1977-78 despite losing to Shrewsbury Town in the Welsh Cup final. Since Shrewsbury were an English club, they could not represent Wales so Cardiff, as runners-up, would play their twentieth Cup Winners' Cup tie.

Adrian Alston: *The game in Tbilisi was a prime example of the difference between playing home and away. We'd won in Cardiff in front of 11,000 Cardiff fans but got smashed in Tbilisi in front of 100,000 of their fans. I remember playing for Australia in a World Cup qualifier against Iran (in 1973). We won 3-0 in Sydney in front of 30,000 Australians, then in Tehran, in front of 119,000 Iranians, we were 2-0 down inside the first 32 minutes. That referee was shitting himself. In Tbilisi there were 100,000 people*

*and the referee for that game was shitting himself too.
It was a difficult situation for us.*

---

*First Round, First Leg
15 September, 1976
Ninian Park, Cardiff*

Cardiff City (0) 1   **Dinamo Tbilisi (0) 0**
Alston 74

CARDIFF CITY: Irwin, Charles, Morgan, Larmour, Pethard, Livermore,
Alston (Sayer), Buchanan, Campbell (Showers), Evans,
Anderson.

DINAMO TBILISI: Gogiya, Khizanishvili, Kanteladze, Khinchagashvili,
Ebralidze, Chivadze, Machaidze, Chelebadze, Gutsaev,
Kipiani, Kopaleyshvili.

*First Round, Second Leg
29 September, 1976
Dinamo Stadium, Tbilisi*

Dinamo Tbilisi (1) 3   **Cardiff City (0) 0**
Gutsaev 22, Kipiani 73
Kanteladze 81 (pen)

DINAMO TBILISI: Gogiya, Khizanishvili, Kanteladze, Khinchagashvili,
Ebralidze, Chivadze, Machaidze, Chelebadze, Gutsaev
(Tsereteli), Kipiani, Kopaleyshvili.

CARDIFF CITY: Irwin, Dwyer, Charles, Larmour, Pethard, Attley,
Livermore, Alston (Sayer), Buchanan, Campbell, Evans,
Showers (Anderson).

(Dinamo Tbilisi won 3-1 on aggregate)

20

Oh, Vienna
Austria Memphis, 1977

'Cardiff are a very tough side and our superior
technique alone will not be enough.'

Hermann Stessl

THE 1977-78 Cup Winners' Cup cast was not short on glamour.
Manchester United were representing England, AC Milan were
flying the Italian flag, and Porto were the entrants for Portugal.
West Germany boasted two clubs in the competition, holders
Hamburg and Cologne. Then there was Anderlecht of Belgium,
winners in 1976 and runners-up a year later. Cardiff, though,
avoided one of the heavyweights. The draw in the luxurious
Atlantis Hotel, situated at the foot of the Alps and overlooking
Zurich, placed the Welsh club with FK Austria Memphis.
Cardiff's representatives at the UEFA draw, chairman Stefan
Terlezki and chief executive Dewi Evans, were more than
satisfied. As they flew to Switzerland, their worry was being
forced to undertake another arduous and costly expedition to
the Soviet Union so both were hugely relieved when Malta's
Valetta were drawn with Moscow Dynamo.

The Viennese club contained six Austrian internationals and
one Uruguayan, Julio Morales, although their star player, the

brilliant 22-year-old midfielder, Herbert Prohaska, was ruled out of both legs through suspension following his red card in a European Cup clash against Borussia Mönchengladbach the previous year. There was another reason for Jimmy Andrews to be optimistic going into the first game at Ninian Park. The Austrians were also without their first-choice goalkeeper, Hubert Baumgartner, who was recovering from a cartilage operation, which meant 19-year-old Hannes Weninger would face the Bluebirds. Andrews sensed the teenager would be a weak link, believing reserve goalkeepers on the continent "often aren't up to the mark".

Andrews' starting XI contained five players who had recently come through the Ninian Park ranks – defender Keith Pontin, midfielders Brian Attley, David Giles and Gerry Byrne, and forward Peter Sayer, a group, said the Cardiff manager, that would form the nucleus of "the new Cardiff City". He was unable to call on £28,000 signing Robin Friday, a replacement for Adrian Alston who had moved to the United States after signing for Tampa Bay Rowdies. The talented but wayward Friday was reported to be out with a virus which then became hepatitis, although medical tests disproved he had been suffering with a liver condition. Nor could Andrews pick new £25,000 signing Keith Robson. The temperamental forward, scorer of one of West Ham's goal in their Cup Winners' Cup final loss against Anderlecht the previous year, was signed after the UEFA deadline so Andrews decided to switch Phil Dwyer to attack alongside Tony Evans.

The Safety of Sports Ground Act had drastically reduced Ninian Park's capacity from 46,000 to just over 10,000. The Canton Stand was closed, the Grange End's capacity was cut from 12,300 to 2,300, the Popular Bank's capacity was slashed from 21,000 to 3,000 and the Enclosure could now hold only 1,350 spectators instead of 6,000. A gate of just over 3,631 turned up to watch Andrews' players tackle Memphis. Cardiff's 67-year-old home was scheduled to stage Wales' crucial World Cup qualifier against Scotland on 5 October but, because of safety issues, the Football Association of Wales moved the game to England, to Liverpool's Anfield. Despite Andrews' pre-match promise that "if they (the supporters) can come along, it will be worthwhile", the 5pm kick-off - due to Ninian Park's new floodlights not being ready - also had a massive impact on attendance. Desperate for a 7.30pm kick-off, the club was prepared to spend £6,000 on a generator to supply emergency lighting but this idea was rejected by South Glamorgan County Council. Aware the club's 20th European tie would be played out in front of a meagre crowd due to the impact of Government legislation and an early kick-off time, Terlezki used the official matchday programme to apologise to the Austrian visitors as "the traditional atmosphere of so many European games here in the past will be absent on this occasion".

By his own admission, Andrews was not one for preparing dossiers and declined to fly to Austria to watch Memphis, although he would have made the journey had the first leg been in Vienna. "A friend has seen them," he explained, "and told me all I want to know." Andrews acknowledged Austrian footballers possessed "a high degree of skill" but perhaps did not relish a physical approach. "If they have a fault it is, as their coach says, that they don't battle enough." Before the first leg Memphis coach Hermann Stessl, an admirer of the "discipline, force and energy" of British footballers, said their Austrian counterparts were blessed with refined skills and good technique "but they lack aggression...they do not like to fight". Andrews hoped Dwyer, a robust defender, would expose that flaw. Attley took Dwyer's place at right-back with Byrne slotting in at left-back alongside central defenders Paul Went, a £30,000 signing from Portsmouth, and Pontin. Behind them

317

was the transfer-listed Bill Irwin, standing in for first-choice goalkeeper Ron Healey who was sidelined with an ankle injury. In midfield Doug Livermore and Alan Campbell were flanked by Sayer and Giles, with Dwyer supporting striker Evans who had missed the last three games with a groin injury and was now struggling with a stomach bug.

Peter Sayer: *I've got a picture of me playing against Memphis at Ninian Park. I'm tussling for the ball with an Austrian guy. In the background you can't see anyone. All you can see is empty terracing, there's nobody there. There was a small crowd at that game which meant there was no atmosphere. Ninian Park could be an intimidating place for the opposition if there was a decent crowd. If there was nobody there then it was a horrible place to play, but that was the case with any ground.*

Gerry Byrne: *There was a strange atmosphere for that game. It was like a pre-season friendly. We didn't have a massive crowd because of the early kick-off and the fact that parts of the ground were closed off. During a game players shout at each other and that night we could hear what was being said quite clearly. Our voices were echoing throughout the ground. Usually that wasn't the case. If you had a decent crowd, you just got the gist of what your teammates were saying. The game was also played in broad daylight as we kicked off at five in the evening and that was weird because you expected to play European games at night, under floodlights.*

The Memphis players were on a £500 bonus to progress to the next round. "Austrian footballers are at their best when they must work for their money," remarked Stessl. Thanks to Robert Sara, a Viennese pay-out appeared likely, the Austrian international defender twice clearing off the line, firstly from Sayer and then Dwyer. Weninger, too, played his part, turning over a shot from Evans. But it was Cardiff who were fortunate to avoid defeat. Earlier, Irwin had twice denied Karl Daxbacker and then Hans Pirkner, but the Ulsterman saved his best for the last 10 minutes with two outstanding stops in the space of 60 seconds, first from Thomas Parits and then Pirkner. Dwyer's physical style caused the Memphis defence problems but the home side – without a win in their first five games - were unable to find a way past Weninger and the first leg ended 0-0.

Bill Irwin: *There was a small crowd at the home game so there was no atmosphere. We always got decent crowds for the European games but not many came to watch Memphis. The turnout was disappointing because we thought we'd get a good crowd since it was a Cup Winners' Cup tie. We wanted the fans behind us. When you had that, it was like having the wind behind you. The supporters can make a difference but the small crowd meant a flat atmosphere which helped Memphis, not us. It made the night easier for them. A decent gate would have made it hostile for Memphis. Instead, they came out, saw a ground that was practically empty and thought 'This is nice!' It might have been different with 10,000 Cardiff City supporters there. It was an even match-up but this was a game we could have won. A bigger crowd would have made a difference.*

Paul Went: *The opposition goalkeeper (Weninger) got injured during the warm-up. In those days there was no substitute goalkeeper so he had to play. Their physio came on and strapped up his leg, which we all saw. We thought we were in the next round because the guy couldn't run or kick a ball and he was slipping about. We were basically playing against 10 men but it was a poor game and neither side created many chances. When we did attack, their goalkeeper had one of those days when he stopped everything. The ball hit him on the head or on his knee. I don't think we would have scored even if the Austrians had walked off and left us alone on the pitch for half-an-hour. We couldn't beat a goalkeeper on one leg and that was disappointing.*

David Giles: *They were a really good side. They had a few internationals and we were delighted their best player, Prohaska, was out. We were looking at the programme in the dressing room before the game and it said he wouldn't be playing. I remember Phil Dwyer saying, 'Thank God he's not playing!' He obviously knew something about Prohaska. But they were still impressive without him and for spells in the game we were chasing shadows because their passing and movement were so crisp. At the end of the game we knew we'd put in a right old shift and Doug Livermore said he must have lost half-a-stone. He was ringing sweat out of his shirt in the dressing room, that's how much chasing about he did. The atmosphere that night was awful. There were parts of the ground which were totally empty. Ninian Park could be a fortress because the crowd was close to the pitch and that would intimidate the opposition but there was a sparse crowd which definitely suited Memphis. It was a weird atmosphere. I played in front of bigger crowds in Football Combination games.*

Tony Evans:

There were no fans behind the goals. It was more like a friendly than a European game. The crowd can be your twelfth man and we didn't have that advantage in the first leg, but we weren't progressing as a side. We had won promotion in 1976 but the club didn't build on that. The nucleus of the side was decent – we had good players like Adrian Alston, John Buchanan, Phil Dwyer, Clive Charles and Willie Anderson. If the club had made two or three quality signings after promotion then we would have kicked on but unfortunately that didn't happen which was a real shame.

The advantage now rested with Stessl's side although Cardiff knew they could profit from the away-goal rule inside the Franz-Horr-Stadion. The Welsh side flew to Vienna minus a chairman – Terlezki had been dismissed for making statements on board policy which had not been agreed by his fellow directors – but they had, more significantly, chalked up their first victory of the season, a 3-1 win over Fulham. There was encouraging news for Andrews after landing in the Austrian capital. Weninger was sidelined with a knee problem so Baumgartner, who had been out for six weeks, would start in goal and Parits, another of Memphis' key players, would not feature because of a groin injury.

Keen for an early goal to upset Memphis, Andrews again switched Dwyer to attack with Freddie Pethard, at right-back, making his first appearance of the season. There was another change, John Buchanan - suspended for the first leg - replacing Giles.

Gerry Byrne: *Memphis played mind games with us over there. We
                 trained at their stadium for an hour or so the night
                 before the game and they stuck us in this big shower
                 room. It was horrible. We weren't given a proper
                 dressing room. They didn't put the heating on for the
                 showers so there was no hot water and there were
                 no benches for us to sit on. There were also people
                 hanging about in places where they shouldn't have
                 been. I know the manager wasn't too happy about it.
                 Memphis were trying to upset us. They were doing
                 whatever they could to win the game.*

The home side, said Andrews, "could crack up" if Cardiff
scored first and his strategy centred on heaping pressure on
Baumgartner, believing the Memphis goalkeeper would lack
mobility and be prone to making errors following his recent
spell on the treatment table. Andrews feared a hostile reception
in Vienna after Swansea-based referee Tom Reynolds enraged
75,000 Austrians by disallowing what would have been a late
winner for Austria in their World Cup qualifier against East
Germany four days earlier but his concern was misplaced as
another referee, Marian Kuston, would play a central role in
the second leg.

David Giles: *The pitches they had in Vienna were beautiful, they
                 were like carpets. They were rolled and flat – it was like
                 training on the surface of a snooker table and we could
                 see why the Memphis lads were so good at passing
                 and moving. We were training on the mud pile that
                 was Coronation Park and also 'dog-shit park' across
                 the road from Ninian Park. It was called that because
                 we'd be playing a five-a-side game and dogs would run
                 into our area and do a shit! That happened quite a few*

322

times. It was totally different in Vienna. The Memphis players were training on these magnificent surfaces and when we were training before the game, I was thinking 'Imagine playing on this every week'. I was on the bench for the second game and we were under the cosh. It was only a matter of time before they got their goal. Jimmy's plan was to try and score from a set-piece as we had players like Paul Went and Phil Dwyer who could do that, and we also knew Memphis didn't like the rough and tumble type of football, but once they went in front they were pretty comfortable. They were content with that, they didn't look to score three or four.

Cardiff's best opportunity fell to Attley after 26 minutes but the midfielder, set up by Dwyer's reverse pass, shot tamely at Baumgartner from 12 yards out. With the tie poised at 0-0, Kuston disallowed Dwyer's strike, chalking off what would have been a vital away goal. The Polish official ruled the Wales international had controlled Attley's cross with his hand before smashing the ball beyond Baumgartner. "I controlled the ball with my chest. It was a perfectly good goal," explained Dwyer afterwards. With Cardiff still reeling from Kuston's decision, Ernst Baumeister scored the winner, the defender dumping the Bluebirds out of the Cup Winners' Cup with a 25-yard shot which beat Irwin after taking a deflection off Went. It was a frustrating night for Dwyer who was also booked seven minutes before half-time and then replaced after 77 minutes, Andrews believing Kuston "was obviously intent" on sending him off. "The referee was always looking for him (Dwyer). He was still looking at him, in fact, after he'd gone off and was sitting on the bench." Andrews described Kuston's display as "very poor indeed" and criticised the Pole for preventing his players from taking quick free-kicks. "My players became exasperated. They felt it was one of those impossible missions."

Phil Dwyer: *Every time I made a challenge the referee awarded Memphis a free-kick. I was getting penalised every time I went for the ball, whether it was in the air or on the ground, and I ended up getting booked. Whenever I made a challenge the Austrians would fall over and put their hands over their faces, and they would complain to the referee. I could see they were trying to get me sent off. It was a real eye-opener for me. My style of play caused Memphis problems in the first game and I don't think they fancied coming up against it at home. Because I was getting penalised all the time I couldn't get involved in the second leg and I was thinking 'Why am I bothering?' The way it was going, I was definitely going to get sent off. Jimmy could see that as well so he decided to replace me with Ray Bishop. I never liked being taken off but I understood why Jimmy made the change. I was going to get a red card if I stayed on that pitch so he pulled me off before I got sent off. I didn't know it at the time but that would be my last game in the Cup Winners' Cup. It was a sad farewell.*

Paul Went: *In effect, I scored their winner. I tried to block the ball but ended up diverting it past Bill Irwin. The home crowd were cheering and I felt responsible for their goal which wasn't a nice feeling. Until then, the game had been fairly even and we were matching the Austrians. I don't like to blame anyone but the referee's performance had a bearing on that game. Memphis got all the 50-50 decisions. If it had been more of a level playing field, the result might have been different.*

OH, VIENNA

Gerry Byrne: *I thought we were unlucky. They scored with a deflected shot. Wenty tried to block the ball, it hit the top of his shin pad and looped over big Bill Irwin. We gave a decent account of ourselves. It could easily have ended 0-0 and gone to penalties. Memphis didn't hammer at us. It wasn't as if they were banging on our door all night. At half-time there was a bit of discord in the tunnel between some of our older players and the referee. They were irate with a lot of his decisions. I know Jimmy Andrews wasn't happy with the referee and he had a few words with him after the game, but we'd lost 1-0 and we were out of Europe. It was just a shame the way they got their winner.*

Tony Evans: *After the game Phil charged down the corridor and started banging on the door of the Memphis dressing room. He was trying to get in and have a go at them because they'd given him a rough time on the pitch. When the game finished he was down the corridor like a shot. It was as if a red rag had been shown to a bull. Their players had tried to get him sent off and that made him angry and upset. That game in Austria was the first time I saw footballers play-acting. It didn't happen in our game, not in those days. If you got whacked, you just got straight back up.*

Memphis caused a genuine surprise by reaching the final in Paris, beating Locomotiva Košice, Hadjuk Split and Moscow Dynamo, but there, in the French capital, the fairy tale ended with Anderlecht crushing the Viennese underdogs 4-0. Cardiff narrowly avoided relegation, Andrews' side finishing 19th in Division Two, just one point above the relegation zone. Aside from poor results, Friday walked out of Ninian Park and retired from professional football while Robson and coach Alan Sealey, former West Ham teammates, were involved in a scuffle in the club car park. This turbulent campaign also saw Cardiff relinquish the Welsh Cup, losing to Wrexham in the semi-final.

David Giles: *Over the two legs we lost 1-0 to a side that reached the final so I think we deserved more credit for what we did against them. They were a quality side, they were no mugs. I remember watching them go further and further in the competition and thinking 'That 0-0 draw at Ninian Park wasn't a bad result.' That evening we had one or two players missing and it was in front of a low crowd so it was a good result, really.*

Paul Went: *In the first leg, Austria Memphis didn't look like a team that would do anything in the Cup Winners' Cup yet they went on to reach the final. Maybe they weren't up to speed when they came to Ninian Park, maybe they hadn't knitted together or maybe that performance was a one-off, but they must have been a good side because you don't reach the final without being one of the best sides in the competition. You also need luck and their luck came against us in the first game. We should have won it because their goalkeeper was injured and we had players who could challenge for the ball at set pieces, but it was one of those nights when we just couldn't score.*

Alan Campbell: *Memphis reached the final that year so going out to them 1-0 wasn't a bad result. Having said that, I was really surprised they went that far. I didn't think they were that good a side. We played them twice and I wasn't too impressed by them. We should have done*

*better at Ninian Park. Had we won by a couple of goals
then that would have put us in a good position flying
to Austria.*

First Round, First Leg
14 September, 1977
Ninian Park, Cardiff

Cardiff City (0) 0 **FK Austria Memphis (0) 0**

CARDIFF CITY: Irwin, Dwyer, Went, Pontin, Attley, Byrne, Campbell, Livermore, Sayer, Evans, Giles (Grapes).

AUSTRIA MEMPHIS: Weninger, Sara R, Obermeier, Baumeister, Parits, Daxbacher, Sara J, Gasselich, Zach, Pirchner, Morales (Drazan).

First Round, Second Leg
28 September, 1977
Franz-Horr-Stadion, Vienna

FK Austria Memphis (0) 1 **Cardiff City (0) 0**

Baumeister 52

AUSTRIA MEMPHIS: Baumgartner, Sara R, Obermeier, Baumeister, Parits, Daxbacher, Sara J, Martinez (Drazan), Zach, Gasselich, Morales.

CARDIFF CITY: Irwin, Pethard, Went, Pontin, Attley (Livermore), Byrne, Campbell, Sayer, Buchanan, Evans, Dwyer (Bishop).

(FK Austria Memphis won 1-0 on aggregate)

21

No Trouble
Derry City, 1988

'We don't expect to beat Cardiff but we're expecting
to give them a good match.'

Jimmy McLaughlin

SINCE their defeat in Vienna in 1977, Cardiff had been kept
out of Europe, reduced to the role of bystanders as Wrexham,
Newport County, Swansea City, Bangor City and Merthyr Tydfil
all represented Wales in the Cup Winners' Cup. Now, after an
11-year absence, the capital's club was back in the competition
it once graced on an annual basis, following a memorable
season which yielded both promotion from the old Division
Four, and the Welsh Cup. The revival was masterminded by
Frank Burrows, a direct and straight-talking Scot in the Jimmy
Scoular mould, who was hired as Cardiff manager in 1986
following a spell as assistant manager at Sunderland.

Inheriting a demoralised side which had suffered two
consecutive relegations, Burrows - a former defender and
member of the Swindon Town side that stunned Arsenal in
the 1969 League Cup final - had displayed admirable adeptness
in the transfer market. On a limited budget, the former
Portsmouth manager assembled a group of players capable not

only of returning to English football's third tier but ending the club's European exile, comfortably dispatching Wrexham in the Welsh Cup final at the Vetch Field. George Wood, the former Scotland and Arsenal goalkeeper, was signed on a free transfer as was centre-back Nigel Stevenson, left-back Nicky Platnauer and midfield trio Alan Curtis, a former Wales international, Paul Wimbleton and Brian McDermott. Terry Boyle, the side's defensive lynchpin and Burrows' lieutenant on the pitch, came from Newport County for £22,000 but the Scot's most astute signing was Jimmy Gilligan. The striker, who fired 19 league goals during the promotion campaign, was a bargain £17,500 buy from Lincoln City.

The Cup Winners' Cup cast for 1988-89 was certainly impressive. Burrows and his players had the chance of facing Johan Cruyff's Barcelona, emerging Italian side Sampdoria, Belgian giants Anderlecht and Greece's most decorated club, Panathinaikos. The draw, though, proved an anti-climax, pairing the Welsh side with the League of Ireland's Derry City. The short journey to Northern Ireland – Brandywell Stadium, in the heart of Bogside, a Republican area, would stage the first leg – also presented the Division Three club with a thumping security headache. Derry was the birthplace of the Troubles, a 1968 clash triggering riots across the city, and was also the scene of 'Bloody Sunday' four years later when British soldiers shot 26 people. Sixteen years on and Northern Ireland's second largest city was still plagued by sectarian violence. Initially, a trip to the troubled province did not greatly concern Cardiff's hierarchy but anxiety surfaced less than a fortnight before the first leg, when a threatening letter, posted in Northern Ireland, arrived at Ninian Park. "It warns us that we're part of Britain and the struggle is against Britain," revealed Tony Clemo, Cardiff's chairman, who took the letter "very seriously". The anonymous, handwritten letter was taken to the nearest police station, in Canton, and Special Branch was alerted.

A nervous Clemo considered asking UEFA to move the game to a neutral venue and even mooted the idea of withdrawing the Bluebirds from the competition altogether. "The players and manager know there's no way I'd place anybody's safety at risk if we weren't happy in our own minds," said the Cardiff chairman. Jimmy McLaughlin, Derry's manager, tried to reassure the Welsh club during his visit to Ninian Park on 30 September, to watch Cardiff's 1-0 defeat in the Littlewoods Cup against his former club, Swansea City. "Things have been blown out of all proportion," he told Clemo. Brandywell, he said, had hosted Arsenal, Nottingham Forest, Oxford United, Leicester City, Sunderland and Red Star Belgrade, all without trouble. "We have a file of letters from these clubs saying they would come back tomorrow," added McLaughlin, born and bred in Derry. Satisfied with the security measures put in place for Cardiff's visit, Clemo sanctioned the trip to Ulster.

Nevertheless, due to a recent increase in unrest in the province – eight days before the first leg, two Catholic civilians were killed by an Irish Republican Army booby-trap bomb in Derry's Creggan area - Clemo and Football Association of Wales secretary Alun Evans both urged Cardiff supporters not to travel to Ulster for the first leg with the Welsh club refusing to sell first-leg tickets. Their pleas were ignored by a group of 30 fans who had asked a Northern Ireland-based contact to buy £105 worth of tickets on their behalf. Their decision to defy the club's advice angered Clemo who remarked, "In my book, they're not true City supporters." The rebels' response was to goad Clemo at Brandywell, chanting 'You'll never ban a City fan' when the chairman appeared on the pitch at half-time to take part in a prize draw.

Jimmy Gilligan: *I didn't have any qualms about going to Northern Ireland. My belief was the club wouldn't have taken us out there if they thought something bad might happen. We had security with us while we were over there and we mostly stayed in the hotel. If we went out, security came with us. We landed in Belfast and didn't know where we were staying. When we were being driven to Derry we could see 'IRA' painted on walls. The things we'd see watching the BBC news, we were now seeing for ourselves. It was real, not something that was on the television. We were mainly confined to the hotel and we did what we were told. The hotel was set in grounds so we could go for a walk but there was no sightseeing or anything like that. As players, we just got on with playing and my focus was on trying to beat Derry. We were a Third Division side so being involved in a high-profile competition was a big thing for us.*

Nicky Platnauer: *Prior to the game the club received written death threats. No specific players were named. The Troubles were never really mentioned and I didn't have any problems going to Northern Ireland. We were there to play a game of football. The first inkling we had of being in a troubled area was seeing armed policemen who were with us at the hotel and on the coach going to the game. We didn't have any problems in Derry. All in all, it was an enjoyable experience.*

The first-round fixture may have lacked glamour yet it offered a faltering Cardiff side a realistic chance of progress. Burrows' side had endured a wretched start to the new campaign, the pre-season optimism quickly blown away by three defeats in the opening eight days. They headed to Northern Ireland smarting from a 4-0 loss at Bolton Wanderers and without their costliest summer signing, right-back Ian Rodgerson, a £35,000 buy from Hereford United, ruled out of both games with a groin injury. That meant a starting role for Phil Bater who had just recovered from a virus which had sidelined the ex-Bristol Rovers player, another of Burrows' free acquisitions, for nearly a week. Gilligan was viewed as Cardiff's biggest threat yet it was Ian Walsh, a former Wales striker signed on a free transfer that summer, who had been finding the net in the opening fixtures, scoring three goals in the first three league games.

George Wood: *We were quite pleased with the draw. Without being disrespectful to Derry, it gave us a good chance of progressing. We weren't worried about going to Northern Ireland. In fact, the hospitality we received out there was fantastic. Our supporters were told not to travel to the game but, as usual, a few turned up! There was no hassle and they were given a great welcome by the Derry fans. While we were in Derry a few of us went for a walk after training. As we were walking I could see these bushes starting to move. All of a sudden soldiers jumped out in front of us. I nearly crapped myself! They were in camouflage and masked-up. You couldn't see them, they were part of the bushes, and they were guarding that particular area. We were wearing our Cardiff City tracksuits so they could see who we were. I think they were just trying to scare us. There were areas of Derry we were not allowed to go to and maybe we had strolled a bit too far.*

Phil Bater: *We had security people with us in Northern Ireland and they had to dress up in our football gear so they appeared to be working for the club instead of looking like security. The iffy thing was, you can tell straight away if someone is an athlete or if someone is just dressing up as one. The security people did stand out – these guys didn't look like sportsmen. There were bulges underneath their tracksuits and obviously they were concealing firearms. When we got to our hotel in Derry we had to stay outside our rooms because they went in first to check everything was OK. I roomed with Brian McDermott and we had to wait while they did their search but, as a group, we never felt threatened in Northern Ireland. We knew Protestants called the city Londonderry and Catholics called it Derry so we had to be careful what we said but the people there really looked after us and Derry gave us something to eat and drink after the game. In the end, we were footballers and we just wanted to play. We were glad to be there and it was nice to see the place.*

Ian Walsh:

I had family in Northern Ireland. My sister-in-law lives in Donegal which is about 50 miles from Derry. I asked them if we should go because there were still problems over there and they said sporting events were left alone so I was quite relaxed about that trip. That said, you're a bit apprehensive when there's a police officer sitting next to you on the coach with a gun in his hand. We stayed on the other side of the river, in the Protestant part, and the ground is in a Catholic area so we saw both sides of the city on the way to the game. We saw motifs on the walls and barricades. We had a great welcome at Brandywell because the people appreciated us being there.

The Cardiff manager described his European opponents as "a good advertisement for football in Ireland" after watching their 1-1 draw with Dundalk at Brandywell. He was also hoping his side had "used up all the bad luck in the opening week". His opposite number, McLaughlin, conceded Derry were underdogs but felt his players could give the Welsh Cup holders a difficult time at Brandywell. "Unlike when you play Red Star Belgrade and Barcelona, we know we have a chance," said McLaughlin, a key figure in the Swansea side that reached the FA Cup semi-finals in 1964. Derry operated a self-stewarding policy so security forces would remain outside Brandywell during the game. However, the Irish club were confident the first leg would pass without incident while the prospect of playing in the troubled province did not, according to Burrows, worry the Cardiff players who were met by Derry officials at Belfast International Airport before being taken to their hotel, the location of which was kept a tightly-guarded secret. Nevertheless, the squad's movements in Northern Ireland would be restricted and there was no sightseeing tour of the city. "We are here to win a football match," the Cardiff manager told the Press. "We are not here to see the beauty of Northern Ireland."

Terry Boyle: *I remember me and Walshy (Ian Walsh) doing an interview before the game as we both had Irish names. My dad was Irish. While we were off-air I was asked if my family was into 'the cause'. I didn't know what that meant but Walshy, who was next to me, gave me a nudge and told me to say nothing, which I did. He told me what 'the cause' was after. I was a little bit surprised to be asked the question. I remember we had the Ulster police with us on the bus – they were wearing Cardiff City gear so as not to look conspicuous. There was also a heavy soldier presence on the night of the game and we had armed guards with us as we were driven to the ground, but the Derry people gave us a good welcome.*

Alan Curtis: *We never felt under threat when we were in Northern Ireland. We didn't think 'We're going into a war zone'. We did have an escort going to the game and we could see tanks on the streets. There were tanks in and around the city. There were lots of British troops about and they were giving us the thumbs-up as we made our way to the ground. It was a slightly surreal atmosphere but the people at the club were terrific, they were incredibly friendly. The Derry supporters were fantastic too. There was never any fear something bad was going to happen. I think the fact we were a Welsh club took the sting out of things. Maybe it would have been different if we were an English club.*

Playing in European competition for the first time in 23 years, Derry's hopes largely rested on striker Jonathan Speak, who had netted 24 goals the previous season but was struggling to rediscover that goalscoring form in 1988-89. "He says he is saving them for Europe," remarked McLaughlin on the eve of the Brandywell showdown. Speak failed to oblige as Derry were held to a goalless draw by the visitors. Backed by a sell-out 10,500 crowd – hundreds of locals watched the game from outside Brandywell and the vantage points included a cemetery on the forbidding Creggan housing estate overlooking the ground – McLoughlin's side was unable to make home advantage count. Their best chance came after 12 minutes when Kevin Brady's cross eluded Platnauer but Noel Larkin,

335

who had scored four goals in the last five games, tripped over his own feet as he went for the ball.

George Wood: *It was a tight game over there. Nobody gave an inch and the game was mainly played in midfield. There weren't many chances and in the end it was a comfortable 0-0 for us. We were happy with the result because we thought we would take them back to Ninian Park and finish them off. It was a good cup tie and I enjoyed it. The Irish crowd was great. Their fans were passionate and they really welcomed us and the small group of Cardiff fans who were inside the ground.*

Alan Curtis: *We were given some information about Derry but going into the game we weren't sure what to expect. They were one of the top sides in Ireland although we weren't bad. We had experienced players like myself, George Wood in goal, and in front of him there were Terry Boyle and Nigel Stevenson. We were all coming to the end of our careers but we were good players. We ended up drawing 0-0 but perhaps that was a game we should have won. I do remember Jimmy (Gilligan) missing a great chance with a header.*

Burrows was satisfied with the result although Cardiff created enough chances to return home with a first-leg lead, Gilligan uncharacteristically wasting three opportunities. "This is only the first half," said Burrows afterwards, "and you never win a game in the first half." McLoughlin, too, claimed he was "not too disappointed with the result". The highlight of an otherwise uneventful first leg was the genial atmosphere at Brandywell. Burrows' players were given a terrific welcome by the Derry public when they appeared on the pitch an hour before kick-off. The visitors reciprocated by gathering in the centre-circle after the final whistle to applaud the home crowd. "People saw for themselves what happened. They are lovely people here," remarked George Cummings, the official UEFA observer who was delighted the evening passed without incident.

Jimmy Gilligan: *It was a tough game. Derry were a well-organised side and they did everything they could to make it difficult for us. The ground was packed but I wouldn't say the atmosphere was intimidating. We were well-received at Derry. There was no booing and nothing was chucked at us. Their fans obviously wanted their team to win but they were decent with us. It was a competitive game and to leave there with a 0-0 draw was a great result.*

Nicky Platnauer: *It was a pretty even game, there weren't many chances. For us, European football was a new thing. We knew an away goal would count double but we couldn't get one. That wasn't on our minds as we came home. We thought we could get the better of them at Ninian Park.*

Cardiff's form had slightly improved by the time Derry arrived in South Wales a month later for the second leg. They had chalked up their first win of the campaign, a 3-0 victory over Huddersfield Town at Ninian Park although this was followed by a 6-1 drubbing at Port Vale. But Burrows' Bluebirds did overturn a 1-0 deficit to overcome arch rivals Swansea City in the Littlewoods Cup and two successive league draws – against Southend United and Bristol Rovers – suggested the Division Three newcomers were becoming a more solid unit. They were expected to dispatch a Derry side missing two key players. Midfield general Stuart Gauld, their captain and described as "half the team", was out with an ankle injury. Also absent was their attacking French full-back Pascal Vaudequin who was nursing a knee and ankle problem. Vaudequin's place was filled by player-coach Jack Keay, coaxed out of semi-retirement for another Cup Winners' Cup adventure. Keay was a member of the Wrexham side that sensationally eliminated Portuguese aristocrats Porto in 1984.

Cardiff were quick to exploit Derry's defensive frailties. McDermott, only picked because Jason Gummer, who had played at Brandywell, Steve Lynex and Rodgerson were all on the casualty list, broke the stalemate after 20 minutes when he headed a Curtis cross past the stranded Tim Dalton. Gilligan effectively sealed the tie two minutes after the restart when he seized onto Brady's backpass and then squeezed the ball between centre-back Paul Curran and the post. Gilligan then notched his second from just a yard out before completing his hat-trick 14 minutes from the end when he headed Bater's cross beyond Dalton. It was the first treble of Gilligan's career and only the second scored by a Cardiff player in Europe, the 24-year-old Londoner following Sandy Allan in 1969.

Phil Bater: *We had sussed Derry out and the second leg was more of a formality. There were no security issues or anything like that, and we got the job done. We had seen what they'd got. They had one or two good players but they didn't have enough of them to beat us. We were playing at a higher level and, at the same time, we didn't want to go out in the first round. Frank was a pragmatic manager and he knew that if we came away without conceding, we'd have a chance at Ninian Park and we beat them 4-0. That Cardiff side was made up of players who had been released by other clubs, who were coming to the end of their careers, or were just starting their careers. We just came together and we had a good two years. We knew our limitations but we'd won promotion and the Welsh Cup, and now we were playing in Europe. Being an Ely boy who joined his hometown club at 31, it was a fantastic way to end my career and Frank was the best manager I ever worked with. He was a different class.*

Nicky Platnauer: *The atmosphere at our place was terrific. It was very, very loud. My son, Leigh, was a mascot that night. He was two at the time and he was frightened by the noise. When we were waiting in the tunnel, we could sense the atmosphere was different and it bounced onto the players. We played well in the second leg. That was a good night for the club. We had a good crowd and we'd also made it to the second round.*

Cardiff's performance, however, did not satisfy Burrows who declined to praise Gilligan after the game, preferring instead to discuss the striker's deficiencies. "Gilligan is too easily satisfied, that is why he is still at this level," commented the ex-Portsmouth chief. "He should be playing in the First Division and if he was a bit more passionate and hungry, he could play there."

Jimmy Gilligan: *We did a good job that night. We dismantled a decent team and we did our job professionally. I was fortunate to score a hat-trick and I made sure I got the match ball at the end but Frank wasn't satisfied and he wouldn't sign the ball for me. All the lads signed it but Frank said, 'No' when I asked him – and when Frank said no, that was that! I didn't say anything back to him. I had to respect his decision but a few expletives came out of my mouth as I walked out of the ground. As a player, I couldn't see where he was coming from and I was fuming with him, but now I'm a coach I can see he was right. He was trying to push me and he did that by caning me. He used to say I was the type of guy he'd like his daughter to marry and that if I had more self-belief, I could have been playing at a higher level. Frank was one of the best managers – if not the best – I played for. As a coach, I like the fact he wasn't satisfied with my performance against Derry.*

Alan Curtis: *We gauged the opposition from the first game and swept them aside at our place but Frank wasn't pleased. That was Frank, he was never happy at the best of times. If we were winning he tended to give us a bollocking. That was his way of keeping people's feet on the ground. After a bad result he would try and lift you. He wouldn't be so critical. Frank was good like that. He was a clever and astute manager.*

340

First Round, First Leg
7 September, 1988
Brandywell Stadium, Derry

Derry City (0) 0   **Cardiff City (0) 0**

DERRY CITY: Dalton, Vaudequin, Brady, Curran, Neville, Doolin,
Hegarty (Carlyle), Larkin, Speak, Gauld, Healy (Keay).

CARDIFF CITY: Wood, Bater, Stevenson, Boyle, Platnauer, Wimbleton
(McDermott), Curtis, Gummer, Kelly, Walsh (Bartlett),
Gilligan.

First Round, Second Leg
5 October, 1988
Ninian Park, Cardiff

Cardiff City (1) 4   **Derry City (0) 0**
McDermott 20
Gilligan 47, 64, 76

CARDIFF CITY: Wood, Bater (Perry), Stevenson, Boyle, Platnauer,
Wimbleton (Morgan), Curtis, McDermott, Kelly, Bartlett,
Gilligan.

DERRY CITY: Dalton, Keay, Brady, Curran, Neville, Doolin, Carlyle
(Quigg), Larkin, Speak, Cunningham, Healy.

(Cardiff City won 4-0 on aggregate)

22

Jutland Destroyers
Aarhus, 1988

'We want to stay in the competition as long as possible
because it brings prestige, pride and money.'

Frank Burrows

THE second-round draw meant Cardiff would return to the
country where their Cup Winners' Cup story began 24 years
earlier. Aarhus, of Denmark, were the next opponents for the
Division Three strugglers, Allan Hebo Larsen's side booking
their place in the second phase with an emphatic 7-2 aggregate
win over Northern Ireland's Glenavon. With television rights
and spin-offs, a place in the third round could earn clubs
between £70,000 and £100,000, money the cash-starved
Bluebirds desperately needed, but it was the Danes who were
favourites to claim this windfall. The comfortable victory over
Derry City three weeks earlier had not sparked the revival
Frank Burrows was hoping for with Cardiff – now third from
bottom in Division Three - failing to win any of the subsequent
three league games.

Floating in mid-table in the Danish top flight and knocked
out of the Danish Cup by Ikast, Aarhus had not hit the
heights expected of them in pre-season although they travelled

342

to Ninian Park for the first leg buoyed by a 5-1 win over Aarlborg, a game watched by Cardiff coach Bobby Smith. Apart from studying Smith's report, Burrows contacted two colleagues for information – Jim Smith, whose Queens Park Rangers side had played Aarhus in a summer friendly, and Glenavon manager Terry Nicholson. Nicholson told Burrows the Danes "would hold their own in the First Division" and were blessed with a ruthless edge. In the first leg at Mourneview Park, said Nicholson, they "created five chances and scored with four of them". But he had spotted a potential weakness for Burrows to exploit. Troels Rasmussen, their Danish international goalkeeper, was uncomfortable dealing with high balls and showed a reluctance to come for them.

Rasmussen was not the only international on Aarhus' payroll. Midfielder Morten Donnerup had played for Denmark as had centre-half John Stampe, the club captain, while Bjørn Kristensen had represented his country at the European Championships in West Germany earlier that year along with Rasmussen. However, the Danes' star man, striker Frank Pingel, was forced to stay behind with a knee injury, news which no doubt delighted Burrows. The goalscoring onus now rested with Danish Under-21 international Henrik Mortensen, a club record £90,000 buy from Anderlecht, who had scored in both games against Glenavon. "We hope to score goals," said Mortensen before the Ninian Park meeting. "Maybe not too many, but we hope for one or two which could be important for the home game."

George Wood: *I'd never heard of Aarhus. I didn't know where it was so I looked them up to get some information and when I saw their squad I thought 'Oh my God!' They were full of Danish internationals and clearly they were*

343

no mugs. Also, Danish football was strong during that period. Rasmussen, the Aarhus goalkeeper, was a Denmark international and they had a few other good players so I knew it was a tough draw. They were a quality side.

Larson, who would soon leave Aarhus to become coach of Esbjerg, tried to do his homework on the opposition, flying over to watch Cardiff's 4-1 Littlewoods Cup defeat against Queens Park Rangers. He did not learn much. Already 3-0 down after the first leg at Loftus Road, Burrows decided to field a clutch of teenagers – Gareth Abraham, a 19-year-old centre-half, and midfielders Chris Fry and Jon Morgan, both 18 - for the second game. Experimentation was not on the Scot's agenda when it came to naming his starting XI to tackle Aarhus at Ninian Park and, for half the game, Burrows' charges were more than a match for the Danes. The opening 20 minutes belonged to the visitors who asserted their authority with their crisp, passing game and incisive breaks. They took the lead after seven minutes when Bjørn Kristensen, playing in midfield, cut inside and placed a neat chip inside the far post following a one-two with Per Beck Andersen. Aarhus, it seemed, were waltzing to an easy victory, but Cardiff regrouped and the pendulum swung towards the Welsh outfit. Nigel Stevenson saw his shot cleared off the line by Jimmy Mørup and a Paul Wimbleton effort was saved by Rasmussen.

Cardiff deservedly – if controversially – equalised four minutes before the interval when Jimmy Gilligan claimed his fourth European goal and sixth of the season. The striker headed Brian McDermott's cross towards Rasmussen; the Dane caught the ball and dragged it back, away from his goal. Gilligan celebrated an equaliser while Rasmussen insisted the ball had not crossed the line. The focus now turned to the

Luxembourg officials, linesman Jean Lemmer ruling in favour of the Cardiff striker, a decision which enraged Larsen.

Jimmy Gilligan: *It was a controversial goal. If there was goal-line technology back then I don't think the goal would have been given but, at the time, I genuinely felt the ball had gone over the line. Then I watched the replay on TV and thought 'Oh, maybe that's a controversial decision'. I was an old-fashioned centre-forward and I took every goal that I could. I was more than happy to do that. I was never going to go up to the referee and say, 'It wasn't in.' Aarhus were a different proposition to Derry but there was a belief we might get a result and when we got it back to 1-1 there was a feeling that we could beat them. We had a right go at them and, looking back, we were punching above our weight in that game because they were a decent side.*

Phil Bater: *When the referee gave us the goal I remember thinking 'You're a lucky boy, Jim!' But that was Jimmy, he'd stick his arm in the air and claim a goal, no matter who had struck the ball. If I hit one from 30 yards and it went in, Jimmy would be the first to raise his arm, that's the sort of lad he was. We gave a good account of ourselves in the first leg, especially in the second half. There were lots of big names in the competition that year and Aarhus wasn't one of them. I thought we had a chance of going through.*

Cardiff now believed a first-leg victory was possible and pressed for a second goal, piling considerable pressure on the Danes in the second half. McDermott almost scored, going close with a header following Wimbleton's cross, but the determination

345

to attack left them vulnerable in defence and, just as they did at Glenavon, Aarhus exposed the space with a clinical raid in the 73rd minute. Burrows' midfielders failed to pick up Bjørn Kristensen who swept forward from just inside Cardiff's half, racing clear of Terry Boyle who was unable to catch the Danish international who beat George Wood from a tight angle. Cardiff could not respond a second time and they angered Burrows with their "hit and hope" football in the last 17 minutes. "We fell into the age-old trap of hitting too many long balls when we should have been showing a little bit more thought," remarked the Cardiff manager afterwards.

George Wood: *They really battered us in the first 20 minutes and we were hanging on. Then we settled down and got it back to 1-1. We then tried to get the second but they hit us on the break and got a late winner. I remember the guy (Bjørn Kristensen) running half the length of the pitch before scoring. Aarhus were fantastic on the break. They played a modern style of football. They would sit back and then hit us – bang, bang. Looking at the game overall, I think a draw would have been a fair result. We deserved a draw for the character we showed.*

Alan Curtis: *We were unlucky in the first game but we showed our inexperience in Europe. We tried to win the game and ended up conceding a second goal. Had it stayed 1-1 then we would have gone to Denmark with something. Instead, we were 2-1 down and it became more difficult for us. When you concede at home in Europe then you're in trouble and we'd let in two. As a team, we weren't experienced in European football and Aarhus were technically good and physically strong.*

JUTLAND DESTROYERS

A draw would have been a terrific result for us but we pushed forward to try and get a winner.

Burrows remained hopeful as his side geared up for the second leg, on the eastern side of the Jutland peninsula. If Aarhus could win 2-1 at Ninian Park, he declared, his side could do the same inside Aarhus' attractive stadium, a 1920s neoclassical building decorated with Doric columns and statues, and situated on the outskirts of the city, in Marselisborg Forest. According to Burrows, achieving a result that would eliminate the Danes was "a difficult but not impossible task" and he took encouragement from the Littlewoods Cup second-leg win over Swansea seven weeks earlier, the Bluebirds advancing to the second round with a 2-0 victory at the Vetch Field. The same scoreline would ensure progress in the Cup Winners' Cup. Gilligan was equally bullish before the return, telling the Press, "We're going all out to win the tie." Cardiff flew to Denmark without centre-half Stevenson, who was nursing a shin injury and had been told to paddle in Swansea Bay's icy water to reduce the swelling. If losing one of his defensive lynchpins was not damaging enough, Burrows' pre-match preparations were strained yet further by a delay at Heathrow which meant a late arrival in Denmark, forcing the Scot to scrap a training session at the Aarhus Stadium.

Cardiff's forward line concerned Larsen – "Bartlett is so quick and Gilligan is very strong in the air" – but the duo soon found themselves peripheral figures as Aarhus, inspired by Per Beck Andersen, a midfielder who would retire the following week to pursue a career in life insurance, chiselled away at Burrows' defence. With Pingel and Karsten Christensen fit, the Danes were at full strength and it was Pingel who fired Aarhus in front after 15 minutes when he smashed the ball into the empty net after Wood had brilliantly saved Claus Thomsen's volley.

Boyle's wayward headed clearance created the opportunity and another mistake allowed the home side to increase their lead 10 minutes later. Mark Kelly was dispossessed as he tried to control Wimbleton's pass, handing possession to Per Beck Andersen who flicked the ball past Wood following a one-two with Pingel which enabled him to cut through the fragile blue wall. Wood then produced a world-class save to prevent a Danish third. Per Beck Andersen looked certain to score when he met Pingel's cross just outside the six-yard box but was left staring at the Cardiff goal in disbelief after seeing the 36-year-old acrobatically push his powerful header over the target. Alan Curtis applauded his teammate while the Dane showed his appreciation of the save by shaking hands with Wood.

George Wood: *I believed we could turn it around in Aarhus - but I'm a Scot and we think we can win every game of football and rugby! After 25 minutes we knew were in for a spanking. They were 2-0 up and they could have scored two or three before they got the first. I had made a few saves and they really did batter us. After they went 1-0 up it was like shooting practice and in the second half it was a case of damage limitation. We did OK after the break. They wore us down and scored two late goals, one of them a penalty. We had a game plan for the second leg. Frank wanted us to sit tight and hit them on the break by trying to get the ball to Gilligan as quickly as we could but it didn't work. They just had more quality. While we tried to hit the ball to Gilligan, they played through us and we were beaten by a better team. Brian McDermott was a winger but he spent most of the night chasing their full-back.*

Alan Curtis: *Aarhus did stamp their authority in the second leg. There was more of an edge to them and they seemed stronger. They got the measure of us from the first game and really stifled us. When they scored the first, our heads didn't drop – Frank wouldn't allow that to happen – but we knew it was going to be a long night. There was a bit of disruption. We arrived in Aarhus late because of a delay at the airport so we didn't do a training session before the game but that really shouldn't have interfered too much. There was a gulf in class and on the night they were too much for us. Denmark was producing good players during that period and their game was on a completely different level to ours. We acquitted ourselves well but they absolutely murdered us.*

Pingel was withdrawn in the 64th minute, but still the pain continued for Cardiff. With a quarter of an hour remaining - and 16 seconds after Nicky Platnauer had pumped a free-kick deep into Aarhus territory - Per Beck Andersen scored his second of the night, turning Christensen's low cross past Wood to finish off a sweeping, exhilarating move. There was yet more misery for Burrows, Stampe converting an 82nd-minute penalty after Boyle was ruled to have fouled Mortensen. "We just didn't get started," said the Cardiff manager afterwards. "We just didn't play." Pingel and Bjørn Kristensen both moved across the North Sea the following year. Their impressive performances for Aarhus had caught the attention of Newcastle United's new manager, Jim Smith, who agreed a £500,000 deal for the duo.

Terry Boyle: *We felt we had half a chance in Aarhus but they showed that on their own patch they were on a different level to us. Frank did everything right but we*

349

were never in the game and as far as the performance was concerned, we didn't deliver and the result was a big disappointment. Our season had not long started whereas in Scandinavia they had nearly finished so they had played a lot more games and their players had a better understanding while we were still adjusting. Still, that game showed Aarhus were in a different class – their passing and movement were much better. Not long after they played us, they sold a couple of their lads to Newcastle for half a million - you wouldn't have got that for our entire squad. When we played Aarhus our results hadn't been good. We hoped to carry on from the previous season but we had a slow start. Some of our lads found the step up into Division Three difficult. They were struggling and were not as consistent as the previous year. That's the way it is sometimes.

Jimmy Gilligan: *We really felt we could do Aarhus at their place but we ended up getting our backsides spanked. They moved the ball about well that night and they were quite aggressive too. We didn't play well but they were too good for us. Sometimes you have to hold your hands up and say the opposition were better and that was the case here. They had decent players and they were a solid team. I don't remember us creating too many opportunities in Aarhus but I do remember having to track back to try and win the ball. I wasn't playing as a forward in that game!*

Nicky Platnauer: *We had great support in Denmark. Lots of our fans made the trip but on the night we didn't do ourselves justice. We took a bit of a hammering and that was no way to go out. If you don't perform and you're up against a better side, then you're going to be on the end of a heavy defeat. Aarhus ran the show over there but you have to put things into perspective – we were in the old Third Division and we were in the bottom half. But we let ourselves down in Denmark. We didn't perform like we could – or should – have done and Frank was disappointed after the game. He wasn't happy with us. We didn't give up, but it wasn't a performance he expected from one of his sides. Managers take things far more personally than players do. I remember the flight home, there wasn't a good atmosphere on the plane.*

The first Cup Winners' Cup campaign in 11 years ended with the club's heaviest European defeat. In the last eight, Aarhus pushed eventual winners Barcelona to the limit, losing 1-0 in Denmark and then drawing 0-0 in the Nou Camp. A forgettable and difficult season saw Cardiff – losing £2,000 a-week - climb away from the relegation zone, eventually finishing 16th, but there would be no European football at Ninian Park the following season. Swansea City won the Welsh Cup.

Alan Curtis: *We should have pushed on after winning promotion but it didn't happen. We were a reasonable side and if we'd kept everyone, and Frank was given a little bit of money to spend, then we may have progressed. Frank was astute in the transfer market. He knew the lower leagues and could get a bargain. But we go up and the first thing we do is sell Mike Ford to Oxford (for £150,000). That's the way it was, all about money. The better players would go and we were always rebuilding. With a bit of investment in that side, we could definitely have pushed on. We had experienced players but we also needed younger legs around us. Frank could see that. I think he became disillusioned himself and the following year he left.*

Second Round, First Leg
26 October, 1988
Ninian Park, Cardiff

Cardiff City (1) **Aarhus (1) 2**
Gilligan 41 B Kristensen 7, 73

CARDIFF CITY: Wood, Platnauer (Rodgerson), Bater, Wimbleton, Stevenson, Boyle, McDermott, Kelly, Lynex (Curtis), Gilligan, Bartlett.

AARHUS: Rasmussen, Wachmann, Kristensen B, Stampe, Rieper, Andersen, Morup (Donnerup), Andersen P, Kristensen K, Lundkvist, Mortensen.

Second Round, Second Leg
9 November, 1988
Aarhus Stadion, Aarhus

Aarhus (2) 4 **Cardiff City (0) 0**
Pingel 15, Beck 25, 75
Stampe 83 (pen)

AARHUS: Rasmussen, Wachmann, Stampe, Rieper, Andersen T, Thomsen (Donnerup), Kristensen B, Andersen P, Christensen, Lundkvist, Pingel (Mortensen).

CARDIFF CITY: Wood, Rodgerson, Platnauer, Wimbleton, Abraham, Boyle, McDermott (Lynex), Kelly, Curtis, Gilligan, Bartlett (Wheeler).

(Aarhus won 6-1 on aggregate)

23

A Tie of Two Halves
Admira Wacker, 1992

'I think we've a good chance of scoring.'

Eddie May

A WORLD Cup finalist had the task of plotting Cardiff's downfall in their first Cup Winners' Cup tie for four years. Siegfried 'Sigi' Held, an attacking midfielder in the West German side beaten by England in the epic 1966 final at Wembley and now coach of Austrian side Admira Wacker, would pit his wits against Eddie May, appointed Cardiff manager in July 1991 and a former centre-half who had plied his trade in the lower divisions with Wrexham, Southend United and Swansea City. While May's playing career may not have been as distinguished as Held's – the German had won the Cup Winners' Cup in 1966 and was a member of the West Germany side beaten by England in the World Cup final two months later – the big man from Essex had sampled success in Europe. May was captain of the Wrexham side that reached the last eight of the Cup Winners' Cup in 1976 when, after disposing of Sweden's Djurgårdens and Stal Rzeszów of Poland, they pushed eventual winners Anderlecht to the limit, losing 2-1 on aggregate.

May's plans, however, were severely disrupted by the absence

353

of defensive duo Jason Perry and Robbie James. Perry had twisted his knee in the 1-1 draw against Hereford United at Edgar Street the previous weekend while former Wales international James was suspended after being booked twice during his last European tie, for Swansea City against Panathinaikos in 1989. But it was UEFA's foreign player ruling, introduced two year earlier, where non-Welsh British players were classed as foreigners, which presented May with his biggest problem. With six non-Welsh players making up his regular starting XI – goalkeeper Mark Grew, defender Derek Brazil, midfielders Paul Millar, Paul Ramsey and Nicky Richardson, and winger Cohen Griffith - May would be forced to field a weakened side against the Austrians. He could name three 'foreigners' and Griffith – signed by May's predecessor, Len Ashurst - eased his selection headache by declaring himself Welsh ahead of the first-round tie. Born on the Caribbean island of Guyana and raised in Leicestershire, the £60,000 signing from Kettering held a British passport and could represent any of the home countries.

Cohen Griffith: *I was born in Guyana when it was part of the Commonwealth so I had British citizenship which meant I could play for any of the home countries. I chose to be Welsh so I didn't count as a foreigner in the Cup Winners' Cup. I probably wouldn't have played otherwise so it was a bit of self-preservation. I wanted to play in Europe – it was a different experience. The club did all the paperwork. I don't think there was much I had to do. I remember Eddie coming up to me before the Admira game and saying, 'You're now a Welshman!'*

Cardiff's foreign contingent consisted of an Englishman, Grew, an Irishman, Brazil, and a Northern Irishman, Ramsey. Grew and Brazil were both new signings, the former arriving from Port Vale and the latter coming from Manchester United in an £85,000 deal. Ramsey, a combative midfielder, had joined the Bluebirds the previous year, signed for £40,000 from Leicester City. Millar, from Northern Ireland, and Englishman Richardson were the foreign players who had to watch from the stands. Without Perry – described by his manager as "Cardiff through and through" – and James, May decided to change his side's formation for the first leg, opting for a sweeper system with Gareth Abraham, the lone survivor from the club's last European game at Aarhus, operating behind Brazil and Lee Baddeley. Cardiff-born Damon Searle, a surging left-back, supported a makeshift midfield of Ramsey, Griffith, Tony Bird and Nathan Blake. The injuries and foreigner rule meant three fringe players – defenders Baddeley and Abraham, and striker Bird – lined up against the Austrian Bundesliga outfit but it was on the bench where the UEFA restriction bit hard. May had no choice but to name five youth-team players as substitutes and if Grew was sent off or forced off with injury, his replacement would be 16-year-old Morgan Williams.

Damon Searle:	*It was a fantastic occasion, playing in Europe. It's something I'll never forget. You'd see Manchester United playing at that level and now we were doing it. At the time we were in the bottom division so we were travelling to places like Rochdale, Bury and Scunthorpe – and now we were going to fly to Vienna to play in the Cup Winners' Cup. The foreigner ruling was a hindrance. It made us weaker because certain players who were playing week in, week out, couldn't play. Nick Richardson and Windy (Paul Millar) had to miss the first leg and that was two first-choice*

> *midfielders gone. We had all young boys on the bench*
> *so if anyone got injured, the manager only had kids*
> *to choose from. But that was the ruling and we had*
> *to abide by it.*

Despite the obstacles, May remained optimistic. Cardiff had enjoyed a bright start to their domestic season and were joint third in Division Three although an inferior goal difference meant they sat in fifth place. May also possessed players who could score goals. Carl Dale, a £100,000 buy from Chester City, had already netted six goals while Chris Pike had tucked away 21 league goals the previous season. Pike and Dale would lead the line against Admira, but May's hopes of unsettling the Austrian defence were very much pinned on Ninian Park's rising star, 20-year-old Blake. The strong and skilful Wales Under-21 international faced Held's charges on the back of scoring a late and brilliant equaliser at Hereford. May was now looking for the gifted attacking midfielder from Newport to "come of age" against Admira who possessed Austrian international midfielder Peter Artner and East German striker Olaf Marschall. "People can make them (Admira) favourites," May told the Press before the game, "but I believe my players are capable of getting a good result." His confidence was shared by Terry Yorath, the Wales manager, who believed Cardiff had enough pace to cause *Admiraner* problems. With his movement and work-rate, Dale, observed Yorath, "is the type of player who can upset the continentals".

Carl Dale: We were happy with the draw and thought we could go through. They weren't Real Madrid, Barcelona or one of the big English clubs and we were a side that could break fairly quickly. Chris Pike was quite fast for a big man. Nathan and Cohen were also pretty quick and

I had a bit of pace. The ability to break quickly was one of our main qualities. We didn't have experience of European football and we knew we had to compete so we prepared well and ended up raising our game.

May's players had an added incentive to progress to the next round. Under a scheme introduced by Cardiff owner Rick Wright, May's players would share 10 per cent of the home gate revenue, and also 10 per cent of the home gate revenue in the second round, if they dumped the Austrians out of the competition. With a crowd of 10,000 expected for Admira's visit, Cardiff would net £50,000, meaning May's players would share £5,000 among them. Roger Ljung, Admira's Swedish international defender, admitted "some people in Austria would laugh if we lose to an English Third Division side". He expected Cardiff to attack in the first 20 minutes in search of an early goal but the Welsh charge never materialised. Instead, Held's side threatened with Johannes Abfalterer shooting wide after Michael Gruber exposed Cardiff's lack of a right-back. The Bluebirds then came to life and Michael Gruber cleared Pike's effort off the line after Franz Gruber, deputising for the injured Wolfgang Knaller, flapped at a Searle cross. Admira, fortuitously, took the lead a minute before half-time. Michael Gruber's cross deflected off Baddeley into the path of Abfalterer and his shot ricocheted off Abraham before rolling beneath the stranded Grew.

Lee Baddeley:

The way Admira played was totally different to what we were used to, it was another style of football. They stood off us and let us play. We weren't used to that. In the league – and we were in the bottom division in those days – the games were more of a battle. You didn't have much time on the ball. They were a decent

*team but we played well and created a few chances
that night. We should have taken a lead to Austria.
We should have gone there with an advantage, but it
was a great experience to play in Europe, especially
for a young lad like me. I was only 18 at the time.*

Held had noted Cardiff's "fighting spirit" after watching their
2-2 draw with Carlisle United at Ninian Park eight days earlier
and this attribute delivered a deserved equaliser shortly before
the hour. Pike - a typically shrewd free transfer signing by Frank
Burrows, from Fulham in 1989 - met Searle's measured free-
kick, beating Admira's vulnerable goalkeeper at the Grange
End with a classic header from just inside the six-yard box.
The momentum was now clearly with the Division Three side
who pressed for a second goal with Dale, Searle and Griffith
all going close.

Damon Searle: *I set up Pikey for the goal. We were awarded a free-
kick on the right side and I just clipped it in with my
left foot. There were a few players lining up outside
the six-yard box but I didn't pick anyone out, I just
tried to put the ball in the right area. It fell to Pikey.
All he had to do was get a touch on it and it was a
goal. He headed it in and he didn't score that many
with his head, despite being a tall bloke. We deserved
the equaliser and then we tried to get the win so we'd
have something to take to Austria.*

Exhausted by their endeavours, the storm generated by
May's players faded 10 minutes before the end, handing the
initiative to an Admira side that always looked dangerous on
the break. Indeed, May had Grew to thank for preventing a
defeat, the former West Bromwich Albion player producing

two excellent saves to deny Gerald Messlender and then Abfalterer. "I think the excitement might have got to us," said Pike, explaining his side's decline towards the end. "A lot of us were whacked by the last ten minutes. If we had got the early goal we deserved, I think we could have won it." Victory may have eluded the Cardiff players but they were praised for a "stirring" display. "Makeshift Cardiff City upheld the best traditions of past Bluebird European campaigns," enthused Robert Phillips in the *South Wales Echo*, and in the *Western Mail*, Karl Woodward wrote, "Eddie May's men preserved their cup-fighting reputation with a valiant display against one of Austria's crack outfits." The biggest compliment, however, came from Held who conceded he was "grateful" to fly back to Vienna with a draw.

Mark Grew: *We were disappointed we didn't take a lead to Austria. We should have won the game at Ninian Park. They got an away goal which helped them but we created enough to win 2-1 or even 3-1. We had a few players who could finish – Chris Pike, Nathan Blake and Carl Dale – but it didn't happen for us on the night so we were under pressure after that because we now had to score in Austria. Had we got a lead then we might have played a different formation over there. We may have tried to hold out and been more cautious instead of having to try and get an early goal, although wherever we went Eddie felt we could win. He wasn't defensive. He would always try and win a game of football, wherever we were playing, and I enjoyed working for managers like that.*

Derek Brazil: *Admira were more scared of us than we were of them. They were happy with the result and they'd scored*

an away goal. After we equalised they just sat back.
Whenever we had the ball, they just dropped into their
own half and looked at us to do something. As a side
in the bottom division, we weren't used to playing that
way.

For the second leg, Cardiff could call on James but Perry was still injured. The central defender travelled to Austria despite being "touch and go" with a knee problem and was ruled out 48 hours before the game following a training session at Admira's Südstadt Stadion, in Mödling, a small town just outside Vienna. While Perry's colleagues took part in a strenuous workout, the defender was able only to jog so May, unsurprisingly, stuck with the same defensive system he used at Ninian Park with Abraham sweeping up behind Brazil and Baddeley. There was only one change with James, a bargain £18,000 capture from Bradford City, replacing Bird in midfield. It would be the 35-year-old's first game in the middle of the park for five years, and May, looking for an away goal, hoped the player capped 47 times by Wales would be a creative influence in that area. "Moving to midfield will be a bit more energetic and will mean a lot more work," said James before the first leg, "but I know I can do it."

Cohen Griffith: *Eddie asked me to play as a right wing-back that night*
and I remember seeing Admira's pitch for the first
time – it was the longest I'd ever seen. It was huge,
really long. Eddie said, 'You've got a job tonight. You're
playing right wing-back.' I knew I was going to have to
run up and down this huge pitch. Then when we went
out for our warm-up before the kick-off, the Admira
fans started chanting, 'Welcome Cardiff! Welcome!'
I wasn't used to that sort of thing. Back home the

opposition's fans had a go at you, they didn't chant, 'Welcome'. The Admira people were being genuine, too. I was quite surprised by that.

May believed his formation would bring "at least one goal" and ordered his players to "go forward from the word go" but it was Admira who landed the first blow. A rare mistake by Brazil allowed Held's team to take the lead just after half-time, his headed clearance falling to Ljung who was positioned on the right-hand corner of the penalty area. Grew went to stop the Swede's shot but the ball took a wicked bounce in front of the goalkeeper, struck him in the face, and then looped up kindly for Marschall to head home.

Mark Grew: *I was blamed for the first goal but the ball pitched up in front of me, hit me on the face and then dropped to one of their lads. The ball we used in Europe was different to the Mitre balls we used in our league. It was lighter and had a plastic coating, and it flew in the air. It was totally different to the ball we were used to. We used these balls in a finishing session the night before the game and they absolutely flew about. I noticed they flew away from you. I'd brought three or four different pairs of gloves with me and I couldn't find any that gave me grip which wasn't ideal going into the game. The weather wasn't great either - it was wet which didn't help. Anyway, on the morning of the game I found an old pair of Sondico gloves which I hadn't used for years and they seemed to work although I wasn't overly happy with them either. This ball we were playing with moved about a great deal and one of their players (Ljung) took a shot. The ball hit the ground and pitched up, hitting me smack in the face.*

Next thing I know the Admira fans are cheering. I was stunned so I didn't actually see the player score.

Derek Brazil: *I made a mistake for the first goal but Eddie didn't have a go at me about it. Some managers jump on players' mistakes but he wasn't one of them. He put his arm around me at half-time and for the rest of the game I was OK although afterwards I did reflect on the mistake. It was a completely different game in Austria. After what happened in the first leg, we went out there feeling quite optimistic but Admira were a different team at home and they caught us by surprise. Looking at the tie as a whole, the first leg lulled us into a false sense of security. We didn't create much in Austria. In fact, we didn't have a chance until after they scored the first goal.*

Cardiff now needed to score twice to progress but Dale and Pike were blotted out of the game by the Admira defence. Blake worried the Austrians with a diving header and Bird, on for Abraham, cut his way into the penalty area only to see his pullback for Dale intercepted. In the 89th minute, the desperate attacking surge was punished by Abfalterer whose tap-in was set up by Marschall. Cardiff, so impressive in the first leg, had failed to produce an encore in Modling, their inability to retain possession and poor final pass aiding Admira's cause. For May, the second leg was a wretched anti-climax. "We had a lot of the ball," he said after the game, "but never looked dangerous up front." The need for discipline in order to avoid conceding another goal had morphed into tentativeness.

Carl Dale: *We were still in it with 40 minutes left and we were pushing for an away goal. We had a good following in*

Austria, a lot of fans came out to support us and that spurred us on but we weren't experienced in Europe and maybe that cost us. If we had more experience at that level then perhaps the result might have been different. Up until their second goal, we still had a chance but when they made it 2-0 at the end we knew we were out. We didn't create much in Austria. There are games when you feel it's not going to be your night and that did feel like one of them. I don't remember having any chances and missing them. They controlled the game more at their place and hit us on the counter-attack. There was a sense of disappointment in the dressing room afterwards, that over the two legs we'd lost a chance to go through. The difference between us and Admira was that they took their opportunities and we didn't.

Lee Baddeley: *We took a few fans to Austria and I remember there was a lot of singing from them throughout the game which really helped us. In his team-talk Eddie told us we had 90 minutes to turn it around, that everybody played well at Ninian Park and there was no reason why we couldn't get a result over here. He was very positive. We were looking for a repeat performance but it didn't work out that way. Admira scored at the start of the second half so we were pushing everybody up to try and get an equaliser. Gareth Abraham was moved up front to help out Pikey and Dale. It was all or nothing and that's how they scored their second. We did OK. We had to push forward and when you do that, sometimes you concede.*

Nathan Blake: *Nobody in the side had any fear about playing in*

*Europe. We were all looking forward to it. Our aim
was to get beyond the first round but we didn't do that.
We had some decent players and we felt we were as
good as Admira but they were more tactically aware
than us. We always went all-out attack and thought
about defending afterwards. Home or away, we only
played the one way. We couldn't play on the counter-
attack. We were tactically naive and that showed in
both games whereas Admira had more experience in
Europe and knew how to play over two legs. Eddie
May prepared us as best he could for those games but
I don't think he was ready for that standard. It was a
step up.*

May could now concentrate on a promotion push. His side,
invigorated by the arrival of striker Phil Stant, a £100,000
buy from Mansfield Town, and Wales defender and former
Everton captain Kevin Ratcliffe, a free transfer from Dundee,
went on to lift the Division Three championship as well as
the Welsh Cup, beating non-league Hednesford Town at the
National Stadium. Admira were eliminated by Antwerp in the
second round, losing a pulsating tie 7-6 on aggregate. Beaten
4-2 at the Südstadt, the Austrians were given little chance in
Belgium yet, remarkably, Held's players reversed the first-leg
scoreline to force extra-time only to be floored by Alexandre
Czerniatynski's 96th-minute effort.

Cohen Griffith: *This was a tie that got away from us. We could
have won the first leg and should have done really.
I remember feeling that way after the game. There
wasn't a gulf in class out in Austria. Eddie changed
things a bit – he felt that was the way to go - but it's
hard to change things and expect it to click straight*

away. I know we needed an away goal so he went with an offensive formation but we had 90 minutes to get a goal. There was no need to be gung-ho from the start. If it was 0-0 with 15 minutes left, then go for it. Having said that, if Eddie went the other way and played 4-4-2 we might have lost by more, we don't know.

Derek Brazil: *We had a brilliant night out after the game. We'd lost but Eddie said we'd given a good account of ourselves and to go out and have a good time. He was a one-off. He respected us and gave us leeway. Eddie was a manager who knew how to handle players. It was like having your dad in charge of the team.*

First Round, First Leg
15 September, 1992
Ninian Park, Cardiff

Cardiff City (0) 1   **Admira Wacker (1) 1**
Pike 58   Abfalterer 44

CARDIFF CITY: Grew, Brazil, Baddeley, Abraham, Searle, Ramsey, Bird (Gorman), Griffith, Pike, Dale, Blake.

ADMIRA WACKER: Gruber F, Dötzl, Zingler, Gruber M, Messlender, Abfalterer, Gutlerderer (Bacher), Artner, Ljung, Marschall.

First Round, Second Leg
29 September, 1992
Südstadt Stadion, Mödling

Admira Wacker (0) 2   **Cardiff City (0) 0**
Marschall 47, Abfalterer 89

ADMIRA WACKER: Gruber F, Dötzl, Müller (Zingler), Gruber M, Messlender, Abfalterer, Bacher, Artner, Temm, Ljung, Marschall.

CARDIFF CITY: Grew, James, Abraham (Bird), Searle, Brazil, Baddeley, Ramsey, Griffith, Pike, Dale, Blake.

24

Dreams and Nightmares
Standard Liège, 1993

'At 2-1, I thought that was it.'

Tony Bird

CARDIFF found themselves drawn with an old enemy for the first round of the 1993-94 competition, pitted against Standard Liège, their conquerors in a bad-tempered – and, at times, violent - tie 18 years earlier. The odds, though, were against the Welsh side claiming revenge. While the Belgians - littered with internationals such as Belgium forwards Marc Wilmots and Michael Goosens, and Brazil defender André Cruz – were challenging for the championship, Cardiff, four months after winning the Division Three title and Welsh Cup, were in turmoil. Desperate to offload the Division Two club, owner Rick Wright was no longer willing to spend money on new signings, as he had done the previous year. Worryingly, in a television interview, Wright – who acquired the Bluebirds in 1991 saying he would stay no longer than two years – warned he would "turn the key in the door" if no buyer came forward. The holiday camp owner believed he would recoup the £2million he had spent on new signings and improving Ninian Park by selling his best players and then winding up the club.

The relationship between Wright and his players had also soured after the owner reneged on a verbal promise to pay each of them a bonus for winning promotion and the Welsh Cup, with a reputed £1m to be shared among the squad. Not even the Professional Footballers' Association (PFA) could end the disagreement, with Brendon Batson, a senior administrator at the PFA, leaving Ninian Park without resolving the dispute. Although Wright eventually reached an agreement with several players, the bonus fiasco caused dressing-room discontent and discord as well as the temporary exile of Phil Stant. The popular striker clashed with Wright after the Cardiff chairman refused to pay a £2,000 bonus. Stant, scorer of 11 goals in 24 league appearances during the promotion charge as well as a hat-trick in the Welsh Cup final win over Rhyl, returned to Mansfield Town on loan at the beginning of the 1993-94 season but was recalled in time for the trip to Belgium after manager Eddie May, recognising the player's worth, urged Wright to end the feud.

There were also problems on the pitch. After securing maximum points in their first two league games, May's side had forgotten how to win and how to keep a clean sheet, losing one and drawing three of their next four league fixtures, leaking 10 goals in the process. Furthermore, six players who had turned down new terms – Nathan Blake, Jason Perry, Kevin Ratcliffe, Cohen Griffith, Damon Searle and Robbie James – were on weekly contracts. Against this uncertain and unhappy backdrop, the Bluebirds travelled to their secluded hotel outside Liège.

Jason Perry: *We'd won the Division Three championship in 1993 but the club was on a downward spiral after that.*

Rick Wright didn't want to invest anymore, saying it was now time for someone from Wales to come forward. Our meetings at the club changed. Before, Rick was talking about investment, now he was saying he wanted to go and there would be cutbacks. Things weren't right off the field, players weren't happy and there was a negative atmosphere about the place. In sport, you need to get rid of any negativity but sometimes it can be too big and that's usually when money is involved. When money becomes an issue at a football club, it's very difficult. We'd won promotion and felt, with two or three additions, we could have gone through the next division but now we were just trying to survive. I don't blame Rick because he was honest. He was a businessman and he said right from the start that he would invest in the club and then leave after two years. He wanted someone else to take it on but unfortunately it didn't happen and we saw what we'd built the previous season being dismantled.

For the second successive year, May was up against another World Cup finalist. Arie Haan, an instrumental figure in Holland's 'Total Football' side beaten in the 1974 and 1978 finals, had been appointed Standard's coach two years earlier and had just guided *les Rouches* (the Reds) to their first piece of silverware in four years, his players beating Charleroi in the Belgian Cup final. As an accomplished player, Haan had won the European Cup on three occasions with Ajax, and the Cup Winners' Cup twice with Anderlecht. Now the Dutchman, who, during his playing career, helped Standard win back-to-back league titles in 1982 and 1983, wanted to steer *les Rouches* to their first ever European trophy.

As was the case against Admira Wacker the previous season, May's team sheet – especially the substitutes - was influenced by the foreigner ruling although a sizeable Welsh presence in his dressing room meant he could pick a relatively strong starting XI. May's three 'foreigners' for the first leg were all Englishmen – goalkeeper Phil Kite, midfielder Nicky Richardson and striker Stant, with the Bluebirds manager omitting two of his non-Welsh regulars, Irish defender Derek Brazil and striker Garry Thompson. Approaching his 34th birthday, Thompson had been the only notable summer signing, the former Aston Villa and West Bromwich Albion player arriving on a free transfer, and his omission in favour of Stant caused a stir. May believed Stant, an ex-soldier who had served in the Falklands conflict, was "likely to get us a goal" and also hoped the switch would wrong-foot Haan. "They (Standard) have watched us a few times but haven't seen him (Stant) play. I'm sure Standard will probably plan for Thompson's aerial dominance." But there was an alarming lack of experience on the Cardiff bench. All five substitutes were teenagers and only midfielder Nathan Wigg had sampled first-team football.

Just as he did against Admira, May opted to play a sweeper system with Ratcliffe operating behind Lee Baddeley, Perry and Searle. The 32-year-old defender, skipper of the Everton side that lifted the Cup Winners' Cup in 1985, had successfully performed the sweeper role in his Wales recall six months earlier, a 2-0 win over Belgium in a World Cup qualifier at the National Stadium. Richardson, James and Blake, who had scored six of Cardiff's 14 goals, formed a three-man midfield with Tony Bird and Griffith supporting Stant up front. May decided to field three forwards after studying Standard's style of football. Haan's players liked to rotate around the pitch which required defenders to have time on the ball. Three strikers, felt May, would put pressure on Standard's defenders.

Cardiff were clear underdogs – before the first leg Haan told the Press, "We are expected to beat Cardiff" - but they would face a Standard side minus four influential players. Régis Genaux, their Belgian international right-back, was suspended for both games. Midfielders Patrick Vervoot, another Belgian international, and Morocco's Mohamed Lashaf were both injured while Haan had suspended Frans van Rooy, a fellow Dutchman, for missing a day's training the previous week. Despite these absences, Standard – led by their brave, hard-working and supremely gifted playmaker Wilmots, the son of a struggling farmer - were still expected to outclass the Welsh side.

They enjoyed the perfect start, Roberto Bisconti punishing Cardiff's early nerves by slotting the ball beyond Kite after being set up by Sascha Rychkov's threaded pass. Haan's men dominated the opening stages and only Kite, Perry and the linesman's flag stopped the Belgians increasing their lead. Cardiff, though, eventually settled and after Gilbert Bodart had superbly saved a Blake header, Bird stunned the Belgians six minutes before half-time with only his third senior goal. The 19-year-old from Cardiff, a product of the Bluebirds' youth programme, dispossessed Cruz and kept his head to beat Bodart. After the interval the Welsh Cup holders were holding their own and in the 62nd minute, from just outside the six-yard box, Bird silenced an angry Stade de Sclessin public with his second, using his right foot to volley Griffith's cross past Bodart. Cardiff were leading 2-1 and staring at their finest result on foreign soil since the indomitable victory in Augsburg 25 years earlier.

Tony Bird: *For my first goal, the guy (Cruz) looked to come in on his right foot. I gambled and went that way instead of left, and the ball rolled straight into my path. I took a touch, the 'keeper came out, and I drilled the ball low and hard under him. The Cardiff fans all went mental. For the second, Cohen dropped his shoulder, moved right and put in a cross with his left foot. I came in with a right-foot volley which went into the roof of the net. During the celebrations, Blakey nearly broke my shoulder! He picked me up and threw me onto the ground with him on top of me. It was like something you'd see in a wrestling match. But we were only in front for about thirty seconds. If they hadn't scored straight from the kick-off I think we would have held out. We needed to hold on for ten minutes. The adrenaline was going when we went 2-1 up but their equaliser burst our bubble and took that second wind away from us. Our defending could have been better. Eddie was upset about what happened and I remember the older boys, people like Robbie James and Paul Ramsey, were disappointed for Eddie. It was a great night for me personally although the result took the shine off it. I knew I was only playing because of the foreigner rule - the following weekend we were at Blackpool and I was back on the bench.*

"For 20 minutes either side of half-time," May later commented, "we did ourselves proud." Their display in the final 20 minutes, however, left him incandescent with anger. The ecstasy generated by Bird's 67th-minute strike – his second goal of the night - lasted barely a minute. Facing an embarrassing defeat and being pilloried by their own public, Standard equalised straight after the restart. With the Cardiff players and the 1,000-strong travelling supporters still savouring Bird's second goal, Wilmots - the game's most impressive player - scythed through the Division Two side to haul *les Rouches* level and calm the restless home crowd. What might have been a famous victory rapidly turned into a nightmare defeat. Cruz, atoning for his earlier mistake, made it 3-2 from the penalty spot after Blake had fouled Patrick Asselman before Cardiff's marking disintegrated, allowing Asselman and Wilmots to inflict further damage.

Cohen Griffith: *We were giving a good account of ourselves and went 2-1 up. The crowd had started to turn on their players and I was thinking 'OK, we're in with a chance here'. Then they went straight down the other end and scored! After that it was like the Alamo. We lost 5-2 but it could have been 8-2. After taking the lead, if we could've held on for another five or 10 minutes, they would have folded. They got hammered by Arsenal in the next round so there were flaws in their defence but we didn't hold on long enough to expose them. After we scored the second, we lined up for the kick-off and the strikers should split the halfway line with one on the left and one on the right. They're the first line of defence but I remember Birdy and Stanty were both on the same side of the centre circle. They were still congratulating themselves on the goal. Standard went down the other side and scored. They went straight through our midfield and defence, and the equaliser got them going. All we had to do was to hold out for ten minutes because their fans were having a go and the pressure was all on them. We would probably have got a third goal but straight away they got back to 2-2 and then battered us in the last 25 minutes. In the end we did well to keep it down to five.*

DREAMS AND NIGHTMARES

Lee Baddeley: *I don't know what happened that night, we just crumbled. We were 2-1 up, then we conceded a goal from the kick-off and heads started dropping. Before we knew it, we were conceding goals and by the end, we'd let in five. It was horrible. It was unacceptable, really. We only had ourselves to blame and I think we lacked experience in Europe. It was a Cup Winners' Cup game so it wasn't a normal stage for us. It was a more nervous situation so you can't afford to lose focus and we weren't able to handle that pressure. They were a good side. There were no mugs in their team and 2-2 would have been a great result for us. Eddie had a go at me at half-time because I was booked for elbowing one of their players off the ball. He said it was a stupid thing to do because it was off the ball and I was now at risk of getting a red card which would have reduced us to ten men, so he gave me a mouthful.*

Nicky Richardson: *We didn't know much about Standard Liège so we went into it a bit blind. Usually you knew the players you were up against or you'd played against them before. This was different because it was a European game although we knew they were a top club. When we went 2-1 up. I remember thinking 'Is this really happening?' The Cardiff fans in the top corner of the stadium were going absolutely crazy but then Standard clicked into gear and Marc Wilmots, who was a top player, equalised straight away. Up until then we had given a good account of ourselves but they took control in the last period and we ended up losing 5-2. We played with a sweeper that night. We hadn't played that system a great deal and when they clicked into gear, they started moving us around. The*

> *speed of their passing was faster than what we were used to and they were finding a few more gaps. Eddie was upset with us after the game but Standard upped their tempo when we went ahead.*

According to Ratcliffe, Standard were "on the rack" after Bird's second goal. "But then they scored so quickly – it left us deflated." From being 23 minutes away from a humiliating loss, Standard would take a commanding lead to Ninian Park. "We feel comfortable now," a relieved Haan commented afterwards. As for May, he was furious with his team's collapse. "If we had held the lead for five or ten minutes," he said, "it might have been different, but we stopped doing the things we had been doing. We collapsed from 2-1 and I learned a lot about one or two of the players." May even claimed players – "I mean anyone, with no exceptions, no matter how big a name" - would be shown the door if they continued to ignore his instructions. His exasperation was understandable. This was the seventh game that season in which Cardiff had taken the lead, and in six of them they had failed to secure victory.

Damon Searle: *Nobody gave us a chance out there yet we were winning 2-1 in the second half and I remember everyone jumping on Birdy when he scored the second. Then we conceded from the kick-off and that was a huge blow. Our second goal was a wake-up call for them. They now had their tails up, and we were deflated, and we ended up conceding five. We were absolutely gutted at the end and I don't think Eddie was pleased with a few of us. This was like a cup final to us and we were leading 2-1 after 62 minutes so Eddie felt it was probably our day. He had a go at me at half-time because I wasn't getting forward. "If you don't cross that effing ball, I'll knock you through that effing wall!' He could see we had a chance of doing something in that game and he wanted me to push forward. Eddie was old school and you knew it when he had a go at you. I saw him kick skips and throw teacups. We called him 'the lion' because he could roar.*

Nathan Blake: *Birdy scored with a volley to put us 2-1 up. It was a world-class goal and it wasn't against the run of the play either. That should have ripped the guts out of Standard Liège but we were still celebrating after the restart and they hit us with a sucker punch to make it 2-2. We just switched off. It was a lack of concentration. After that, they had the wind in their sails and it was like trying to stop an avalanche. We didn't do anything to change things and Standard gathered more and more momentum. Tactically, we didn't make any changes. We didn't put an extra man in midfield to shore things up. Soon we were 3-2 down, then 4-2. That was game over. They went on to score a fifth. I was absolutely gutted at the end. I had my hands on my head because I couldn't believe we'd lost the game like that. We were in control, then we got slapped. You had to give Standard credit but we hadn't learned from our experience against Admira the previous year. Tactically, we didn't know what to do. We were still naive and we collapsed after Birdy scored the second.*

Kevin Ratcliffe: *We were over-achieving, playing in the Cup Winners' Cup. We were a Third Division side, Standard were playing in Belgium's First Division. They had international players and their star was Marc Wilmots. He was quick and he wasn't bad in the penalty area! His all-round game was excellent and his record speaks for itself (Wilmots is Belgium's leading goalscorer with 28 goals in 70 appearances and he scored 72 goals in 142 outings for Standard). Playing in Europe was a great experience for us and for a while we made a game of it but at 2-1 we were in a false position. They were on a different level and they showed that towards the end.*

The defeat in Liège completed a dark 24 hours for the Welsh club, which saw its name on the European stage blackened by supporter violence in Liège. After the game, more than 150 Cardiff fans were arrested following ugly clashes with Standard's notorious hooligan element, 'Hell Side'. Most were released without charge and deported. Before the first leg, the 1,000 visiting fans were escorted to the Stade de Sclessin by riot police following a series of skirmishes with Standard supporters earlier in the day, which forced the Belgian police to mobilise water cannons.

Nicky Richardson: After the game we went into the centre of Liège and a group of us were walking down the street when this guy, standing outside a bar, started shouting at us. It turned out to be Arie Haan. There were about three or four of us and he invited us into this bar. He got us something to eat and drink, and he had a chat with us. I started talking to Arie, which made the night for me because I remembered him scoring this great goal against Dino Zoff in the 1978 World Cup. That was the first World Cup I saw on television and I asked him about that goal. I watched the 1978 final during a school camp in the Lake District – it was my final year in primary school – and I was cheering for Holland in that game. He also talked to us about the great Dutch team of the 1970s and his exploits with that side. He was a nice guy, very down-to-earth and approachable. It was a great memory from that night, and certainly a better memory than the game.

Jason Perry: *We were winning 2-1 but in the end we lost 5-2 which shows we weren't good enough. The result was probably a fair reflection of the difference between us and Standard Liège and shows where Cardiff City was at that time. The continental clubs were ahead of us in terms of training and facilities. We didn't have the greatest facilities. They were also way ahead of us with diet. Our typical pre-match meal was beans on toast and after a game we'd have fish and chips. That was the way our game was in those days. It's no excuse but the scoreboard in Liège reflects the difference between how we prepared and how continental sides like Standard prepared.*

By the time Standard arrived in South Wales for the second leg, Cardiff's situation had worsened. May's side had now gone eight games without a win, losing their last four. The latest setback was a 3-2 home loss against a Plymouth Argyle side managed by former England goalkeeper Peter Shilton. Standard had every reason to feel confident of progressing. Not only did they hold a comfortable lead – a Cardiff side low on morale would need to win 3-0 or 4-1 to eliminate the Belgians – but, with Lashaf and Vervoort fit again, and van Rooy back in the fold, Haan was able to field virtually a full-strength side for the return. It was a different scenario for May who had to pick a team containing eight Welshmen. He was also unable to select the injured Richardson and Blake, and new signing Alan Knill since the central defender - capped once by Wales, in 1988 - was signed after the UEFA deadline.

In public, the Cardiff manager was buoyant, insisting his struggling players could overturn the deficit on home soil. If the players could score two in Liège, reasoned May, they can score three at Ninian Park. In a bid to try and ruffle the Belgians, he made a bold decision, omitting his first-choice goalkeeper, Kite, and handing 18-year-old goalkeeper Steve Williams, from Powys, his first-team debut. This meant he could pick three 'foreign' outfield players; Stant and Thompson, both physically strong forwards and both English, led the attack with striker-turned-midfielder Paul Millar, from Northern Ireland, taking the third 'foreigner' spot. May hailed Williams' performance as "brilliant" although the young goalkeeper conceded he was at fault for Standard's 14th-minute opener, a goal that ended any hope, albeit remote, of a dramatic Welsh comeback. A moment's hesitation from the teenager and Wilmots met van Rooy's corner at the far post, his header flying in off the frame of the goal after eluding Searle, who was standing on the goal line.

Damon Searle: *They had been a bit lax in the first game but away from home, they were more professional. We had to go for it because we were 5-2 down and Eddie increased our artillery, picking Stanty and Thommo (Garry Thompson). We needed an early goal but the tie was over after 14 minutes when they scored. At the time I thought 'Now we've got to score four!' It wasn't going to happen, not against a team of their quality. We were going for it because we were looking for a couple of early goals, but instead they got the early*

goal and that was that. Looking back, we lost the tie
in Belgium in those last 20 minutes.

Ragged at times inside the Stade de Sclessin, Haan's players had no intention of presenting Cardiff with any gifts in the second leg, and nine minutes before the break Lashaf capitalised on Baddeley's mistake, tapping the ball into the net after Williams had stopped the defender's clumsy clearance. "They were good coming forward and their passing was unbelievable,"said Williams, reflecting on his first senior game. "The way they were passing the ball around, we just couldn't get a touch." Bisconti added a third early in the second half, Lashaf inviting his teammate to slice through Ratcliffe and Baddeley before producing a neat finish. James did score a spectacular consolation goal for the Bluebirds just before the hour, a wonderful volley from just outside the penalty area after Griffiths' deflected cross dropped kindly to the 36-year-old. Haan, who scored two breathtaking, long-range goals at the 1978 World Cup in Argentina, against West Germany and Italy, admired the strike, describing it as "very nice". It proved to be James' final goal for Cardiff. Five days later, he played the last of his 782 league games, an ignominious 5-0 defeat at York City, before dropping into the Conference to join Merthyr Tydfil. In February 1998, at the age of 40 and as player-manager of Llanelli, James collapsed and died while playing for the west Wales side in a Welsh League game against Porthcawl at Stebonheath Park.

Lee Baddeley: *The second game was always going to be tough but*
you never knew what might happen – we could score
an early goal or one of their players could get sent off.
We went into it needing to score early. There wasn't
much of a team-talk from Eddie. It was basically go

*out, enjoy yourselves, don't let yourselves down and
see what you can do. We had a job to do and that was to
try and turn the tie around but they got the early goal
instead of us and that was the nail in the coffin. It was
a long night after that, but we had to be professional
and keep plugging away. It wasn't nice knowing you
were out and still had 75 minutes left to play but we
tried to get something out of the game. If I was being
honest, the tie was over before a ball had been kicked
at Ninian Park.*

Cardiff, crushed 8-3 on aggregate, feared sanctions from
UEFA after coins and cigarette lighters were thrown from
the Grange End at Jacques Munaron, Standard's substitute
goalkeeper, before the start of the second half. To the Welsh
club's relief, referee Graziano Cesari declined to report the
incident. "Everybody was getting excited but nobody got
hurt," explained the Italian, while Haan assured Cardiff there
would be no complaint from Standard who had condemned
the Bluebirds to their heaviest aggregate defeat in the Cup
Winners' Cup. "The gulf in class, evident during long periods
of the first leg, was crystal clear throughout this one," wrote
Robert Phillips in the *South Wales Echo*. Standard had given
May's players "a lesson in the art of retaining possession"
with Wilmots, Lashaf and Thierry Pister dictating the game.
Haan summed up the second leg perfectly. "We had everything
under control."

Kevin Ratcliffe: *The home game was my last appearance for the club.
Before the next game (at York) Eddie said he didn't
need me and that was the end of me at Cardiff. Looking
back, I think Eddie kept me on because he wanted me
to play against Standard Liège. It wasn't a good time at*

the club. There was a lot of bad feeling between players and the owner because we were getting messed about over our promotion bonus. We were also struggling in the league. The season before, we'd won the Division Three championship but during the summer the club didn't invest so there was only one way things were going to go. It was always going to be a long struggle. Had Rick Wright spent £200,000-£500,000 on new players, the team could have pushed on but he wanted out.

Standard met another British side, Arsenal, in the second round and Haan used the draw as a platform to dismiss the British game with the Dutchman singling out Cardiff. "I think British clubs all play the same style," he remarked before the first leg at Highbury. "We have played Hearts, Portadown and Cardiff in the last two years – all the same. Cardiff could not play football so they kicked us." Arsenal were a different proposition, smashing Standard 10-0 on aggregate. Haan was sacked days after the 3-0 first-leg loss, with René Vandereycken presiding over the 7-0 reverse at the Stade de Sclessin. Despite losing their last three league games - the losses included a wretched 7-2 home defeat at the hands of Cambridge United - Cardiff retained their Division Two status, finishing just two points above the relegation zone. There was, however, despair and embarrassment in the Welsh Cup where May's charges were beaten by Barry Town in the final, the Welsh League Division One champions winning 2-1 at the National Stadium. A turbulent season saw a public row between Wright and Stant, Blake sold to Sheffield United for £300,000, and Ratcliffe depart Ninian Park. Wright eventually offloaded the club, in 1995 to Samesh Kumar. By then, Cardiff were back in Division Three.

First Round, First Leg
15 September, 1993
Stade de Sclessin, Liège

Standard Liège (1) 5   **Cardiff City (1) 2**
Bisconti 13, Wilmots 63, 84   Bird 39, 62
Cruz 71 (pen), Asselman 76

STANDARD LIÈGE: Bodart, Smeets, Leonard, Bisconti, Cruz, Pister, Hellers, Asselman, Bettagno, Rychkov, Wilmots.

CARDIFF CITY: Kite, James, Searle, Baddeley, Perry, Ratcliffe, Bird, Richardson, Stant (Evans), Griffith, Blake.

First Round, Second Leg
28 September, 1993
Ninian Park, Cardiff

Cardiff City (0) 1   **Standard Liège (2) 3**
James 59   Wilmots 14, Lashaf 36, Bisconti 50

CARDIFF CITY: Williams, James, Searle, Baddeley, Perry, Ratcliffe, Bird (Wigg), Millar (Bartley), Stant, Thompson, Griffith.

STANDARD LIÈGE: Bodart (Munaron), Smeets, Leonard, Bisconti, Cruz, Pister, Hellers, Asselman, Bettagno, Rychkov, Wilmots.

(Standard Liège won 8-3 on aggregate)